Economic Stability

in

a Changing World

Economic Stability

in a Changing World

ESSAYS IN ECONOMIC THEORY AND POLICY

JOHN H. WILLIAMS

NATHANIEL ROPES PROFESSOR OF POLITICAL
ECONOMY, HARVARD UNIVERSITY

NEW YORK

OXFORD UNIVERSITY PRESS

1953

PRINTED IN THE UNITED STATES OF AMERICA

Preface

THE central theme of the book is the relation of economic theory to public policy. Economic theorists have always, I believe, had economic policy as their objective, even if their policy were merely laissez faire. The increased importance of the role of government in our complex modern society has greatly heightened this emphasis. Yet I have long been preoccupied with the limitations of traditional theory as a guide to policy, and from this point of view have been more impressed by the essential similarity in method of classical and Keynesian economics than by the differences in the conclusions reached. I have felt, too, that the current attempts to 'dynamize' static equilibrium analysis suffer from much the same kinds of limitations. Some of the essays in this book are largely concerned with the nature of my discontent. I hope, however, that they will not be found merely negative.

In arranging the contents, I have put in Part I three essays dealing expressly with some of the fundamental current issues of theory and policy, essays which I regard as setting the tone for the book as a whole. Part II is a series of papers on the Marshall Plan. These papers are to a considerable extent the outcome of my experiences as an adviser to the Organization for European Economic Co-operation in Paris and as occasional consultant to the Economic Co-operation Administration in Washington and Paris. Part III begins with a paper 'Free Enterprise and Full Employment.' This was my contribution to a symposium of six American economists on postwar economic policy, published by The Twentieth Century Fund under the title, *Financing American Prosperity*. In preparing this very long paper for the book I have cut it down by nearly half, chiefly by omitting statistical material, and without, I hope, leaving out anything essential in the analysis. I have also included here my old review of Keynes's *Treatise on Money,* partly because some of my colleagues and students have urged me to do so and also because of the fairly frequent references to it in my later papers and the opportunity this book affords to bring together my views about Keynes at different stages in his thinking.

I wish to thank the editors of the various publications in which my papers originally appeared for permission to republish; credit is given on the copyright page and in the footnote accompanying each essay. I also wish to thank Miss Katherine McKinstry, who has assisted me in preparing these essays for the press, has read the proofs, and made the index.

J. H. W.

Cambridge, Massachusetts
October 1952

Contents

Part I

Economic Theory and Policy

1

An Economist's Confessions

ONE advantage of a presidential address is that one can appear on our program with a topic of his own choosing. It is however a dubious advantage. As I have proceeded with the job of program making (and I am sure my predecessors will testify to what an arduous job it is), I have been asked what topic I was reserving for myself. But programs are not made in that way, and as one works on a program so extensive as ours, he is apt to find that he has assigned about all the topics that interest him, and that, far from having reserved anything, his question becomes what can he possibly find to say that does not trespass too much on others.

I have decided to make mine a kind of personal confession. I came into economics at a later age than most, with virtually no undergraduate training in it and after several years of college teaching in a different field. Yet I had had for some time a genuine, if quite untutored, interest in some of the economic problems of the times, and before entering the Graduate School I carefully scanned the catalogue. I think I have never fully recovered from the shock of having practically all my choices crossed out, partly on the ground that some of the things that had seemed important to me were by then thoroughly understood and agreed upon by professional economists — I could read about them later — and even more on the ground that one must have a thorough indoctrination in 'theory' before doing anything with 'applied fields' or special 'problems.'

I am not criticizing my advisers and, now that I am somewhat indoctrinated, I would probably give similar advice. This experience, however, not only gave me a feeling of strangeness that I spent most

Presidential address delivered at the Sixty-fourth Annual Meeting of the American Economic Association, Boston, 27 December 1951; published in *The American Economic Review,* March 1952.

of my first year trying to overcome, but also set in motion a process of wondering about the content, purposes, and methods of economic inquiry that has remained with me ever since. One result was that (though I have taught it and worked in it ever since) I never did have a course in money and banking. This was one of the fields, according to my advisers, in which the theory and the problems had been pretty well worked out and agreed upon. Looking back (it was just after the Federal Reserve System had been established, and before wartime monetary problems — not to speak of postwar problems — had emerged), it does appear to have been a time when old controversies had grown sterile and most men thought they knew where they stood and found little worth debating about. Yet we were on the threshold of a period of revival of interest which has outstripped all preceding periods, and which has I think had more effect upon economic theory and policy, including the Keynesian 'revolution' and a vast literature on the monetary aspects of the business cycle, than any other development of recent times. In international trade, which has been my other main interest, I did have a course. I was singularly fortunate to have Professor Taussig as a teacher and guide in research, and to have as friends and fellow students such men as Jacob Viner and Frank Graham. But in this field also it was a relatively quiet time, and I heard frequently the comment that international trade theory was the part of classical economics, more than any other, that had withstood the buffetings of time and change and, along with its handmaiden, the gold standard, had come down to us virtually intact and unscathed.

II

One strong impression from those days, which has remained ever since, is the relativity of economic principles and policies to changing conditions. Keynes remarked on the 'Ricardian victory' as 'due to a complex of suitabilities in the doctrine to the environment.' [1] This was surely no less true of the Keynesian victory; and since then time has moved on again, and even the Keynesians are becoming changed men. A fair question is how much does our thinking lead and direct, and how much does it merely follow, the changes in environment. Very much in the literature of economics strikes me as rationalization

[1] J. M. Keynes, *The General Theory of Employment, Interest, and Money,* Harcourt, Brace & Co., New York, 1936, pp. 32-3.

after the event. This is not, however, necessarily a belittling comment, provided we know what we are doing and recognize the limitations.

The alternation of periods of comparative quiet with periods of intense intellectual ferment has been characteristic of the development of economic thought. Eighteenth-century English economic thinking had been relatively sterile before Adam Smith, the founder of classical economics, produced his *Wealth of Nations* in 1776. That book, to which I find an increasing inclination to return in the discussion of some of our current problems, particularly those of international economic growth, came after a long period of decay of mercantilistic doctrines. The question is not whether mercantilist theory was wrong in some absolute sense. Indeed, in our time there has been a considerable revival of some of its ideas. But it clearly lacked a 'complex of suitabilities' for the environment of the eighteenth century, and before Adam Smith there had been a long period of chipping it away. Smith had had a succession of forerunners in such men as Hume, Locke, North, Steuart, Petty, and Cantillon; he wove together the separate strands of thought which he had found and in the process revealed for the first time their full significance for the modern age.

The *Wealth of Nations* was, pre-eminently, the product not only of the man but of the times. It was the product of the great economic changes which, through their successive phases of geographical discovery, colonization, and commercial and industrial revolution, were sweeping away old doctrines, laws, and institutions — themselves the products of their times — and creating the modern world. This close relation of ideas and events is of course understandable and desirable. There appears to be a fairly well defined pattern. Times change, old ideas are undermined, the time span depending upon the importance and the rapidity of economic change; and on occasion, when the time is ripe, new leaders come forward to produce their 'revolutions.' Such a process is not confined to economics but has characterized every field of human inquiry. This is not the source of my unrest. In economics, however, there have been some features of the process which have left with me, since graduate student days, the abiding sense of wonder, to which I referred earlier, about the progress of our thinking, and particularly whether we are making some progress toward doing the leading, or are merely being led on by events which, after the fact, we seek to rationalize into some plausible pattern.

Adam Smith has been described as a great observer, and even as a great thinker, but not as a great theorist. Baumol's very interesting recent book *Economic Dynamics* [2] begins with a chapter on 'classical dynamics.' It makes not a single reference to Adam Smith, but gives an excellent analysis of Ricardian economics. Yet surely Smith deserves a high place, and perhaps the highest, in any historical account of dynamic economics. The point evidently is that, while Smith provided the rationale of the new expanding economy, which had already broken its mercantilist fetters, he did not produce a consistent theory of value and distribution. This Ricardo did, writing forty years later. And so it has come about that Ricardo is known, not only as the greatest exponent of classical economics, but as the real founder of the classical 'system.' By the time the theory had passed through the hands of his followers, particularly J. S. Mill, it had indeed achieved a triumph. By the middle of the nineteenth century, most economists, at least in Britain, undoubtedly were convinced that the basic principles of economics had been fully worked out, though doubtless much work would always remain for lesser minds to do in the 'applied fields.'

III

It is interesting to reflect on the nature of this triumph. Ricardo carried over intact Smith's philosophy of freedom. I think there can be little doubt that this fact, together with Ricardo's attack on the landlords, was primarily the reason for the triumph. The policy implications were thoroughly in accord with that particular phase of British economic development. Statesmen, industrialists, and merchants could readily understand and heartily endorse them. Indeed, they had by then long been living by these rules, and were doubtless delighted to find that they had all along been right, and even scientific.

But few laymen could have known much about Ricardo's theory of value and distribution, any more than most laymen today (who like to divide us all into Keynesians and anti-Keynesians) have any understanding of the Keynesian system, but base their bias, for or against, solely on what they conceive to be the policy implications. For me the great paradox of classical economics is that, whereas it

[2] William J. Baumol, *Economic Dynamics,* Macmillan, New York, 1951.

began with dynamics, providing the rationale for revolutionary economic changes, it wound up in a tight system of static equilibrium theory, which in striving for logical consistency became increasingly remote from reality. This I think we can ascribe mainly to Ricardo's theory of value and distribution. Economics had taken a major turn in the road — a turn away from Smith's causes of wealth, and a turn which I think has mainly characterized economic theorizing ever since.

Immediately following his striking single-page first chapter, in which he promises to reduce classical economics to the status of a special case under his own general theory, Keynes begins his Chapter II, 'The Postulates of Classical Economics,' with the statement: 'Most treatises on the theory of Value and Production are primarily concerned with the distribution of a *given* volume of employed resources between different uses and with the conditions which, assuming the employment of this quantity of resources, determine their relative rewards and the relative values of their products.' In the accompanying footnote, he adds: 'This is in the Ricardian tradition. For Ricardo expressly repudiated any interest in the *amount* of the national dividend, as distinct from its distribution. In this he was assessing correctly the character of his own theory.' Keynes then quotes from Ricardo's letter to Malthus: 'Political Economy you think is an enquiry into the nature and causes of wealth — I think it should be called an enquiry into the laws which determine the division of the produce of industry amongst the classes who concur in its formation. No law can be laid down respecting the quantity, but a tolerably correct one can be laid down respecting proportions. Every day I am more satisfied that the former enquiry is vain and delusive, and the latter only the true object of the science.'[3]

In earlier papers, covering a span now of over twenty years, I have criticized the Ricardian assumptions, with special reference to the theory of international trade — the given amounts of resources already known and in use, the constant costs — and the conclusions which so readily follow as to inherent equilibrating tendencies, mutually beneficial to the trading countries. In view of the origins of classical economics as an intellectual response to an expanding world, a world expanding on a revolutionary scale, I have never been able to understand how our thinking could have come to such a pass, and why as a

[3] Keynes, op. cit. p. 4.

graduate student my teachers should have sought to impress upon me that this was the one part of classical economics which we could still accept as adequate, undamaged by time and change. To my mind, it was never realistic, even for its own times, and certainly not for ours.

But as the quotations from Keynes indicate, and as Allyn Young showed in his brilliant British presidential address in 1928, 'Increasing Returns and Economic Progress,' [4] the limitations of the Ricardian kind of theorizing applied not only to international trade but to the whole field of economic inquiry. It had ceased to be a study of growth and had become static equilibrium analysis.

IV

Now I must make a second confession. In embarking upon Keynes's *General Theory,* I was again for a few pages mystified and misled. In view of the passages quoted above, I thought it was going to be a book about the causes of wealth, based not on the given resources, already known and in use, but on the forces and incentives which increase them, and provide the growing real income and increased voluntary leisure which in our kind of society should be the primary aims of economic inquiry. But this book too turned out to be static economics, with the difference — and this is what explains classical economics' being a 'special case' — that static equilibrium has now given way to 'comparative statics,' and partial equilibrium analysis has now become total equilibrium analysis. This latter, as it turned out, was what Keynes meant by the quantity of resources employed, as distinct from their distribution among uses and their relative rewards.

But surely the basic method is precisely on all fours with the classical analysis. It is again a purely logical contrivance which proceeds from certain assumed relationships to conclusions which inexorably follow so long as the assumptions are maintained inviolate and 'other things' remain unchanged. In its essentials, the Keynesian system, like almost any consistent theory, is simple. Several times in the course of the book, Keynes sums it up very well in a few sentences. To my mind, it is a recast version of the quantity theory of money, which he seeks to 'push back toward becoming a theory of output as a whole.' He does this by converting the quantity equation into an income equation and applying concepts mainly derived from refinements on the

---

[4] *The Economic Journal,* vol. xxxviii, December 1928.

Marshallian k (demand for money), including as the really unique feature of his theory, on which its whole validity depends, his 'law' of the propensity to consume. The core of the theory is his conclusion that an advanced capitalistic society suffers from a combination of a declining marginal propensity to consume and declining opportunities for investment. This and other parts of the theory, such as the assumption that costs and prices will remain constant or neutral as effective demand rises to a full-employment level of income, represent the effect on Keynes of the Great Depression of the 'thirties; and it is not to be wondered at that his American disciples, in particular, elaborated his theory (though I think without adding anything not already there) into the stagnation thesis. Once again, as with Ricardo, we have the 'complex of suitabilities to the environment.'

One interesting point in common, as between Keynes and Ricardo, is their attitude toward 'laws.' Ricardo had rejected an inquiry into the quantity of wealth because no 'law' could be laid down. Keynes's analysis of the level of employment turns primarily on his assumed 'law' of the propensity to consume. Herein lies a real dilemma for economic theorizing. We are constantly searching for 'laws' or 'regularities' or 'normal' or 'stable' relationships. Without them we are reduced to what Bagehot called the 'All Case' method of the German historical school. But at the other extreme lies what he called the 'One Case' method of the British classical school. We are all too apt, seizing upon the conditions of a particular period of time and applying the simplifying processes of selection and emphasis to which economic theorizing seems all too prone, to come forth with a system of universalized 'laws,' a system which is perhaps not implausible at its time of origin, but which, as it becomes increasingly concerned about the consistency of its internal logic, turns in upon itself, and grows more and more remote from reality. This is precisely the sense in which Adam Smith has come to be referred to as not a great economist, whereas Ricardo was. And it was because Keynes presented a logical system, based on a 'law' which seemed not implausible in the conditions of the 'thirties, that he was greeted as the founder of the 'new' economics.

No one was better aware than Keynes of the need of qualifying general principles to accord with the realities of particular situations. His work, including also his earlier books, and particularly the *Treatise on Money,* is full of passages in which he recognizes complicating circumstances which do not fit his theories. In the *General Theory,* one of the best examples is his passage on mathematical economics, in which he recognizes how much farther formal logic (and the unrealities inherent in it) can be carried in symbols than in words.[5] Or, again, his chapter on prices, in which he gives five excellent reasons why costs and prices will rise, and inflation emerge, well before his full-employment level of effective demand has been reached. No better analysis could be desired as to why we experienced the inflationary conditions of 1936-7 on a comparatively low level of employment; and nothing further would be needed to explain the much more serious inflation of the postwar period. But it was characteristic of Keynes — and this may be inherent in the nature of economic theorizing — that after stating his qualifications he always swept them aside as 'not affecting the rigour' of his conclusions. As he said of his qualifications about prices and wages: 'They have . . . a good deal of historical importance. But they do not readily lend themselves to theoretical generalizations.' [6] So, like Ricardo in his particular context, he swept them from his mind, and proceeded with his theory.

But we have been living in a period of very rapid change. Since the war, we have been faced with a condition of inflation, seemingly as intractable as the deflationary conditions which found expression in Keynes's theory. We may still argue, as many Keynesians do, that the income equation is still as applicable as it appeared to be in the beginning. But to my mind this is either mysticism or the familiar confusion between an identity equation and a law. It was over this same sort of confusion that the long controversies about the quantity-of-money equation became so sterile. Certainly, in recent years, Keynesian economics has been undergoing fundamental changes. We have become dissatisfied with the 'law,' as Keynes gave it to us. One form that this

---

[5] Keynes, op. cit. pp. 297-8.

I have never been sure how much he really meant this passage (though surely he did when he wrote it) and how much, perhaps unconsciously, he felt the need of taking the curse off his own essentially similar kind of presentation. He, probably more than anyone else, provided the impetus for the mathematical model-building which has become a kind of economists' refuge since the *General Theory* appeared. As one of my younger mathematical friends once said to me: 'I don't know whether Keynes's system is right or not, but it is a beautiful thing to play with.'

It was, I think, in connection with this sort of interest and technique that the word 'elegance' came into economics.

[6] Ibid. p. 302.

has taken has been the further analysis of the consumption function. It seems now agreed among econometricians that the 'simple relation' between income and consumption, as Keynes stated it, is unstable, and in searching for a more complex relation which may have some promise of greater stability various hypotheses have been introduced which contradict Keynes's own theory. For example, liquidity is now commonly accepted as a factor influencing consumption, whereas in Keynes's theory it affected only investment. We have been working with various hypotheses, including saving out of past income, liquid assets, capital gains, the last highest income reached during a boom, expectations of future income, and other possible factors affecting the income-consumption relation. The broad fact seems to be that we have nothing left of this basic concept of the Keynesian theory other than that consumption is an important component of income and deserves all the study we can give it.[7]

One over-all criticism of Keynesian economics that seems to me justified is that Keynes's emphasis on the demand side — his principle of effective demand — sins quite as much in its taking for granted the adaptability of supply as the classical economists did in their reverse emphasis. This has interested me particularly in connection with problems of international trade adjustment, and how to effect the grand reconciliation between internal full-employment policies and a country's balance-of-payments position by some method other than mere grants of aid. But its applicability is general and the place to begin the correction would be in the internal economy, even if we were considering, as Keynes mostly did, a closed economic system. Assuming, as Keynes did, constant technique, and confining himself to short-period analysis, with no analysis at all of economic processes — *how* we get from one state of static equilibrium to another — Keynes's theory has always seemed to me peculiarly inapt as a starting point for an analysis of growth and change, and in this regard inferior to the classical theory it was intended to supplant.

It is not surprising therefore that one major feature of contemporary economic thinking is the attempt to dynamize the Keynesian statics. We now have, for example, from ardent Keynesians, books with such titles as *Towards a Dynamic Economics,* which on inspection turn

---

[7] I have taken part of this paragraph, and some scattered comments elsewhere, from my earlier paper, 'An Appraisal of Keynesian Economics,' see Chap. 3 below.

out to be business-cycle theory. Here again, I must make a confession. I had thought that while comparatively few theorists, notably Schumpeter and Marx, had tried to do anything with long-run theories of change — long-run change has been left mainly to the historians and the statisticians — the business-cycle theorists had for half a century and more been concerned with the dynamics of short-run change. I had not thought it unfortunate that, as business-cycle theory developed, its relation to classical equilibrium theory had become increasingly tenuous. This seemed to me one of the major ways in which economic thinking had been seeking to come once again in touch with the realities of economic life; and one of my main questions about Keynes had been whether he had done economics a service or a disservice in attempting to push the analysis of economic fluctuations back into an abstract framework of equilibrium theory. As I said in my paper four years ago, I hoped and believed that we would find ourselves bringing back the things he temporarily submerged, the study of the processes of short- and long-run change, the emphasis on growth and productivity, and on price-cost-profit relationships.

Now this process is in full swing, and classes in the colleges that earlier had dealt mainly with Keynes's *General Theory* are wrestling with the business-cycle theories of Hicks, Harrod, and other leading Keynesians. In the process, Keynesian thinking has undergone further pronounced changes. It comes with rather a start to find men, who probably still regard themselves as Keynesians, or as having drawn their main inspiration from him, writing books about the economic characteristics of an expanding economy, and to find, as is true of both the Hicks and the Harrod versions of the cycle,[8] an assumption of a rising floor of autonomous investment. Surely this is a far cry from the 'thirties. It is true that the language remains, and the income equation still stands, as it always must as an identity equation, but I am not able to reconcile the assumption of a rising level of autonomous investment, providing ever higher bottoms for depressions, and springboards for bigger booms. To explain the booms, induced investment and the acceleration principle are assigned the major

[8] See J. R. Hicks, *A Contribution to the Theory of the Trade Cycle,* Oxford University Press, London, 1950; and R. F. Harrod, *Towards a Dynamic Economics,* Macmillan, London, 1948.

role.[9] To make the transformation complete (but still presumably in the name of Keynesian economics), Hicks leaves out money entirely, except for a couple of supplementary chapters which he clearly regards as of very secondary importance. What now has become of Keynes's effort 'to push back' the theory of money toward becoming a 'theory of output as a whole'? Clearly, the new environment of the postwar period has sent us upon a new search for an acceptable 'complex of suitabilities'; and Keynes's theory, as theory, is becoming rapidly submerged.

One of the most interesting aspects is the treatment of investment. What, some of the critics are now asking, is autonomous investment? Is there any such thing really? How distinguish between autonomous investment and induced investment? Is there not a continuous interplay?[10] Is there any such thing as a rising rock-bottom consisting purely of autonomous investment? And does it not seem ironic that in dynamizing Keynesian theory we find it necessary to transform his whole treatment of investment, and turn it round and make it walk in the opposite direction from that which he had assumed? In Keynes's own theory, there was no place for induced investment. Investment was the independent factor, tending to decline, and consumption was the induced factor, dependent upon income, in accordance with the fundamental law of the propensity to consume.

V

Economic theorizing seems to me pointless unless it is aimed at what to do. All the great theorists, I think, have had policy as their central interest, even if their policy were merely *laissez faire*. Keynes's greatest virtue, I have always felt, was his interest in economic policy; and it has been said, despite the paucity of discussion of specific

[9] Probably, along with the rising bottom of autonomous investment, Hicks would regard as the most unique feature of his theory the concept of a full-employment ceiling which provides the downward turning point in induced investment. The autonomous investment floor remains throughout as an unexamined assumption, and the full-employment ceiling is purely formal logic, which (as in the case of Keynes's full-employment 'equilibrium') would probably rarely conform to reality, except under direct controls and in special circumstances, such as war or defense. It is interesting to note, too, how the full-employment 'equilibrium' has now become merely a 'turning point.'

[10] And a continuous interplay between investment and consumption?

policies in the *General Theory,* that he started with what he regarded as the policy requirements of the time and built his theory around them. I find this quite understandable, and my main objection, as outlined above, is to the pretension to universality which seems to be the inescapable bane of theorizing.

We do not escape this bane when we turn from 'general theory' to some more limited field. I have long since ceased to be interested in *the* theory of international trade; and I have long thought it naïve to speak of *the* theory of the business cycle. I strongly sympathize with Trevor Swan, the Australian economist, in his recent review of Hicks's book.[11] Hicks begins his book in his characteristically disarming way, describing it as a 'progress report,' with 'weak links'; but it soon becomes apparent that his hope is that this may be *the* theory of the trade cycle, the next stage (after the theorists have approved) being 'the concern of the statisticians, econometrists, and economic historians' to do the detailed verifying. This is a not unfamiliar division of labor suggested by the theorists. Swan, in concluding one of the best criticisms of the book I have seen, says: 'I suspect that the search for *the* theory of the trade cycle . . . is the economist's equivalent of the search for the elixir of life or the philosopher's stone.' But 'each hopeless effort adds its quota of knowledge and understanding.[12] If the truth of the trade cycle is many, policy directed against

[11] T. W. Swan, 'Progress Report on the Trade Cycle,' *Econ. Record,* vol. xxvi, Dec. 1950, pp. 186–200.

[12] I pause over this sentence. Possibly it is true, but in business-cycle theorizing so much depends upon selection and emphasis that theories can even be misleading. Recognition of such defects then induces some other theorist to present a counter-theory, and so the game goes on endlessly. I have long preferred J. M. Clark's 'strategic factors' approach, based on the data rather than on any system of internal logic.

As the theories pile up one on another, we find ourselves forced to classify (and also to sift and discard), to the point where this process of classification becomes itself a form of business-cycle theorizing; the results are almost certain to have stamped upon them the selection and emphasis which seem most acceptable to the classifier and interpreter. Such work performs an invaluable service for the graduate students, whose success in their doctoral examinations turns so much upon the compendiousness of their knowledge of the literature. (I had wanted to say 'compendiosity,' but cannot find it in the dictionary.)

There is, at the opposite extreme, the all-inclusive type of business-cycle theory (for which Swan nominates Kaldor's theory) into which almost any particular theory can be fitted; but this sort of theory is apt to be so generalized as to be merely truistic.

the trade cycle must reckon not with one, but with all its theories. Is it not time . . . to forget the glittering prize of achieving *the* theory of the trade cycle, and concentrate upon the systematic and pedestrian attempt to discover how the economy works and grows in its parts and as a whole?' [13]

We do not escape the limitations of the systematizing process when we embark on theories of long-run growth and change, as Schumpeter and Marx have done. This, however, does seem to me the kind of theorizing we stand most in need of, and I regret that it would go far beyond the limits of my paper to discuss it.

I come back then to the question with which I began my paper. Are we, through our economic policies, making headway toward doing the leading, or are we merely the victims of our changing environment, desperately hanging on and seeking, after the event, to rationalize as best we can? I have spent a good part of my life, half inside and half outside the university, but trying in both places to deal with questions of economic policy. My difficulties may be due in part to an innate attitude of mind, which seems always to have included a vein of skepticism, and a desire to try to look all round a problem rather than to plunge forthwith for the bold solution. But the real point of my paper is that, as I think, the difficulties are largely due to the kinds of reservations I have been making about the dependability of theory as a guide to policy.

In any event, I cannot remember when policy questions did not present themselves to me as dilemmas, which I would have to go outside formal theory to try to get my bearings on, and even then would find very heavy going. About the practical usefulness of theory, I have often felt like the man who stammered and finally learned to say, 'Peter Piper picked a peck of pickled peppers,' but found it hard to work into conversation. I will not discuss whether this attitude of mind makes for good or bad policy making. Probably we need a mixture of minds and temperaments and biases to function effectively. But I will say that I think the most dangerous policy maker is the man who knows the answer, because he feels he can take it literally from his theory.

[13] Swan, op. cit. p. 200.

VI

I had not meant in this paper to deal primarily with specific questions of policy, but some comments may have illustrative significance. We are again living in a period of revolutionary economic change. In the domestic field, I have been mainly interested in monetary and fiscal policy. I am hopeful that the sessions on these subjects in our present program will add to our understanding, and I hope too that the forthcoming Patman sub-committee hearings, following on those of the Douglas sub-committee two years ago, will throw further light on the interrelated postwar problems of monetary control and debt management.

But I must confess that, despite all the discussion and the accumulated experience here and abroad since the First World War, this range of problems still impresses me as being one of the great dilemmas, political as well as economic. There are few economists today who favor unadulterated *laissez faire*. But about the kind and degree of intervention there is endless debate. In our kind of economy — apart from war or defense — the main emphasis has been on general monetary and fiscal controls. But central banking in its heyday did not prevent the booms of the 'twenties or the Great Depression of the early 'thirties. The result was a shift in emphasis toward fiscal controls. I still believe that the first phase of this shift, which we called pump-priming, and which involved a combination of monetary control and a cyclically unbalanced budget, represented, if we could have held to it, the most promising approach. But this seems to me to have been a case, par excellence, of theory's being carried along by its own internal momentum to the point where fiscal policy threatened to submerge monetary policy, without having proved its own effectiveness. Deficits, instead of being merely cyclical, became continuous; monetary policy became burdened with the dual and conflicting roles of stabilizing the debt as well as stabilizing the economy, and the emphasis on the former role increasingly overshadowed the latter. This was the kind of problem that I felt some economists overlooked when they belittled the significance of an internal debt on the ground that 'we owe it to ourselves.' [14]

[14] See J. H. Williams, 'The Implications of Fiscal Policy for Monetary Policy and the Banking System,' *The American Economic Review,* Supplement, vol.

We can only speculate as to what the further developments might have been but for the war. My own view was that we had had one of the longest and greatest recoveries on record from the Great Depression, and that, though we had let it get out of hand in 1936–7 on a still low level of employment, the new recovery from the steep but short depression of 1937–8 might well have carried us to a more normal level of output and employment, and have provided the setting for a more effective co-ordination of monetary and fiscal policies.

But the war greatly changed the dimensions and even the character of the problem. By attempting to freeze the pattern of interest rates and by allowing automatic access by banks to central bank reserves, we found that it is not possible to freeze interest rates except in one direction, and that longer-term rates fall toward the shortest and the debt is freely monetized, as bankers and others 'play the pattern.' Since the war, the great problem has been how to restore some effective degree of freedom to the monetary authority to perform its role as an economic stabilizer, with due regard also for maintaining a properly functioning government securities market. This is the problem of monetary policy and debt management. I shall not attempt to discuss it here — it is being dealt with in two of our sessions [15] — except to say that after slow progress earlier we may now be witnessing something like a monetary renaissance, with the Treasury-Federal Reserve accord of March 1951 unpegging the long-term rate, and with a demonstration of the security market's ability to stand pretty much on its own feet in December 1951 — with a minimum of support through open-market operations — and to stage a revival of rediscounting up to nearly a billion dollars, for the first time in eighteen years, and with no visible signs of panic. These seem long steps toward a revival of a flexible interest-rate policy, without which no general monetary control seems to me possible.

One source of confusion still in our thinking is the distinction between the flexibility of interest rates and the level of rates. Many a red herring has been drawn across this trail. When the emphasis was

---

xxxii, March 1942, pp. 234–49; reprinted in my book *Post-War Monetary Plans and Other Essays,* Basil Blackwell, Oxford, 4th ed., 1949, Chap. 14.

[15] See Woodlief Thomas, 'Recent Experience with Monetary-Fiscal Measures,' and R. V. Roosa, 'Integrating Debt Management and Open Market Operations,' *The American Economic Review,* Supplement, vol. xlii, May 1952.

greatest on fiscal policy and deficit financing in the late 'thirties, some economists emphasized most the level of rates, and this emphasis has persisted. One can trace it all the way from Keynes's 'euthanasia of the rentier' to some of the recent statements by the Council of Economic Advisers. Keynes changed his mind, and almost the last time I saw him was complaining that the easy money policy had been greatly overdone and interest rates were too low both in England and here. When I suggested that this was being done in his name, and that he ought to write another book, he was much amused, and said he did think he ought to keep one jump ahead.[16] What most interests me is not the level of rates — the present level may well be the long-run average — but the flexibility of rates. I cannot sympathize with the view that we had better not alter rates because any upward shift might be permanent, and that to avoid such a shift we should fight inflation entirely by other means.[17]

Despite, however, some recent steps in the right direction, the problem of co-ordinating debt management and monetary control still remains a dilemma. We shall be at best for some time in the pioneering stage, working under conditions for which earlier monetary theory and policy provide little guidance. To pose the problem as merely one of defining spheres of jurisdiction (though that is not unimportant) is to miss the true nature of the dilemma. It can be solved, if at all, only through co-ordination of policies, covering a range that goes even beyond the Treasury and the Federal Reserve System. We have, I think, made important progress from the thinking of the 'twenties, which

[16] One of Keynes's great virtues was that, despite his propensity to theorize, and to project each new theory into universal time and space (which suggests the analogy of the detective story writer who becomes absorbed in the internal consistency of his plot, until he becomes absorbed in another plot), Keynes was ever sensitive to the changing conditions of his time and country. Some of his postwar utterances in particular suggest that in some fundamental respects he had come almost full circle in his thinking. See, for example, in addition to his changed views about the interest rate, his article on 'National Self-Sufficiency,' *Yale Review,* vol. xxii, Summer 1933, as contrasted with the posthumous article on 'The Balance of Payments of the United States,' *Economic Journal,* vol. lvi, June 1946.

[17] Including fiscal policy, direct monetary controls, and quite possibly other direct controls. There is not space to deal with direct monetary controls, but I do favor their permanent retention, as probably the most acceptable form of direct controls, and among the most effective provided reasonable discretion is given to the monetary authority.

ran mainly in terms of controlling investment through the effects of interest rates on borrowers, and which assumed that banks would always be 'loaned up.' While we should not swing to the other extreme — the borrower will always be important — the conditions of the 'thirties, characterized by large excess reserves and a mounting public debt, shifted the emphasis toward the lender; and, as I said earlier, it was under these conditions (the pump-priming phase) that we began to appreciate the possibilities of the combination of deficits and easy money as instruments of recovery.

A debt, however, of the present size presents new problems — problems of debt structure and of debt holding, as between bank and non-bank investors, problems of how to control the great institutional investors, such as the insurance companies, while at the same time making efficient use of them for Treasury financing, problems as between marketable and non-marketable debt, of finding proper instruments of debt for small savers, problems of achieving a correct pattern of maturities, so that the debt will not pile up unduly in the short or long or intermediate sectors.[18] All of these questions in the sphere of debt management have a bearing on the effectiveness of monetary control, for the less the debt is capable of self-management, the greater becomes the need for central bank support of it, and the more monetary control as an economic stabilizer becomes submerged by the conflicting need of supporting the government security market. Thus inevitably it is a dual problem rather than a problem of jurisdiction.

My mind for a long time has run chiefly on the thought that with a large debt, widely held, small changes in interest rates could be effective in creating uncertainty, preventing the monetization of the debt and 'playing the pattern'; and that, combined with a proper fiscal policy, such a policy of flexible interest rates could be developed into an effective instrument of economic control. But without adequate fiscal co-operation, the task, to say the least, would be most discouraging. As experience since the war has taught us, even when the budget is balanced, monetary control has to step aside temporarily when the Treasury is engaged in refunding operations, and the main emphasis

[18] As an example of what happens when there is an undue proportion of short-term debt, we may observe the experience of England, where short-term rates, even after the war, had to be frozen completely. It is significant that in its recent measures attempting to regain some control over the money supply, Britain has had to unfreeze its short-term rates, and at the same time to make efforts toward reducing the amount of such debt relative to longer-term debt.

has to be placed on providing an adequate security market. It needs to be emphasized therefore that, though we may have been making some progress recently, we shall be facing quite a different set of circumstances when, as now seems most probable, the Treasury begins again to incur substantial deficits. Shall we then be forced back into the frozen pattern of rates, and shall we find ourselves again providing automatic access by the banks (and others) to central bank reserves? Though we did last year unpeg the long-term rate by the Treasury-Federal Reserve accord, we did it largely by converting the long-term marketable debt into non-marketable debt.[19] It remains to be seen what we shall find ourselves doing once we get into substantial deficit financing. This is what I meant earlier by the need for a wider co-ordination of policies. The size of the budget and of the deficits depends upon Executive and Congressional action.

VII

What seems certain is that we need a more rounded monetary-fiscal policy, in which each part plays its proper role. The experience of other countries as well as our own has indicated that the fiscal policy by itself is by no means the cure-all that in the first flush of enthusiasm it was thought to be. For one thing it seems highly improbable that the Congress, in any country, would ever accord as great a degree of discretion and flexibility — or could possibly — as in the monetary field. Through the use of an increasingly progressive individual income tax and the corporate income tax, we have achieved a substantial degree of built-in flexibility on the revenue side of the budget; perhaps what we most need now is a broader and more flexible use of regressive taxes (in the form of indirect taxation) if we really want to use taxation contra-cyclically. Since the war, we have, up to now, avoided deficits, and in the earlier years have even had surpluses. We have moderately reduced the federal debt, though this was partly due to the fact that we had previously overborrowed for war purposes. But these achievements, noteworthy though they are in the circumstances,

[19] Or rather, into convertible debt, giving an option of converting the $2\frac{3}{4}$ per cent non-marketable bond into a marketable $1\frac{1}{2}$ per cent five-year note; a policy which I feel may cause us added difficulties, if this should become the chief new technique for tapping long-term funds. In my view, to get true sensitivity through moderate changes in interest rates, we shall need particularly to increase our intermediate and long-term marketable debt relative to the short-term debt.

have been due mainly to the retention of taxation at virtually its wartime level and, since Korea, to an increase in the tax burden by some
fifteen billion dollars. The level of expenditures has remained high
and intractable, despite vigorous efforts by some Congressmen in
both parties to reduce less essential or wasteful expenditure; and
now, since Korea, it is climbing back toward a level not much below
that of the war period. There is no real indication in this postwar
experience that we are making progress toward a truly contra-cyclical
use of fiscal policy; though perhaps, in view of the extraordinary
circumstances of the cold war and now rearmament, such an achievement was hardly to be expected.

One aspect of fiscal policy that I felt was underemphasized in the
discussions of the 'thirties was the dangers that may be inherent in
the growing size of the budget as distinct from its variability. Keynes,
for example, said in 1940: 'It appears to be politically impossible for
a capitalistic democracy to organize expenditure on the scale necessary
to make the grand experiment which would prove my case . . . except in war conditions.' [20] This point of view was widely prevalent
among American economists, who laid our failure to achieve full
employment in the 'thirties to the fact that the yearly deficits were only
three or four billion dollars instead of ten or fifteen billions. As the
war drew to a close, there was much misgiving among government
economists, as well as academic, that the reduction of expenditures
from the wartime level would recreate large-scale unemployment.
Predictions to this effect were freely made and postwar policies were
based upon them, reinforcing the inflationary tendencies that have
since proved so intractable. This whole experience in prediction — one
of the most striking failures in the history of economics [21] — was
clearly due to the Keynesian bias in favor of large public expenditure.
It was accompanied by such a show of 'scientific' technique, with
much making of mathematical models, projections, and regression
lines (and much scoffing at business men as 'armchair economists')
that the plain man, though he might distrust the conclusions, could
scarcely be blamed for being bewildered and misled.

[20] *The New Republic,* 29 July 1940.
[21] A good parallel was the joint meeting of the American Economic Association and the American Statistical Association in December 1929, when the most
optimistic forecaster said the 'recession' resulting from the stock market crash
of 1929 was already over, but the public would not realize it until February
1930; and the most pessimistic said it would end about Labor Day 1930.

As I have indicated, the bias toward high public expenditure tends to load the task of contra-cyclical variation onto the revenue side of the budget. Instead of the diamond-shaped pattern of change which the budget should have, with the two sides moving in opposite directions, we tend to have a rising burden of taxation to counter the persistent upward tendency of expenditures. Such a process, if long continued, would be likely not only to undermine any true contra-cyclical budgetary policy but to change the character of the economy. The sheer size of the budget raises serious questions about the viability of the economy — its vitality, its productivity, its flexibility and adaptability — to a far greater extent than was appreciated in the 'thirties. We tend to accept maladjustments as a sort of *force majeure* which can be overcome only by increasing doses of public intervention. The economy becomes harder to stabilize, and budgetary policy becomes a less effective stabilizing instrument.

I have long sympathized with the thesis of Colin Clark, the Australian economist, that a burden of taxation beyond some percentage of the gross national product (he puts it at 25 per cent) turns upon itself and, instead of having the deflationary effects intended, becomes an engine of inflation, partly through pushing up wages and other costs and thus pushing up prices to the point where the tax burden, in real terms, has been brought back within the limits of tolerance, and even more through undermining incentives to produce and to save. The Cripps budget of 1948, which created a substantial surplus, was regarded as a miracle of austerity and self-discipline in the harsh conditions confronting Britain. But there are now many British economists who question whether the losses in incentives to workers, business men, and investors have not more than offset the deflationary effects intended. There are now suggestions in Britain that the way to get more work is to tax-exempt wages for specific kinds of work or beyond some standard schedule of work-time. In countries like Britain and Sweden, and even here, rising corporate taxation is accompanied by rising depreciation allowances which also tend to undermine the intended effect. Even we discuss various forms of tax exemption, and make proposals for legislation, in order to get more work, or more output of particular kinds, or more saving (and more investment of savings in government securities). It seems generally agreed that the British tax burden has reached and probably passed the limits of tolerance; and it seems more than a coincidence that the disillusionment about the big budget is being accompanied by a return to general monetary control in Britain and many other European countries.

As I said earlier, we clearly need a better-rounded monetary-fiscal policy; and failing this, we should recognize that the next turn of the road would be toward direct controls, the alternative, in the present context of events, being more careful scrutiny as to the amount of inflationary pressure the economy can tolerate. One of the main fears in Britain today, for example, is that the rearmament program, if it overtaxes British capacity, may result in permanently fastening upon Britain the direct controls which since the war they have been seeking to relax, at least internally. The American answer traditionally has been to seek relief through increased output. In the war, we got a wholly new vision of the expansibility of our economy. But we must not forget that the extraordinary expansion of output in the war, though it was an important factor in postponing inflation, did not prevent our getting it later on. Perhaps equally impressive has been the expansion of output since Korea, even though the defense program seems to be lagging in some important respects. Industrial production in 1951 was 10 per cent above 1950, and 25 per cent above 1949; it surpassed every other year except the two peak war years. Total output of goods and services, in real terms, was even larger than in the peak war year 1944. This is all the more noteworthy, in that we embarked upon the rearmament program from an already very high level of employment and production, whereas at the outset of the war there was still large unutilized capacity.

Since recovering from the initial shock of Korea, and the later Chinese intervention, we have managed to maintain a precarious balance between inflationary and deflationary forces. How long this balance may continue will depend largely upon two factors, the size and speed of the rearmament program, and the public behavior as to saving. Saving, from a low point of 2.2 per cent of disposable income after taxes in the buying panic after Korea, rose last year to about 10 per cent. Against this anti-inflationary factor (and the further one that we may not soon repeat the great increase in inventories that followed Korea), we have to set the size and speed of the armament program, combined with a continuing high volume of investment. Though I am of course quite incompetent on the military side, it must be emphasized that this will be our most serious economic problem, if we are not to dissipate our defense effort through renewed inflation;

and if this is a difficult problem for us, it is of course much more so for our Allies. We should not rely too much on mere increase in output. Though less serious than a scarcity inflation, the expansion of output is an inflationary process, in that incomes are paid out before goods appear in the market; and military expansion means that incomes are paid out to produce goods not available for civilian consumption. Unless the program is kept within feasible bounds, or unless we can count on increased saving (than which nothing is less predictable), we may find ourselves undoing with one hand what we are trying to do with the other, and also creating a grave prospect of recession when we come to the period of leveling off the rearmament program.

VIII

If domestic problems raise questions about the relation of theory to policy, this is even more the case in the international sphere. Since, however, this paper is already long, and my paper at last year's meeting was on this subject,[22] my comments will be brief. Throughout its history, international trade has played a leading role in economic growth and change. In modern times, it has been a process of growth from a center in which the countries outside the center have owed their development (and often their very existence) to the movement of factors, as well as of goods, from the center; and the center countries have in turn owed their further development primarily to this movement. Such a world was inevitably heterogeneous, with countries in markedly different stages of development. Any theory of international trade which does not approach the subject matter in this way must have very serious limitations as a guide to policy. Here particularly, we should feel the inadequacies of static equilibrium analysis.

One of the greatest paradoxes of recent times is that, while since 1914 the world has been in a state of profound and virtually continuous disturbance, formal international trade theory has continued to emphasize equilibrating tendencies. This has been true even of non-Keynesian theory, but even more true of the Keynesian type of analysis of international trade adjustment in terms of income. There has been, I think, a tendency to run away from the actual problems by putting them under an expansible umbrella labeled 'short run' or

[22] See Chap. 2 below.

ascribing them to wars and periods of transition. The broad fact is that after nearly forty years we find ourselves in a very different kind of world, with most of the problems still remaining to be solved, and new ones continually appearing.

Though I cannot sympathize with the tendency of theorists to throw out everything that does not fit long-run theory under a general label of 'short run,' I do feel that we have been troubled all along by two basic problems, one of which is relatively short run and the other secular. But the main point about them is that they are interrelated in the sense that the former would probably not exist (or recur so persistently) but for the latter. Since the end of the First World War, much has been said about maldistribution of reserves. This was Keynes's complaint in his *Tract on Monetary Reform* in 1923, when he said that the world's gold was buried in the vaults of Washington. There has been a persistent bias toward gold absorption by this country. Owing in large part to this bias, it has not been possible either to restore the gold standard or to work out any other feasible international system. The International Monetary Fund has up to now been almost wholly inoperative, and it remains to be seen how successful will be the much more limited experiment of the European Payments Union set up under the Marshall Plan, unless some provision is made for feeding dollars into it. The maldistribution of reserves has played a major role in the deterioration of multilateral trade, which even before the Second World War had become pronounced. This is a short-run problem only in the sense that it has given rise to frequent short-run crises. Since the last war, European reserves, and particularly British reserves, have displayed a biennial pattern, with crises in every odd year. There is some truth in the view that if European, and particularly British, reserves were larger, some of these storms could be ridden out. The alternative, as experience has already shown, is further emphasis on exchange controls and other discriminatory practices, and on further exchange-rate adjustments, and, quite probably, further deterioration of multilateral trade.[23]

[23] This subject played a major part in the United Nations' special report on *National and International Measures for Full Employment,* United Nations, Lake Success, 1949. It is discussed anew in the most recent United Nations' special report on *Measures for International Stability,* United Nations, New York, 1951.

These problems are symptomatic of deeper-seated maladjustments arising out of long-run cumulative changes in the relative positions of the trading countries. The great commercial revolution for which Adam Smith provided the rationale remade the internal economies of the Western European countries. This was the great movement from the center. It bestowed on those countries enormous advantages. Through export of capital, labor, and entrepreneurship, as well as goods, they were able to concentrate capital and labor on a small amount of land, resulting in a population density now four times ours, in increasing return industries and to buy the products of increasing cost industries from abroad. But in doing so, they have become committed to a particular organization of their productive effort. As such countries lose their initial advantages and foreign markets are cut off or seriously reduced through the growing productivity advantages of other countries developed in the process, it becomes increasingly difficult to find alternatives, either domestic or foreign. This is the basis of the urge for European integration, which has been present under some form or name ever since the Marshall Plan began. Whether we have been making any headway with this problem in its long-run aspects, as against mere reconstruction from war, still remains a much unsettled question; and one now confused anew by the rearmament program.

Meanwhile the United States, which in earlier stages of development absorbed European labor and capital and provided an expanding market for European manufactures in exchange for our food and raw materials, to our great mutual benefit, has in its later stages of development presented a growing threat of chronic world imbalance. Occupying a great and diversified land area, the United States has developed a rounded economy, marked by rapid technological progress, on a scale never previously witnessed. It produces over 40 per cent of the world's manufactures, but still relies predominantly on home supplies of food and raw materials. Over the last hundred years, our imports have declined from about 10 per cent to less than 5 per cent of our national income, compared with percentages of 10 to 30 or higher for Western European countries. Since the 1870's, the composition of our foreign trade has undergone pronounced changes, with imports of manufactures showing a large relative decline and exports of manufactures a large increase (from about one-seventh of our exports to about one-half). In the process, the share of Europe in our trade has undergone a marked secular decline, and the pattern of our trade has shifted toward the non-European world. Though the wars have undoubtedly accentuated these changes, they were already apparent before 1914. They raise a question whether Western Europe, if much more vigorous measures toward increasing productivity are not taken (and it must be remembered that increasing productivity is a race — this country cannot be expected to stand still), is not in danger of being pushed into a backwater.

Meanwhile a great change appears to be under way in the relation of industrial production and trade to foods and raw materials. For perhaps three-quarters of a century, the problem had been whether the industrial countries could absorb the food and raw materials which they had been instrumental in developing in other countries, on terms of trade tolerable to the latter. Now the imbalance appears to be swinging the other way. Owing partly to the expansion of industrial output in Europe under the Marshall Plan, and even more to our own absorption of raw materials (in the consumer durable goods industries as well as in the capital goods industries), there is a general world problem of availability of supplies. Again, this problem has been much accentuated by the rearmament program; but it was becoming apparent even before Korea. World industrial production since 1938 has grown by some 50 per cent, while the output of food and raw materials has at most increased by 10 per cent. Some experts have estimated that, apart from the United States, the world's food production is now lower than before the war; and if we take out a few items, such as petroleum and aluminum, this may well be true also of the raw materials.

This problem of the changing balance in production points up the need, on the economic side, of an effective program for the underdeveloped countries. It comes, however, at a time when sharply divergent views are developed as to the purposes of international investment (or grants). The less developed countries, with their recently won sovereignty and their growing social welfare consciousness, often do not welcome the nineteenth-century kind of foreign investment, which they regard as 'exploitation,' a process of extraction at low cost of what the industrial countries wanted, while doing little or nothing toward creating a better rounded economy and a better scale of living. Thus, the urge for a mixed economy collides with the world need for primary production. Moreover, the number of countries is limited from which good results could be expected from any large-scale program of investment. Probably what we need in many countries is pilot experiments, such as the International Bank might undertake (and has already); and in any event any general investment program would have to be planned or controlled by governments, not only because private capital is still timid (after the mistakes of the 'twenties) but because we would not otherwise know how the parts might fit together.

These are surely not short-run problems. Nor are they problems for which good policy answers can be derived from formal theory.

IX

As I look back over my paper. I have some misgivings. The discussion of current problems has taken more space than I intended, and it may well be a mistake to try to cover such large areas of policy in what can at best be only thumb-nail sketches. It may well be too that some readers who might not be unsympathetic to the general thesis of this paper, and might want to join me in some of my confessions, may fall out with me when it comes to the specific policies. For I have often felt that, whether we agree or disagree in our formal theorizing, it is when we come to policy making that we really find out how we stand. But in any case, I did feel the need of attempting some kind of illustration of what I was driving at in the earlier portions of the paper.

Now that I have somewhat eased my mind of some things that have long been on it about economic theory and method and the purposes of economic inquiry, I should like somewhat to smooth the troubled waters — though I do hope I have troubled them. If any theorist takes my remarks too much to heart, I can only say that I never get much beyond being in a quandary. As Keynes said, without theory we are 'lost in the woods.' We must of course have hypotheses for testing. But it is a close question whether it is any worse to be lost in the woods than in one's theory, pursuing its internal consistency to the point where contact with reality is lost. This, I think, is the biggest of all our dilemmas, and there may be no escape from it. I do not pretend to have provided an answer; but it should do us no harm to be aware of the limitations under which we work.

2

International Trade Theory and Policy —
Some Current Issues

WHEN my participation in this program was suggested, there was a question whether I should present a theoretical paper or one dealing with the present situation. It set me thinking, as often previously, about the relation between theory and current problems. Since 1914 there has been a greatly heightened interest in international economics. It has resulted in a voluminous literature, embracing the greatest advances in our thinking since Ricardo and Mill. The main drift in theory, until recently at least, seems to have been toward further emphasizing equilibrating tendencies — whether through refinements on the classical analysis, or through the use of more modern value theory, or by introducing more countries and commodities. This is what the writings of such eminent international trade theorists as Taussig, Ohlin, and Graham have in common. The so-called 'modern,' or Keynesian, approach has carried this emphasis even further through its analysis of international trade adjustment in terms of income.

Yet the period has been one of profound and virtually continuous international disturbance. The central question is how to reconcile theory and fact, or how to build a bridge between theory and current problems. Are the theories misleading; or are the forces they (rightly) emphasize temporarily submerged; or does the fault lie with economic policies pursued?

One of our chief needs today is to clarify the distinction between long and short run. Equilibrium analysis almost inevitably introduces a bias toward calling maladjustments short run, even though they may endure for years. In a recent article Metzler, after bestowing

The American Economic Review, Supplement, May 1951.

well-deserved praise on Graham's *The Theory of International Values,* remarks on Graham's underemphasis on short-run forces: 'Graham's theory . . . is entirely a long-run theory of adjustment, whereas most of the balance-of-payments problems, including the disturbances of the interwar period as well as the current dollar shortage, are essentially short-run problems.' And later on he says: 'A movement of capital and labor from one industry to another frequently requires a protracted period of time. Indeed, adjustments of this sort sometimes continue over several generations.' [1] G. A. Elliott's excellent review of Graham's book, though in general highly favorable, similarly concludes with questions about the short run. 'Should not some consideration be given to the obscuring garments in which the eternal verities are currently clothed? May not the path to equilibrium affect the equilibrium position itself?' [2]

I have picked out these comments because they raise the kinds of questions that have always interested me most with regard to international trade theory and have seemed to me particularly relevant to policy. I recall in 1919 having the great privilege of discussing at our annual meeting Professor Taussig's paper on Germany's reparation payments and of being brash enough to question the conclusion that the completion of the reparations process would lead, theoretically, to a 'stage of equilibrium identical with that which prevailed at the very start.' But Professor Taussig made it clear in his paper that he was merely applying the Ricardo-Mill analysis, and not making a prediction: 'Only if the assumed premises hold good, is it to be expected that the consequences will ensue as predicted'; and his paper concluded with the query: 'Who can say what sort of world we shall find ourselves in ten years hence?' [3] Surely most people would agree that the events of our times have changed the equilibrium positions. But is that not a way of saying that the so-called 'short-run' changes have enduring effects? And if that is so, are we not really asking whether a method of analysis which treats the 'problems' of international trade as outside the scope of (long-run) 'theory' is useful

[1] L. A. Metzler, 'Graham's Theory of International Values,' *American Economic Review,* June 1950, p. 320.

[2] G. A. Elliott, 'The Theory of International Values,' *Journal of Political Economy,* February 1950, p. 29.

[3] F. W. Taussig, 'Germany's Reparation Payments,' *American Economic Review,* Supplement, March 1920, pp. 35, 49, and my comment, pp. 51–2.

as a guide to policy, or indeed for any purpose other than the intellectual pleasure derived from exercises in internal logic?

As Taussig said, it is a question of the premises. Apart from the Keynesian emphasis on income and effective demand, international trade theory has always turned primarily on adaptability of resources, and particularly on the assumed contrast between internal and external mobility of factors. Assuming full employment as given, a high degree of internal adjustability to external changes, constant costs, and given amounts of resources in the trading countries, it follows readily that changes in demand among the trading countries for each other's goods could have only mild results, affecting as Mill said the 'division of the gain' from trade, but only within the narrow limits set by the unchanging zone of the comparative costs and only briefly disturbing the unchanging equilibrium position.

Without attempting to trace the development of more recent theory, my impression, as I said earlier, is that the main drift has been toward rather than away from the Ricardian analysis. This seems to me true even when writers are specifically attacking the comparative cost doctrine, as Ohlin and Graham have done. Their main purpose has been to supply a more modern value theory. But the effect of this modernizing (and also of introducing into the analysis more countries and more commodities) has been to strengthen rather than weaken the basic classical emphasis on adaptability of the internal economy to external changes.[4]

The fault still lies with the assumptions. In a paper some twenty years ago, I tried to express my doubts about the classical assumptions.[5] Perhaps what they added up to was a protest against attempting to apply static equilibrium analysis to an ever changing world. One paper to which I have often returned is Allyn Young's brilliant presidential address before Section F of the British Association in 1928, 'Increasing Returns and Economic Progress': 'No analysis of the

[4] One might add much else in the literature pointing in the same direction, but I will mention only Paul Samuelson's recent demonstrations, which have attracted wide attention, that, following up on Ohlin's approach, one may prove that even factor returns are equalized as between the trading countries. See his papers on 'International Trade and the Equalisation of Factor Prices,' *Economic Journal*, June 1948, and 'International Factor-Price Equalisation Once Again,' ibid., June 1949.

[5] 'The Theory of International Trade Reconsidered,' *Economic Journal*, June 1929; reprinted in *Post-War Monetary Plans*, op. cit., Chap. 2.

forces making for economic equilibrium, forces which we might say
are tangential at any moment of time, will serve to illumine this field,
for movements away from equilibrium, departures from previous
trends, are characteristic of it.' [6] Of course the answer that is now
fashionable for all such criticism, whether in international trade or
other fields, is that we must 'dynamize' the static theory. But I as yet
have little faith. May this not be merely another form of question
begging? Is not the essential problem whether international trade
changes are sufficiently systematic to lend themselves to any sort of
equilibrium theory?

The difficulty seems to me inherent in the nature of the subject
matter. International trade is so complex, so subject to heterogeneous
conditions and to ceaseless changes in conditions, that it seems to me
almost as naïve to speak of *the* theory of international trade as I
have long thought it to be to speak of *the* theory of the business cycle.
But we can study processes of change, and are more likely to do so
usefully if we do not have to put everything that does not fit the
long-run 'theory' under an expansible umbrella labeled short-run
'problems.' This should not, however, mean dispensing with the concept of balance, as something to be striven for by conscious policy.
The concept of balance could be defined more loosely and at the same
time more usefully, since it would take its meaning from the actual
problems in question. Since 1948 (at least before Korea), we have
had as our working concept Western European 'viability,' or freedom
from the need of 'extraordinary outside assistance.' But Point Four
has broader implications; and so very likely there will always be a
changing target and a changing conception of the practical meaning
of balance. What it comes to, I think, is that once we attempt to deal
with the world as it is rather than on the simplified assumptions of
traditional theory, there can be many and varying conceptions of balance, and the answer depends on what we are striving for rather than
on inherent tendencies arising out of limiting assumptions which, in
large part, rule out the actual problems that we face.

II

The questions I am raising, for both theory and policy, have since
the war been brought into sharp relief by the debate about the dollar
shortage. It has been a good debate, because it has been about a live

[6] *Economic Journal,* December 1928.

issue, of world-wide importance, in which theoretical analysis and policy prescriptions must come to grips. One thing it has brought out is that all or most of us have felt more strongly than the classical economists ever did, or perhaps ever had occasion to, the need of doing something. Even those who have held to a *laissez faire* conception of international trade have felt the need of creating through policy the conditions under which free market forces might work. At the other extreme are those who draw the conclusion that the only remedy is full economic planning.

What has interested me especially has been the varying emphasis on internal and external factors. This difference is largely based on adherence to the traditional type of international trade theory on the one hand and to various degrees and kinds of dissatisfaction with it on the other hand. Much has been very rightly said about the need of overcoming internal inflation in the deficit countries. The effects on the balance-of-payments position, once this was done in Western Europe, were striking. This is the familiar process of adjustment to external forces through internal change. But it hardly justifies the view, in any but a very doctrinaire sense, that the dollar shortage could have been cured at any stage by simply cutting off the dollar aid. External deficits were at once a cause and an effect of the inflation, and without external aid no politically or socially tolerable internal adjustment could have been made.

The point at issue here is one of international trade theory. What the classical economists did not recognize is that there are limits of productivity and real income beyond which international trade adjustment through the play of internal forces cannot, in the general interest, be tolerated. That we in our time do recognize this fact is shown in various ways: by our greater emphasis on international investment (and even grants), by our much greater awareness of the importance of the terms of trade, by the modern insistence on internal high employment, and by our recognition of currency devaluations as in some circumstances the preferable, or unavoidable, method of adjustment. Do not such qualifications leave wide open the question of how much emphasis to put on internal and external forces? And is it possible to embrace them all in any systematic theory?

III

Besides the distinction between long and short run, but interwoven with it, is the effect of wars. Could it not be said that war has been, overwhelmingly, the source of the really serious maladjustments, seemingly intractable at times but still short run in the sense that we have only to recover from them in order to see emerge once more the 'eternal verities'? Even allowing for the undoubted fact that wars do change the 'equilibrium position,' this would still leave the fundamental theory intact. But there is much in the literature and in the facts which suggests that this answer provides too easy a way out. I am much impressed, for example, by the fact that the deterioration of multilateral trade was much greater in the 'thirties than in the 'twenties, and stemmed much more from the Great Depression than from the First World War. Of course, if we could ascribe the depression to the war, we would complete the circle; but this again seems to me too easy, and I have regarded the depression, particularly in this country, as due primarily to internal causes.[7] A more tenable view is that the wars hastened a process of change already under way, and by completing the destruction of the nineteenth-century pattern of trade revealed deep-seated international maladjustments which had their beginnings much farther back.

I have long been impressed by the relativity of economic ideas and principles to changing conditions. On this ground any system of universals (eternal verities) is suspect. It was on this ground that Keynes attacked Ricardian economics; and it is on this ground that we today may question Keynesian economics.[8] International trade, looked at over time, provides a particularly fertile field for this kind of questioning. It has been a process of growth from a center in which the trading countries outside the center have owed the development of their trade, and indeed their very existence, to the movement of factors from the center; and the center countries have in turn owed their development primarily to this movement. Any theory of international trade which does not approach the subject matter in this way must have very serious limitations as a guide to policy. Western Europe created the modern world and was in turn remade by it. The internal mobility on which traditional theory is based was itself a product of external trade,

[7] See Chap. 4 below.
[8] See Chaps. 1 and 3.

including pre-eminently the external movement of capital, labor, and enterpreneurship to produce the goods which comprised the trade. Such a world was inevitably heterogeneous, with countries in markedly different stages of development and subject to markedly different conditions as regards relative internal and external mobility of factors.

In such a world there was much room for cumulative processes of change. The old analysis of the barter terms of trade, concluding that an investing country, for example, must worsen its terms of trade, entirely missed the cost and productivity effects of the investment process on both the lending and the borrowing countries. Foreign investment is a dynamic process which operates on both ends, and there is no ground for saying that it (or labor migration), without reference to the particular case, tends to equate factor returns or the benefits from trade (and of course much less ground for saying that trade in goods will do so). Particularly is this true if we take away the further Ricardian assumption about given amounts of factors, and count among the potential factors not merely physical resources awaiting development but also the potential technological developments. In this context, also, the assumption of constant cost seems peculiarly inapt, and with that, as Allyn Young showed, goes much of the traditional theory's reliance upon inherent equilibrating tendencies.

Associated with such changes is the development of the pattern of trade, which is a product not only of the natural distribution of resources but of commercial policy, investment, labor movements, trade and financial organization, and everything that has gone into the making of the history of trade. Hilgerdt has described how slowly the nineteenth-century pattern emerged, mainly about England as a center. He characterizes it as a 'formation only about three generations old,' and describes its marked deterioration in the last generation, particularly in the 'thirties.[9] One of the questions most debated in recent years, especially in the discussions of the dollar shortage, has been the role of the American economy in the deterioration process. In the earlier nineteenth-century stages, when our development absorbed European labor and capital at better returns than they could find at home and at the same time provided an expanding market for European manufactures in exchange for our food and raw ma-

[9] Folke Hilgerdt, *The Network of World Trade*, League of Nations, Geneva, 1942, pp. 84, 89.

terials, the results were mutually beneficial, and were part of the great dynamic changes which through their successive phases of colonization, commercial and industrial revolution, and expansion of complementary trade between Europe and the widening exterior have created our modern world.

But in its later stages our development has presented a growing threat of chronic world imbalance. Occupying a great and diversified land area, the United States has developed a rounded economy, marked by rapid technological progress, on a scale never previously witnessed. It now produces over 40 per cent of the world's manufactures but still relies predominantly on home supplies of food and raw materials. Over the last hundred years our imports have declined from about 10 per cent to less than 5 per cent of our national income, compared with percentages of 10 or 30 or higher for Western European countries. From the 1870's until the last war, United States imports of manufactures dropped from about 38 per cent of all imports to less than a quarter, while manufactured exports grew from about one-seventh of all exports to about one-half. In the process, the United States has looked increasingly to the non-European world for imports, largely in direct exchange for exports, and the share of Europe in the United States trade has undergone a pronounced secular decline. The effect of the war has been to accentuate this shift, with the result that since the war the United States has been getting not only the bulk of its food and raw material imports from outside Europe but also a substantially larger part than previously of its manufactured imports, while the proportion of manufactures to total imports has diminished further.

I have long puzzled over not only how such phenomena can be reconciled with traditional theory but, what is more important, by what measures maladjustments of this character can be resolved. For one thing, this is surely not the many countries case with which the modern theories deal, but the case of the one against the many. If our development only indicated an increasing trend toward autarky, it might suggest that with Europe rehabilitated by the Marshall Plan (and apart from the new threat of war) there might be room for the rest of the world to achieve viability within itself. This is the case for the much discussed 'two worlds.' But, even though the discriminatory policies which such a view envisages were carried much further than they have been, it would still in all likelihood be true that the outside world's need of our markets and of our exports would be so great that changes in the volume and in the terms of trade, though they might have comparatively small effects on us, would have greatly magnified effects on others. If our objective is a better balanced world, we must reverse our tendencies toward autarky by conscious policies of a more complex and sophisticated kind than those derivable from traditional theory.

One of the most difficult aspects of the problem of change over time is that progress in comparative productivities must be regarded as a race. Since the war, with external aid, Western Europe has made substantial progress not only in volume of output — now more than 20 per cent over prewar — but also in productivity. The American economy, however, cannot be expected to stand still, and we shall probably continue to be confronted with the question of comparative advances in productivity over time. Foreign investment, as I indicated earlier, is not necessarily an answer to such a problem. In the nineteenth century, the great movement of capital and labor to this country did not tend to equalize incomes internationally, but greatly contributed to the geographical expansion of the American economy and set in motion a cumulative rise of productivity, creating even greater disparities in incomes. But in a later phase it could well occur that foreign investment might stimulate a more rapid rate of advance of productivity in the lending country than in the borrowing countries, and thus create further disparities of income. Basically, what the world now requires is a flow of American capital accompanied by a flow of European exports. Such a development is not only unprecedented historically, but presents new and complex theoretical problems. It is not a question of 'tied loans' but of an organic relation between the flow of capital and of goods. The danger lies in a further strengthening of trade ties between the United States and the less developed parts of the world, leaving Western Europe in a backwater.

From this point of view it would seem advisable for Western Europe to co-operate as fully as possible with her own resources in international investment, as Britain has been doing in the sterling area. As regards American investment, it is quite unlikely that the main reliance can be on private foreign investment. A part of our puzzle has been that, while the role we should play in the world is that of creditor country, the conditions are often more favorable for investment here, not only for Americans but for others. The history of the interwar period is full of perverse capital movements of this kind, which disturbed rather than restored international equilibrium. The kind of development program now needed for a better balanced world would require planning, whether or not we like that word, because it would not be at all certain otherwise how the parts might fit together.

The classical economists would dispose of differences in comparative productivity by having them reflected in comparative money wages and prices. Once this process is worked out, no trade problem remains; the trading countries have comparative cost differences which result in balanced trade. But the difficulty with such reasoning is its static character. Once time is introduced and the possibility of divergences over time, the traditional explanation of how adjustment comes about, through money flow and its effect on comparative price levels or through income changes, misses the point that these adjustments would be at the expense of real income, the only corrective (in a free market) being reverse order changes in productivity — or a division of the world into hard and soft currency areas. The classical economists got round any such difficulties by not seeing them as possibilities; with them the costs and terms of trade were fixed and predetermined. There is an element of illusion involved in making comparisons in which physical productivity differences are washed out by cost and price differences. By such analysis one could doubtless, at any point of time, draw up tables indicating which goods (barring tariffs or other interferences) countries should buy and sell. But over time, if there are divergent rates of growth of productivity, the trade will be progressively less favorable to the countries less rapidly advancing in productivity. Thus there develops a question as to how trade can be equilibrated at a tolerable level of real income.

One important aspect of this kind of analysis is the effects of such processes upon countries, such as those of Western Europe, which in an earlier phase themselves experienced cumulative advantages from trade. This reminds me again, as it did in my old paper referred to earlier, of Mill's comment on Adam Smith's 'vent for surplus' principle of foreign trade, which he characterized as a 'surviving relic of the Mercantile Theory':

The expression, surplus produce, seems to imply that a country is under some kind of obligation of producing the corn or cloth which it exports . . . if prevented from exporting this surplus [the part not consumed at home], it would cease to produce it, and would no longer import anything, being unable to give an equivalent; but the labor and capital which had been employed in producing with a view to exportation would find employment in producing those desirable objects [previously] brought from abroad; or . . . substitutes for them . . . And capital would just as much be replaced, with the ordinary profit from the returns, as it was when employed in producing for the foreign market.[10]

But of course the difficulty is that countries such as England or those of Western Europe have specialized over a long period in production for world markets, fostered by export of capital and labor, and have thereby been able to concentrate capital and labor on a small amount of land (resulting in a population density now four times ours) in increasing return industries and to buy the products of increasing cost industries from abroad. In the process they have reaped enormous cumulative advantages of territorial division of labor; but in doing so they have become committed to a particular organization of their productive effort. What Mill failed to see was that, in a later phase of change, as such countries lose their initial advantages and foreign markets are cut off or seriously reduced through the growing productivity advantages of other countries developed in the process, it becomes increasingly difficult to find alternatives, either domestic or foreign. This is the basis of the urge for European integration, which has been present under some form or name ever since the Marshall Plan began, and has found expression in such ideas as 'the one big market,' 'co-ordination of investment,' the Schuman Plan; and on the monetary side the European Payments Union. These are surely not short-run problems or short-run solutions.

IV

Though I may be exceeding my allotted space, I must say something about the short-run problems. I have already mentioned the Great Depression and its effects on world trade. During and after the depression we witnessed a renewed collapse of the gold standard and a wave of currency depreciations, the beginnings of the drive for internal stability at full employment, and, closely related thereto, the growth of external controls, bilateral trading, and discriminatory practices, which even before the war had gone far to undermine the kind of trading that traditional theory assumes.

[10] J. S. Mill, *Principles* (Ashley ed.), Book III, chap. XVII, pp. 579–80.

The over-all result has been a changed conception of how world trade stability must be achieved. Instead of adjustment through internal change, there has developed the view that external stability must depend on maintenance of internal stability at full employment in the leading countries, and particularly in the United States. In the ITO discussions there was much insistence that countries could not adhere to a multilateral trading system without some kind of guarantee of stable high employment in the United States, and many of the 'escape clauses' in the Charter stem from this view. Since the war we have had further striking demonstrations of how fluctuations in our economy produce magnified effects throughout the world. Our very mild recession of 1949 created a new reserve crisis in England and the sterling area, requiring drastic cuts in imports from us, and precipitated the world-wide series of devaluations relative to the dollar (which probably would have been necessary in any case). Since then, owing partly to the devaluations and partly to the boom here, accompanied by stockpiling and other preparations for defense, we have seen another great turn of the wheel. Our huge postwar export surplus has disappeared; we have lost substantial amounts of gold; European reserves, especially Britain's, have been built up; and ECA aid to Britain has by mutual consent been suspended.

There is not space to discuss, as I recognize the theme of my paper would logically require, how much of this improvement may be permanent and what the implications would be for theoretical analysis. Even less can I discuss the new threats to European viability now arising from the military program. But what is clearly indicated by the experience of recent years is the magnitude of short-run changes and their close relation to changing conditions here. One aspect of this is again the difference between a world with one predominant country and the traditional conception of many countries mutually held in balance through compensatory internal adjustments. But there is also the profound change in the attitude of many countries toward internal adjustments.

For the classical economists the problem of full employment did not exist, since they assumed it away and discussed international trade only from the standpoint of best application of resources, given and in use. Full employment theory and policy in our time have been developed as 'closed economy' economics, and the reconciliation, I feel, has never satisfactorily been made. As I said earlier, Keynesian economists have further emphasized equilibrating tendencies through income changes, even if prices are insensitive. But by putting the primary emphasis on internal stability at high employment and on 'effective demand' as the guide to internal policy, they have gone to the opposite extreme from the classical economists, who made external equilibrium depend upon the free play of internal forces.

Carried to its logical results, as Keynes in an earlier phase in his thinking was quick to see, the emphasis on internal stability (for countries much subject to external strains) would mean striving for national self-sufficiency, or at least for an economy sheltered by some kind of combination of direct external controls and of successive currency devaluations which would, while preserving internal rigidities, enable a country to break off from and tie on to external price levels, gaining temporary trade benefits (if others did not retaliate) but at the risk of inflationary pressures which might undo them. Keynes in his last phase had gone a far cry from this, the Keynes who insisted that exchange-rate changes must be the rare and last resort, or the Keynes of the posthumous article.[11] Perhaps had he lived his next effort might have been the reconciliation.

Though no satisfactory way out, in my judgment, has been found, this conflict between internal and external policy aims has in recent years come increasingly under discussion. I have not now much confidence in the suggested formula that we can have the best of both worlds if only the nations will combine on common domestic policies for maintaining high employment. Though I made such a suggestion regarding this country and England in 1943,[12] I was relying heavily on the intimate wartime co-operation we then had. I would question now its feasibility even for those countries; and any general extension of the idea of common domestic policies to a large number of countries in such a mixed world seems visionary, at least until some decisive steps are made toward common sovereignty.

During the past year, the standard text on how to achieve and maintain both internal and external stability at full employment has been the United Nations' report, *National and International Measures for Full Employment*. There is not space in this paper to discuss it, except

[11] J. M. Keynes, 'National Self-Sufficiency,' *Yale Review*, 1933; and 'The Balance of Payments of the United States,' *Economic Journal*, June 1946.

[12] 'Currency Stabilization: The Keynes and White Plans,' *Foreign Affairs*, July 1943; reprinted in *Post-War Monetary Plans*, op. cit., Chap. 8. See also R. G. Hawtrey, *Bretton Woods for Better or Worse*, Longmans, Green, London, 1946.

to say that I have been sympathetic at many points with some of the excellent reviews it has received.[13] While in many ways an excellent report, to have been turned out by five economists from different countries in a few weeks' time, it still leaves me dissatisfied with the reconciliation. As I tried to point out in my paper at our meeting three years ago,[14] one of the greatest difficulties of Keynesian economics (and this report is mainly Keynesian) is how to achieve a full employment level of effective demand without precipitating inflation well before that point is reached. If this is a serious problem even in 'closed economy' economics, it becomes much more so when internal economies are exposed to external strains. If, for example, export industries are threatened with unemployment through decline of foreign demand, attempts to protect full employment by increasing internal effective demand could only raise costs and prices and make a bad matter worse; or if we start from some lower level of employment, there is increasingly the danger that as effective demand is increased toward the full employment level, it will go, at least in part, into costs and prices rather than output, again creating an external deficit. The formula whereby the report would make countries suffering from a decline in effective demand responsible for the deficits thereby produced in other countries seems to me an arithmetic rather than an economic solution of the problem. Surely responsible policy makers would not be content with such a generalized, mechanical formula without examining the circumstances of the particular case. Perhaps what my impression adds up to is that, as I said earlier, the Keynesian kind of prescription sins quite as much in its emphasis on effective demand as classical trade theory does in its emphasis on internal adjustability of factors and output. But we are making headway in recognizing what the problem is and the need of reconciling the conflicts that lie within it. At any rate, we seem to be making progress toward recognizing that policy must have a higher place than the classical economists would have assigned to it and, I hope, toward directing our theoretical analysis more to this end.

[13] See C. P. Kindleberger, 'International Disequilibrium,' *Canadian Journal of Economics and Political Science,* November 1950; W. W. Rostow, 'The United Nations' Report on Full Employment,' *Economic Journal,* June 1950; Jacob Viner, 'Full Employment at Whatever Cost,' *Quarterly Journal of Economics,* August 1950; and H. C. Wallich, 'United Nations Report on Full Employment,' *American Economic Review,* December 1950, p. 876.

[14] See Chap. 3.

3

An Appraisal of Keynesian Economics

THE topic assigned to me is, I am afraid, much too ambitious. I cannot do more than select some questions that seem to me important for an appraisal of Keynesian economics. I shall in part be going over ground I have already tried to explore at some of our earlier meetings and elsewhere, but I do hope to make some further progress.

Keynes's greatest virtue, I have always felt, was his interest in economic policy. Economic theorizing seems to me pointless unless it is aimed at what to do. All the great theorists, I think, have had policy as their central interest, even if their policy was merely *laissez faire*. If, nevertheless, I have been skeptical of theory, in its traditional form, it is because of its pretension to universality. Economic theory is an exercise in logic, involving abstraction from what the theorist regards as nonessential. Added to the simplifications of selection and emphasis is that involved in the one-thing-at-a-time method of analysis. Our dilemma is, and has always been, that, as Keynes said, without theory we are 'lost in the woods.' Without hypotheses for testing, we have no basis for economic inquiry. But one can reject with Bagehot what he long ago called the 'All-Case' method of the German historical school, while questioning, as he did, the range of validity of what he called the 'Single-Case' method of English political economy.[1] This is the kind of question that has chiefly interested me with regard to Keynesian, as well as classical, economics.

As the reference to Bagehot indicates, Keynes was not the first great English critic of classical economics. As a graduate student, nothing interested me more than the writings of the heretics. I found

American Economic Review, Supplement, May 1948; *Post-War Monetary Plans* (Blackwell edition, 1949).

[1] Walter Bagehot, 'The Postulates of English Political Economy,' in *The Works of Walter Bagehot,* Hartford, Conn., 1889, vol. v, pp. 249, 253.

no more penetrating discussion of the relativity of economic concepts than Bagehot's *The Postulates of English Political Economy;* and I returned repeatedly to ponder over Cliffe Leslie's savage outcry against 'generalizations . . . which have passed with a certain school of English economists for economic laws . . . generalizations which were once useful and meritorious as first attempts to discover causes and sequence among economic phenomena, but which have long since ceased to afford either light or fruit, and become part of the solemn humbug of "economic orthodoxy." ' [2] The weakness of such men, from the standpoint of the impression they made on later generations of economists or their own, was that they set up no rival system.[3] By the nature of their objections they could not, and had no interest in trying. The strength of Keynes, again from the standpoint of the impression he has made, stems from the fact that he did set up a rival system, for which, like his classical predecessors, he claimed universal validity. To reduce classical economics to the status of a 'special' case under his 'general' theory, as he so dramatically did in his single-page first chapter, was to stake out his claim on what he undoubtedly regarded as the highest conceivable level; it probably has no parallel in economic literature. But the questions remain: how valid is his system as a picture of reality, what is the range of its application, how useful is it as a guide to economic policy?

In one of the most interesting essays in *The New Economics,* Arthur Smithies, whom I have always considered a good Keynesian, says that Keynes's theory must be regarded as the beginning rather than the end, and calls upon us to construct a really 'general' theory, in which Keynes's theory would be a 'special' case.[4] This is welcome evidence — and one could cite much besides in the recent work of men who have been ardent Keynesians — of a willingness to appraise Keynesian economics more critically than was apparent in the first wave of enthusiasm that greeted the appearance of *The General Theory* in the 'thirties. Perhaps it will help us to get away from the

[2] Thomas Edward Cliffe Leslie, 'The Movements of Agricultural Wages in Europe,' *Essays in Political Economy,* Dublin, 1888, p. 379.

[3] How they affected my own thinking about international trade theory I tried to show in my old paper, 'The theory of International Trade Reconsidered,' *Economic Journal,* June 1929. Reprinted as Chap. 2 in my book, *Post-War Monetary Plans,* op. cit.

[4] 'Effective Demand and Employment,' in *The New Economics: Keynes' Influence on Theory and Public Policy,* New York, 1947, Chap. xxxix.

tendency to classify everyone as Keynesian or anti-Keynesian. That never seemed to me a helpful starting point for considering objectively either what Keynes's contribution has been or what its limitations are. I doubt, however, whether 'dynamizing' Keynes's static equilibrium analysis, which is what Smithies, Klein, and other mathematical economists seem to have in view, will remove the limitations. To my mind, they are inherent in the nature of equilibrium analysis, especially when applied to income as a whole.[5]

II

Keynes leaves no room for doubt that, in his view, his principle of effective demand revolutionized traditional economic theory. In the preface to *The General Theory* he speaks of 'treading along unfamiliar paths,' and of his long 'struggle of escape.' It is clear, too, that he regarded his contribution as monetary. The evolution of his thinking covered the greater part of the interwar period, and the stages in it were marked by the *Tract on Monetary Reform* (1923), the *Treatise on Money* (1930), and *The General Theory* (1936). It is clear all the way through that he was intensely concerned with the problems of his day, and particularly with those of England. In this sense all his books are dated. The first deals with the monetary disturbances of the early 'twenties, with a large emphasis on international monetary policy; it is dedicated to the 'Governors and Court of the Bank of England, who now and for the future have a much more difficult and anxious task than in former days.' [6] The second is a monumental work — analyti-

---

[5] The limitations of mathematical economic theory were never better expressed than by Keynes himself: 'It is a great fault of symbolic pseudo-mathematical methods of formalising a system of economic analysis . . . that they expressly assume strict independence between the factors involved and lose all their cogency and authority if this hypothesis is disallowed; whereas, in ordinary discourse, where we are not blindly manipulating but know all the time what we are doing and what the words mean, we can keep "at the back of our heads" the necessary reserves and qualifications and the adjustments which we shall have to make later on, in a way in which we cannot keep complicated partial differentials "at the back" of several pages of algebra which assume that they all vanish. Too large a proportion of recent "mathematical" economics are mere concoctions, as imprecise as the initial assumptions they rest on, which allow the author to lose sight of the complexities and interdependencies of the real world in a maze of pretentious and unhelpful symbols.' *The General Theory of Employment, Interest and Money*, London, 1936, pp. 297–8.

[6] Preface, p. vi.

cal, statistical, historical — whose central theme is a monetary theory of the business cycle (mainly on closed economy lines) and a policy of control of the cycle by the central bank. There is no evidence as yet of preoccupation with unemployment as a chronic tendency, booms are emphasized quite as much as depressions (nothing interested him more than our stock market boom), underconsumption and over-saving theories are given only passing reference.

In a famous passage of *The General Theory,* every sentence of which has a special relevance for his own theory, Keynes refers to 'the completeness of the Ricardian victory' as 'due to a complex of suitabilities in the doctrine to the environment into which it was projected.' [7] It was, I have always felt, a similar complex of suitabilities that accounted not only for the great impression made by Keynes's theory but also for its origin. It was not a coincidence, or a misinterpretation of Keynes, that the first great development of the theory by his disciples was the stagnation thesis, that the war was regarded as a superlative demonstration of what could be accomplished to sustain employment by a really adequate volume of effective demand, and that the weight of expectation of Keynesian economists was that we would relapse after the war into mass unemployment unless vigorous antideflation measures were pursued. There is no better short statement of the stagnation thesis than that given by Keynes: 'The richer the community, the wider will tend to be the gap between its actual and its potential production; and therefore the more obvious and outrageous the defects of the economic system . . . Not only is the marginal propensity to consume weaker in a wealthy community, but, owing to its accumulation of capital being already larger, the opportunities for further investment are less attractive.' [8] In an article in the *New Republic* which I have often quoted, Keynes concluded: 'It appears to be politically impossible for a capitalistic democracy to organize expenditure on the scale necessary to make the great experiment which would prove my case . . . except in war conditions.' [9]

I find it increasingly suggested that we should distinguish between Keynes's 'personal opinions' and his 'theory.' I agree there is often a real point in the distinction between what Keynes says and what his theory says. The book contains many *obiter dicta* which do not fit

[7] Pp. 32–3.
[8] P. 31.
[9] 29 July 1940.

into the skeleton of his theory, and indeed provide in some cases valid grounds for objection to it. But it has been my belief that the stagnation thesis constitutes the essential content of the theory, and that as we move away from the circumstances that thesis envisaged, the difficulties for the determinancy of the theory are increased and its force as a formula for economic policy is decreased. I have, however, been skeptical of the stagnation thesis, and some of my reservations about Keynes's theory date back to that phase of the discussion.

III

Keynes's main interest was in monetary theory and policy. The development of his thinking was directed toward 'pushing monetary theory back toward becoming a theory of output as a whole.'[10] His progress can be traced in the transition from $MV = PT$ to $I + C = Y$. There is the question in each case of distinguishing between the truism and the theory. In the traditional quantity theory (which Keynes endorsed without reservation in the *Tract*),[11] V and T were assumed constant, or independently determined, though in the later writings on the subject this is qualified by such statements as 'normally,' 'except in transition periods,' 'apart from the business cycle.' On these assumptions M affected only P (though some thought the connection often ran the other way), which was a complete demonstration that money was merely a *numéraire* and could be ignored in real analysis.

The main concern of business cycle theory, whether monetary or non-monetary, has been with fluctuations of income, output, and employment. In this sense, we had half a century and more of 'macroeconomics' before *The General Theory* appeared. But there have been formal difficulties with both sides of the quantity equation. In Keynes's *Treatise,* so far as the 'fundamental equations' were concerned, the effects of monetary changes were registered exclusively

---

[10] *The General Theory*, Preface, p. vi.

[11] P. 81: 'This theory is fundamental. Its correspondence with fact is not open to question.' But in the accompanying footnote he quotes with approval a statement by Pigou which seems to me to raise rather than settle the essential question: 'The Quantity Theory is often defended and opposed as though it were a definite set of propositions that must be either true or false. But in fact the formulae employed in the exposition of that theory are merely devices for enabling us to bring together in an orderly way the principal causes by which the value of money is determined.'

in P. As he later said, the equations 'were an instantaneous picture taken on the assumption of a given output.' [12] Moreover, as his critics pointed out, they were identities, his excess of investment over saving (via the quantity of money and the interest rate), his windfall profit rise, and his price rise being the same thing, with no causal relationship disclosed, so far as the equations were concerned.[13] There has been difficulty also in the business-cycle literature with MV. V has often been treated as a constant (whatever the writer may have said about it in chapters outside his formal theory), or as reinforcing the effects of changes in money quantity. But there is also discussion of demand for money as a factor to be offset by control of the supply, and of the concept of the natural rate of interest as the equator of saving and investment. All these versions, I think, appear in the *Treatise*, though the last undoubtedly interested Keynes most and constitutes a main theme of the book. But the chief emphasis is on business deposits. Regarding income deposits, so crucial for his later theory, his statement in the *Treatise* is: 'I incline to the opinion that the short-period fluctuations of V^1 (velocity of income deposits) are inconsiderable,' which appears to mean that consumers' demand for money is not a determinant of prices or output (consumers spend what — or in proportion to what — they get), and contains no hint of the later marginal-propensity-to-consume analysis.[14]

[12] *The General Theory*, Preface, p. vii.

[13] I agree with Lawrence Klein's statement (*The Keynesian Revolution* [New York, 1947], p. 17), though it comes oddly from a mathematician, that there is more to the *Treatise* than the equations. In my own review (see Chap. 11 below), I referred only briefly to them, though pointing out their truistic nature, and dealt chiefly with the responsiveness of investment and the price level to the interest rate (which seemed to me the core of the book), his monetary analysis, and my reasons for doubting the effectiveness of his central bank policy.

[14] *Treatise*, Chap. 15, p. 246. It is not possible to find a consistent monetary analysis in the *Treatise*. Sometimes he speaks of business deposits A as interacting with income deposits, as though it were merely the quantity of the former (in response to the central-bank-determined interest rate) that mattered; at other times the main emphasis is on business deposits B (a part of the financial circulation); at other times, and particularly in the statistical and historical chapters, it is on transfers between 'cash deposits' and 'savings deposits,' a part of the analysis that always seemed to me particularly oversimplified and unrealistic; see my review, Chap. 11. In the 'bear position' there is some anticipation of liquidity preference, but, as Keynes pointed out, they are by no means the same thing (*The General Theory*, p. 173). For an interesting and suggestive inter-

In *The General Theory, MV = PT* is replaced by $I + C = Y$, but one can readily see the old equation underneath. *Y* is *PT*. Investment and consumption are the components of income through which monetary changes register their effects. Though not in the equation, the quantity of money (together with 'liquidity preference') determines the interest rate, which (in relation to the expected profit rate — 'the marginal efficiency of capital') determines the volume of investment. The demand for money is broken down into the three strands that had been implicit in the analysis since Marshall. Velocity becomes the multiplier, command-over-consumption-units becomes the propensity to consume, and the distinction between the decision to save and the decision to invest becomes liquidity preference. The identity equation $I + C = Y$ becomes the causal equation $I + C(Y) = Y$. It is the development of the analysis of demand for money which constitutes, I think, the chief innovation of *The General Theory,* and upon it, and the use Keynes makes of it, mainly turns the answer to the question •whether he has succeeded in 'pushing back the theory of money to becoming a theory of output as a whole.' But a question hardly secondary is what has become in the new theory of *P*. In the *Treatise,* as I have said, *T* was constant; in the new theory it is *P* that has become constant, or neutral.

Having shown the development of Keynes's income equation out of the quantity equation, I must add a brief statement of the theory in his own terms. As he sums it up on page 29, 'the essence of *The General Theory'* is that 'the volume of employment in equilibrium depends on (i) the aggregate supply function, (ii) the propensity to consume, and (iii) the volume of investment.' The supply function is the supply price of total output, measured in unit labor costs, assumed (up to full employment) to be constant or neutral. With the cost-price level thus stabilized, changes in effective demand are registered in output and employment. Of the two components of effective demand, the schedule of the relation of consumption to income is a stable function (which may, however, have a characteristic cyclical pattern) determined by the 'psychological law' of the 'marginal propensity to consume,' which is that as income rises a part of the increment is saved. It follows that for every point on the schedule a multiplier can

---

pretation of the extent to which the *Treatise* foreshadowed *The General Theory* (as Keynes thought it did), see John Lintner, 'The Theory of Money and Prices,' *The New Economics,* op. cit. pp. 515–26.

be computed. With consumption and the multiplier thus given, changes in investment (the 'autonomous' factor), together with their multiplied effect, determine changes in the level of output and employment, which may settle at any point (up to full employment as the limiting case) determined by the quantity of effective demand. Thus, the lower the marginal propensity to consume, at a full-employment level of income, the greater will need to be the volume of investment if that level of income and employment is to be maintained. As a society grows richer, its marginal propensity to consume grows 'weaker . . . but, owing to its accumulation of capital being already larger, the opportunities for further investment are less attractive.' Therefore, the state must intervene, through monetary and fiscal policy, to compensate for the widening 'gap between actual and potential production' and maintain a full employment level of effective demand.

IV

I have stated the theory baldly because that, I think, is the only way to get at its logic. After that has been done, the rigor of the assumptions may be relaxed, but this is a process of relaxing also the conclusions, and leads back to the questions I asked earlier about the validity of the theory as a picture of reality and a basis for policy.

The paradox of the book (and one of its chief weaknesses) is that while its central thesis is long run, its formal analysis is short run, not in the business-cycle sense (to which Keynes devoted only a chapter of 'Notes'), but, as Hicks pointed out, in the sense of Marshall's short-run equilibrium. It is in this sense a special rather than a general theory, and a theory more static than the classical theory it was intended to supplant. Moreover, as has been shown by various writers,[15] some of the more novel features of Keynes's interest and wage theory rest on special assumptions, and are less damaging to classical theory (on the appropriate 'level of abstraction') than he supposed. In this sense, too, he falls short of presenting an acceptable general theory.

But much of the formal wage and interest theory seems to me secondary. Keynes's main concern was monetary, and it was the quantity equation, and particularly his long meditation over the Marshallian k (plus the impact upon him of the Great Depression), that led him to formulate his income equation and his income theory. Having done so,

[15] E.g. Schumpeter, Hicks, Lange, Leontief, Tobin, Modigliani.

he worked out the interest theory that seemed to him appropriate, took over such parts of traditional wage theory as seemed to fit, and rejected those that seemed not to fit. His great contribution was in focusing attention upon income and in challenging on monetary grounds the assumption, implicit in classical economics, of a full employment level of income automatically sustained. But the important question to ask, I think, is not how much his theory differs in its formal logic from classical economics but how much it differs from business-cycle theory, the relation of which to classical equilibrium theory had been becoming increasingly tenuous for at least half a century; and whether in attempting to push the analysis of economic fluctuations back into an abstract framework of equilibrium theory he has done economics a service or a disservice.

As I said earlier, the study of economic fluctuations had of course been concerned all along with 'macro-economics.' But the main emphasis had been placed on fluctuations in investment. To this Keynes adds little that is conceptually new, unless it is the emphasis on expectations, which comes oddly in a book that is otherwise not only static, with constant technique, but very short run. The emphasis on declining investment opportunities, though part of his central thesis, is certainly not new; it had made its appearance in each preceding major depression. As a practical problem it seems remote today, as it has in each previous period of renewed expansion.[16] Yet as a statement of a long-run tendency (wars apart) it has seemed to me not only plausible but desirable that new investment should become a decreasing part of total income in an advancing society, with qualitative technological change taking over more of the role of progress on the side of supply, and the benefits going increasingly to consumption on the side of demand. But Keynes himself did not discuss technology, and in any case the real seat of his pessimism and the core of his theory lie in his views about consumption. It is here, too, that his theory differs fundamentally from business-cycle theory.

[16] The reader is doubtless familiar with the literature of the controversy over declining opportunities for investment. In addition to the references elsewhere in the paper, I should mention (among others) G. Terborgh, *The Bogey of Economic Maturity,* Chicago, 1945, and D. M. Wright, 'The Future of Keynesian Economics,' *American Economic Review,* June 1945, and ' "The Great Guessing Game": Terborgh versus Hansen,' *Review of Economic Statistics,* February 1946.

V

Keynes's law of the propensity to consume is the important novel feature of his theory. It has been also the most controversial. It was the main question raised by my paper on 'Deficit Spending' at our meeting in 1940,[17] by Kuznets' review of Hansen's *Fiscal Policy and Business Cycles* in 1942,[18] and (along with his attack on equilibrium economics generally) by Burns's recent papers on Keynesian economics.[19]

As a first statement, apart from the business cycle or other special circumstances, Keynes's 'law' that as income rises consumption rises by less than unity is a plausible hypothesis; but it does not mean, necessarily, that consumption is the 'passive' factor or that the consumption function is stable. These two assumptions — (1) that consumption is dependent on income and (2) that there is a 'regular' or 'stable' or 'normal' relation between them, such that the consumption function can be derived as a given datum of the system and used as a basis of policy and prediction — constitute the essence of Keynesian economics. They bear a striking resemblance to the basic assumption of the quantity theory, that demand for money could be treated as a given factor, with the difference that, whereas that assumption was used to support the classical conclusion of full-employment equilibrium (apart from the business cycle), the new law of demand for money becomes the basis of the new equilibrium theory in which full employment is merely the limiting case. The whole structure rests upon the validity of the new law of the demand for money.

Historically, there seem to me to be ample grounds for doubting both the assumptions I have stated. They do not, for example, account for the effect of the rise of the automobile, a consumption good — or of new products generally — upon the growth of national income, where we have had a dynamic response of consumption and investment, each to the other. The application of an investment 'multiplier' to consumption as a passive, given factor in order to account for such changes seems wholly unrealistic. Nor would, I think,

---

[17] *American Economic Review*, Supplement, February 1941; see my *Post-War Monetary Plans*, op. cit., Chap. 13.

[18] *The Review of Economic Statistics*, February 1942, pp. 31–6.

[19] Arthur F. Burns, *Economic Research and the Keynesian Thinking of Our Times*, New York, 1946, and also his paper on 'Keynesian Economics Once Again,' *Review of Economic Statistics*, November 1947, pp. 252–67.

any 'dynamizing' of Keynes's technique by mathematical methods get us much further. Keynes's proposition that autonomous changes in investment determine changes in income, and hence in consumption (according to the 'law'), is probably no better than its opposite, that spontaneous changes in consumption determine changes in income, and in investment. The *interdependence* of consumption and investment, each responding to the other — and both responding (spontaneously rather than systematically) to changing ideas, methods, resources — seems to me to be the essence of economic progress. But it does not lend itself readily to equilibrium analysis, which is probably the reason why it has been the concern of the historians and the more imaginative kind of statisticians rather than of the pure theorists. As between Keynesian and classical economics, however, the latter provides, in many respects, a more realistic point of departure for a study of progress.

The rise of consumer durable goods has been the outstanding economic phenomenon of our times. From the standpoint both of long-run growth and of business-cycle behavior it raises serious questions for Keynesian analysis. Between the two wars expenditures on such goods were fully as large as those on capital goods, and their fluctuations fully as great; nor can we make any clear generalization as to which played the greater role in initiating cyclical changes. As 'outlets for saving' they played as large a role, and the same kind of role, as new investment; nor is there any more reason for applying a 'multiplier' to the one kind of expenditure than to the other. They make the Keynesian statements about 'oversaving,' or 'institutional factors which retard the growth of consumption,' or consumption as the 'passive' factor, seem much less realistic than they might otherwise.

Historically, however, the growth of consumer durable goods accounts only in part for the rise in real consumption. Kuznets' paper, 'Capital Formation, 1879–1938,' at the University of Pennsylvania Bicentennial Conference, constitutes an important landmark in the modification of Keynesian theory.[20] He demonstrated that, while national income rose greatly during that period, standards of living rose correspondingly, and the great bulk of the increase in income went into consumption. Saving, as measured by real investment, re-

[20] *Studies in Economics and Industrial Relations,* Philadelphia, 1941, pp. 53–78.

mained a constant fraction of income, with an apparent moderate tendency in the 'twenties (on which he does not insist) for consumption to increase relative to income.[21] In England before the war, according to Colin Clark's data, saving had been a diminishing fraction of a growing national income for at least a generation.[22] Since Kuznets' paper, the 'secular upward drift' of the consumption function, to which no reference is made in Keynes,[23] has become a standard part of the statement of the consumption function. Its practical effect has been to bring the plane of discussion (the possible 'gap between actual and potential production') back pretty much to where it had been before Keynes wrote, by disposing of the more serious version of his law and the one which I think he himself believed — that consumption, as a society grew richer, became a diminishing fraction of income — and limiting the stagnation thesis to a discussion of declining opportunities for investment.

But while the 'secular upward drift' is now regularly included in consumption function formulae, its implications for the analysis have not been sufficiently examined. One thing it means, I think, is the point mentioned earlier, the dynamic interaction of consumption and investment. No application of the growth of investment and a multiplier to the consumption existing at the beginning of Kuznets' period, on the assumption of passivity (in the way that was so commonly being done in the 'thirties) could ever account for the income-consumption relation at the end; and if instead we take a historical regression of the previous relation and project it forward, we are merely begging the question.

[21] Had residential housing been counted as consumption rather than investment, the upward tendency of consumption would have been more marked.

[22] His figures on net investment as a percentage of national income show a decline from 12.2 per cent in 1907 to 8.1 per cent in 1924, 7.2 per cent in 1929, and 6.9 per cent in 1935. His conclusion was: 'I believe the facts have destroyed the view up till now generally prevalent, that the rate of economic growth was primarily dependent upon the rate at which capital could be accumulated. The very rapid expansion at the present time [before the war] is taking place at a time of heavily diminishing capital accumulation. What is more remarkable, practically none of the capital which is being saved is being put into productive industry proper.' *National Income and Outlay*, New York, 1938, p. 270.

[23] Hansen's *Fiscal Policy and Business Cycles*, New York, 1941, Chap. 11, p. 233, contains, so far as I know, his first reference to it. It is accompanied by a footnote referring to Kuznets' forthcoming data (the paper mentioned above); they were both present at the Pennsylvania Conference.

Another part of the explanation, without doubt, has been the cost-reducing function of investment, with which, because it is too short run, Keynes's analysis does not deal. As I tried to show in an earlier paper, investment is significant, not primarily because of the money income and the employment provided by the capital-goods industries themselves, but because of the fact that by producing consumer goods in more efficient, and therefore cheaper, ways it releases consumer income for expenditure on other goods and services, and by increasing productivity per worker makes possible upward adjustments of income and increased voluntary leisure. This has been the heart of the productive process under the free-enterprise system. It points to the importance of price-wage-profits relationships which in the Keynesian system become submerged, and to the inadequacies in these directions of the Keynesian monetary and fiscal policies as the means of sustaining full employment in an advancing society.[24]

VI

Since the war Keynesian economics has undergone a number of significant shifts. Faced with a condition of inflation as alarming, and seemingly as intractable, as the deflation Keynes faced when he wrote his book, the stagnation thesis has receded into the background of the theory. This is mainly what is meant by distinguishing between Keynes's opinions and his theory. But, as I said earlier, the difficulties for the determinacy of the theory have been increased by the new conditions, and its applicability to policy has become less clear cut. One of the new questions is the relative importance of monetary and fiscal policies — control over the broad aggregates of the income equation — as against more specific (including direct control) policies. Is Beveridge's program for full employment,[25] and that of the six Oxford economists,[26] a logical following out of Keynesian theory (as they assume) or a contradiction of it? Keynes did not favor a planned

---

[24] See Chap. 10 below, pp. 199–211; see also William Fellner, 'The Technological Argument of the Stagnation Thesis,' *Quarterly Journal of Economics*, August 1941; and E. D. Domar, 'The Prospect for Economic Growth,' *American Economic Review*, March 1947. This is a point I have emphasized in virtually all my papers on Keynesian economics since my review of the *Treatise*, see Chap. 11 below.

[25] Lord Beveridge, *Full Employment in a Free Society*, London, 1944.

[26] *The Economics of Full Employment*, Oxford Institute of Statistics, Oxford, 1944.

or regimented economy (except in war), and regarded his theory as a defense against it. Another important set of questions relates to the cost-price effects of monetary expansion, which seemed secondary in deep depression when there were large unemployed resources. Another relates to the longer-run relations of costs, prices, profits, productivity which Keynes's analysis ignores, but which seem to me more important for stability and progress than the short-run monetary factors which his theory selects for emphasis.

Most interesting has been the postwar development of the consumption function. Keynes's book, despite his distrust of mathematics, has undoubtedly given a great impetus to the study of econometrics, and the consumption function in particular has given the mathematicians, whether Keynesian or non-Keynesian, an ideal concept for building models of national income and making forecasts. Thus far, the forecasts have been almost uniformly bad. Though I am quite incompetent to judge, my suspicion has been that the explanation is twofold: first, the stagnation bias carried over from prewar Keynesian economics; second, the fact that in the depressed 'thirties the income-consumption relation (as well as investment) was abnormally low, reflecting consumers' insecurity and pessimistic expectations. In any event, it does seem significant that the chief error made in the forecasts has not been in the estimates of postwar investment but in the consumption function, the one element theoretically derivable from within the Keynesian system.

After the appearance of the 'secular upward drift,' the emphasis was on the assumed short-run stability of the consumption function. But postwar experience has cast doubt also on this. It seems now to be agreed among econometricians that the 'simple relation' between income and consumption, as Keynes stated it, is unstable. In searching for a more complex relation which may have some promise of greater stability, hypotheses have been introduced which contradict Keynes's own theory. For example, liquidity is now commonly accepted as a factor affecting consumption, whereas in Keynes's theory liquidity affected only investment. Such a change strikes at Keynes's whole structure of demand for money, with its elaborately worked out separation into the three distinct strands I discussed earlier. Instead of the simple relation between current income and current consumption on which Keynes built his theory, we are today working with various hypotheses, including saving out of past income, liquid assets, capital gains, the last highest income reached in a boom, expectations of future income, and other possible factors affecting the income-consumption relation. That expectation should be brought in to explain consumption, whereas with Keynes it affected only investment, is surely a major departure. But it seems unnecessary, and even misleading, to pick out any particular points of difference. The broad fact seems to me to be that we have nothing left of this basic concept of the Keynesian theory other than that consumption is an important component of income and deserves all the study we can give it. The same is of course true of investment, the other component of income. That this is not now being studied with equal intensity by the econometricians is doubtless due to the fact that the changes in it are not derivable from within the system and do not lend themselves as readily to mathematical manipulation.[27]

Scarcely less significant among the postwar developments is the growing recognition of Keynes's underemphasis on the price aspect of monetary changes. As I said earlier, in deep depression this could be ignored, but the practical problem that confronts us, except in that unique condition, is that a volume of effective demand that is adequate for full employment appears to have cost-price effects which not only expand money income at the expense of real income but cre-

[27] Lawrence Klein has recognized that for a true equilibrium system both investment and consumption should be determinable from within the system, see 'A Post-Mortem on Transition Predictions of National Product,' *Journal of Political Economy,* August 1946, pp. 302–3. He lists the relations we must know before we can make good forecasts: 'A principal failure of the customary models is that they are not sufficiently detailed. There are too many variables which are classified as autonomous when they are actually induced . . . The surplus of autonomous variables results from a failure to discover all the appropriate relationships constituting the system. In addition to the consumption function, we should have the investment function, the inventory function, the housing function, the price-formation equations, etc.' In *Econometrica,* April 1947, he made his own forecast for the fiscal year 1947, and said that if he were wrong the reason would probably be his failure to take account of the further rise of prices. (Why should not prices be predictable from within the system?) The actual price level was not significantly different from the one he chose to use; his estimate of investment was too high (though not seriously so); but his forecast of national product was too low because he underestimated the consumption function.

ate a highly unstable economic situation. In other words, Keynes's stable equilibrium (even if we could concede it on other grounds) would seem not to include full employment as the limiting case, but something substantially short of that. This seems to me our most serious practical dilemma. It has both short- and long-run aspects. It presents a question whether we have to make a choice between allowing for a certain amount of slack (and fluctuation) in our use of resources, in a free-market system, or, if we insist on continuous full employment, recognizing the need for more specific controls. But this leads on to the question, not only of our scheme of values (political and social as well as economic), but also of the vitality of the system, whether in a more planned and controlled system we would not weaken the dynamic forces which promote growth and which might, with further study, be directed toward the achievement, not of stable equilibrium in any exact sense, but of a less unstable economy than we have had hitherto. Much, I think, could be accomplished through the further study of price-wage-profit practices and policies. As I said in an earlier paper, though these relations have long been a main concern of (classical) economic theory they have been overlaid in recent years by preoccupation with monetary and fiscal analysis, and the tendency has been to regard price-cost behavior as a kind of *force majeure* to be 'offset' rather than corrected. It is surprising how little we know, and can agree upon, with regard to these relationships, and what course to steer in order to avoid merely (a) letting them take their course, (b) compensating for them by monetary and fiscal manipulation, or (c) subjecting them to direct control.[28]

Chapter 21, on 'The Theory of Prices,' is for me one of the high spots of *The General Theory*. One of Keynes's characteristics was that while he was as sharp as anyone could wish in seeing possible qualifications and objections to his theory, he never permitted them to interfere with his conclusions. Chapter 21 (in which occurs the passage on mathematical economics) is an excellent discussion of the reasons why before full employment is reached, monetary expansion affects prices and costs as well as output and employment. It is interesting that the chapter runs in terms of the quantity theory of

---

[28] See my statement on 'The Employment Act of 1946' before the Joint Congressional Committee on the President's Economic Report, 2 July 1947, reprinted in my book, *Post-War Monetary Plans,* op. cit. Chap. 12, p. 212.

money, which suggests again that his own theory is a recast version of the quantity theory.

If there is perfectly elastic supply so long as there is unemployment, and perfectly inelastic supply so soon as full employment is reached, and if effective demand changes in the same proportion as the quantity of money, the quantity theory of money can be enunciated as follows: 'So long as there is unemployment, *employment* will change in the same proportion as the quantity of money; and when there is full employment, *prices* will change in the same proportion as the quantity of money.' [29]

Inserting Keynes's new concept of demand for money, this is not a bad statement of his own theory. But he goes on to introduce five qualifications: effective demand will not change in exact proportion to the quantity of money; resources are not (a) homogeneous, and (b) interchangeable, so that their supply elasticities vary; the money wage-unit will tend to rise before full employment; the remuneration of the factors entering into marginal cost will not all change in the same proportion. I cannot reproduce the discussion here. It contains references to bottlenecks, collective bargaining, boom and depression psychology, and other factors. One would need nothing more than this chapter to explain not only the kind of dilemma that confronts us today, but the inflationary conditions of 1936-7 on a comparatively low level of employment.[30] But so far as I can see, Keynes does nothing to resolve the dilemma, and this chapter has no place in either the logic of his theory or his policy prescription. It is on a par with similar qualifications of his fundamental equations in the *Treatise*, which he said did not 'affect in any way the rigor or validity of our conclusions.' [31] In distinguishing between what Keynes says and what his theory says, it is this kind of difference that seems to me significant. I can offer no explanation of it except that it is what equilibrium analysis seems to do to us. The key, I think, lies in what Keynes says

[29] *The General Theory*, pp. 295-6.

[30] One of the peculiarities of an inflationary volume of effective demand is, apparently, that the slope of the consumption function is no longer necessarily less than unity. For a discussion of this and other aspects of the behavior of the consumption function under war and postwar conditions, see R. V. Roosa, 'Use of the Consumption Function in Short Run Forecasting,' *Review of Economics and Statistics,* vol. xxx, May 1948.

[31] See Chap. 11 below, pp. 230-33.

about the rise of money wage rates before full employment (he might equally have said it of any of the other qualifications) : 'They have . . . a good deal of historical importance. But they do not readily lend themselves to theoretical generalizations.' [32]

VII

I am afraid I am outrunning the space assigned to me, but some other topics must be briefly mentioned. Keynes's claim to having put monetary analysis into real terms depends largely on his assumption of constant prices; price and wage changes would affect the consumption function, liquidity preference, and investment. He overstated his point (with which I have long sympathized) that the interest rate does not determine saving. He was wrong in saying that investment does not affect the interest rate but is only affected by it, though we had a striking demonstration during the war of how far an easy money policy can go in freezing the rate at a low level. His point that there is a minimum rate below which liquidity preference will not permit the rate to be driven is valid but needs elaboration. So far as the time risk is concerned, our experience with a frozen pattern of rates demonstrated that rates on long-term governments would fall progressively toward the shortest. But so far as the income risk is concerned, an easy money policy widens the gaps in the interest-rate structure and suggests the need of other methods of attack. An all-out easy money policy, such as some Keynesians have favored, designed to saturate liquidity preference, carries both short-run inflationary dangers (as we are now recognizing) and longer-run dangers of undermining the whole fabric of the private capitalistic economy.[33]

[32] *The General Theory*, p. 302.

[33] In my last talk with Keynes, a few months before his death, it was clear that he had got far away from his 'euthanasia of the rentier.' He complained that the easy money policy was being pushed too far, both in England and here, and emphasized interest as an element of income, and its basic importance in the structure and functioning of private capitalism. He was amused by my remark that it was time to write another book because the all-out easy money policy was being preached in his name, and replied that he did think he ought to keep one jump ahead.

How greatly Keynesian fiscal policy (and war finance) have complicated the problem of varying the interest rate as an instrument of cyclical control (because of the public debt), we are only now beginning to recognize fully.

For a discussion of these and other aspects of the interest-rate problem, see my paper, 'Implications of Fiscal Policy for Monetary Policy and the Banking

Keynes's emphasis on wages as income and on the downward rigidity of money wage rates and his insistence that unemployment could not be cured by a policy directed primarily at cutting wage rates are among his most important contributions from a practical standpoint, whatever their theoretical merits on some abstract level. But as related to monetary business-cycle analysis they have always seemed to me less novel than he supposed. Monetary policy had not run primarily in terms of wage cuts but in terms of compensating for wage and price rigidities. His conclusion, moreover, is subject to two large reservations: the effect of cost reduction on investment and its effect (which he recognized) on foreign trade. Moreover, from a purely economic standpoint, there is no reason why cost-reduction policies should not be combined with monetary policies of expansion, as Sweden and Australia did with notable success in the Great Depression.

One of the points most commonly agreed upon, even by Keynesians, is that the aggregates of the income equation must be broken down. A point that has especially interested me is the need of breaking down the saving function to differentiate between business and consumers' saving. I have never understood how Samuelson's findings could be offered in verification either of Keynes's propensity to consume or of Hansen's chapter to which they are appended. His analysis yielded the striking conclusion that consumers in the aggregate spent virtually all their increases in money income and that any additional saving accompanying rising income almost wholly took the form of business saving.[34] The implications of such a conclusion for economic policy are of course very great.

Finally, there is the now familiar point that the Keynesian saving-

----

System,' *Post-War Monetary Plans,* op. cit. Chap. 14; see also H. C. Wallich, 'The Changing Significance of the Interest Rate,' *American Economic Review,* December 1946.

[34] See Alvin H. Hansen, *Fiscal Policy and Business Cycles,* op. cit. Chap. 11, Appendix, pp. 250–60, by Paul A. Samuelson.

Samuelson's analysis is based on Kuznets' data (1919–35). For consumers he finds a marginal propensity to consume of 0.97, and for business enterprises a marginal propensity to save of 0.49. 'This [business saving] accounts for most of the leakages incident upon net investment: as far as these data go, the leakages incident upon household savings are much smaller and possibly negative' (p. 257). In his conclusion (p. 260) he again emphasizes 'the very sensitive relation of consumption to aggregate income payments.'

investment concept (like so much else in the analysis) has tended to submerge the study of the *process* of economic change. We have again, as in the *Treatise,* 'instantaneous pictures.' How saving and investment must always be equal in real terms, and yet how sometimes the equality denotes equilibrium and sometimes it does not, has caused endless confusion. We can make some headway by differentiating between a 'normal' income-saving relation and a process of adjustment to the normal relation. But Keynes does not discuss process, and 'normal' saving begs the questions I raised earlier. For a study of change the Swedish *ex ante, ex post,* or Robertson's time-period analysis seems much more realistic.[35]

VIII

As I look back over my paper, my appraisal of Keynesian economics seems to be mostly critical. The most difficult thing to appraise is one's own bias. No doubt my appraisal has in it some element of unfavorable reaction, both to Keynes's own showmanship and his tendency to oversimplify and overstate his case, and to the sheer mass and exuberance of the claims made by his followers in his behalf. I admit all this has been working on me for a long time. Economic instability is equaled only by the instability of economists; what we need most, and often seem to have little of, is perspective. While I have no fondness for prediction, I do believe that the wave of enthusiasm for the 'new economics' will, in the longer perspective, seem to us extravagant. And perhaps it will be only then that we shall be able to appraise objectively Keynes's contribution.

Beyond question it was very great. No one in our time has shaken up economists as much or been as influential in bringing economic analysis to bear on public policy. What he has given us, in particular, is a much stronger sense than we had before of the need for consumption analysis. It was the combination of the man and the times that did it. But I do have to insist again that it was policy, in Keynes's case, that led to theory, and that the weakness (as well as the strength of the impression made) lies in the overgeneralization. What we shall probably find ourselves doing is bringing back the things he temporarily submerged, the study of the processes of short- and long-run change, the emphasis on productivity, and on price-cost-profit relationships.

[35] See, among recent discussions of this point, David M. Wright, *The Economics of Disturbance,* New York, 1947, Chap. 2.

If the conditions to which his theory was mainly directed should re-appear, we shall probably find ourselves swept far beyond the kinds of remedies he favored, and forced into things he thought his theory and policies would avoid. But if we can maintain reasonable stability and, by the study of forces and relationships he largely ignored, continue to promote growth, his policies should play an effective role in a more rounded economic policy. I have sympathized all along with the idea of a cyclically unbalanced budget and with tax policies designed to promote stability and growth. But these, for Keynesians, at least before the war, were relatively mild objectives. Moreover, these are not exclusively Keynesian policies, but have been quite as popular with economists in Sweden, for example (where Keynesian economics has never really taken hold), as anywhere else.

What I find increasingly said, as the stagnation thesis recedes into the background, and the postwar questions about the consumption function, the price effects, and the like cast further doubts upon the theory as Keynes stated it, is that (and here the analogy with the quantity equation is striking) he has arranged the elements affecting the income equation in a useful form. This, I think, is true, with all the qualifications I have made. Undoubtedly, his formulation has greatly intensified the study of national income and its composition, though it is interesting that, as I indicated earlier, men like Kuznets and Colin Clark, who have pioneered such studies, dissented from his theory.

What it comes down to is that Keynes's analysis would appeal to me more if he had not claimed too much for it. As with his predecessors, it is the pretension to universality, and the equilibrium technique, that offend me, with the further point that in his case the defect seems to me worse. There is a legitimate and important role in economics for partial equilibrium analysis but the analogy with it of the Keynesian type of total equilibrium analysis seems to me most imperfect, be-cause in the nature of the case the 'other things equal' condition is invalid. Consumption, investment, total income interact, and they comprise all the 'other things.' Until, at least, the econometricians make more headway in deriving them (and their parts) from 'within the system,' this will be the nature of my skepticism.

Part II
Marshall Plan Papers

4

Economic Lessons of Two World Wars

THERE has been this year a growing sense of crisis in world affairs. In April the Moscow Conference ended in stalemate. In May, with the Truman Doctrine and the grants to Greece and Turkey, we took a stand against further Russian penetration in Europe, and presumably in Asia. On 5 June, Secretary Marshall's Cambridge speech, a month after Dean Acheson's Mississippi speech, revealed our Government's recognition of the increasing gravity of the European situation and the need for prompt co-ordinated action. The Secretary's speech was seized upon on both sides of the Atlantic and overnight became the Marshall Plan.

Since then events have moved swiftly. Sixteen European nations, on the invitation of England and France, have accepted Secretary Marshall's suggestion that Europe must study its own needs and present a program of self-help which would provide a basis for planning further American aid. Russia has further revealed her hand by rejecting the invitation and forcing her satellites to do likewise, though some of them clearly wanted to accept, and she has threatened the rest of Europe with dire though vague consequences for their acceptance.

The European Committee is to report in September. Congress will not reconvene until January. But in the meantime, as I write, three committees (one a nonpartisan, nongovernmental group under the chairmanship of Secretary Harriman) are analyzing the American aspects of the problem, our available resources, the impact of fur-

Foreign Affairs, October 1947; *Postwar Monetary Plans* (Knopf edition, 1947).

ther foreign aid upon our economy, and what our policies and actions should be.

With this time-schedule, American aid under the Marshall Plan cannot begin until next year, but since June it has become increasingly clear that the situation in some countries cannot wait. England and France have been rapidly running out of dollars. Our loan to Britain of 15 July 1946 ($3.75 billion) and the Canadian loan ($1.25 billion) had been designed to cover a five-year breathing spell in which Britain's trade position might be restored. According to the tentative time-schedule submitted by the British, it had been expected that the loans would be used up at a diminishing rate during the first three years, leaving two years more in which to develop a surplus in Britain's balance of payments before interest and loan repayments would begin. But by 1 August all but $1 billion of the American loan and half a billion of the Canadian loan had been used up, and the drawings on our loan in June and July alone had amounted to the astonishing total of $1 billion. It was this situation which, after a week of continuous Cabinet meetings, forced the British Government to bring in a drastic plan of self-help — involving the reimposition of wartime controls over labor and management and very substantial further reductions of imports and of government overseas expenditure — and to request a conference with our Government concerning the convertibility and nondiscrimination clauses of the Anglo-American Financial Agreement.

The position of the French international balance has been even more critical. Though since May 1946 France has received foreign loans and credits of $3.2 billion (of which nearly two-thirds was furnished by our Government) only $600 million remained unused at the end of July, and the prospective deficit by the end of the year, after allowing for exhaustion of the loans, mobilization of French-held foreign investments, and the restitution of gold by Germany, was estimated at $600 million.[1] Such a deficit would more than exhaust the French gold reserve, which now has shrunk from $3.2 billion in August 1939 to $540 million, in contrast with the British gold reserve which at $2.4 billion is somewhat higher than before the war.

Meanwhile in Germany, where Allied policy has never really got out from under the Morgenthau concept of the 'pastoral state,' pro-

[1] *The Economist,* 3 August 1947, p. 199.

duction is running at 35 to 40 per cent of the prewar level. There is recognition that this situation also cannot wait for the Marshall Plan. In July a new and much more liberal directive was given to General Clay supplanting J.C.S. Order 1067, which with amendments has been in effect in the American zone since April 1945; and a British-American conference in Washington was scheduled for mid-August on the vital question of expansion of coal output in the Ruhr, which has been only half of prewar.[2]

II

While the Marshall Plan is being worked out — and the steps are being taken that cannot wait — we must try to clarify our understanding of the problem and our part in it. American reactions have been varied and have, I think, shown some confusion and misunderstanding. It is certainly true that our aid already has been large, some $10 billion in loans and credits and $5 billion in outright gifts. Our postwar exports (in part financed by these means) have equaled, and this year even exceeded, those of the war period, when our exports were financed mainly by lend-lease. During the first half of this year the outflow was at an annual rate of about $20 billion (nearly 10 per cent of our gross national product), and the monthly surplus over imports was about $1 billion. Nothing like this has happened before in time of peace, though after the last war — for about a year and a half, when it ended in a serious slump — the outflow was relatively about as large.

One widely prevalent assumption seems to be that aid under the Marshall Plan will be put on top of these figures and will raise the level of exports and the export surplus to some higher magnitude. Can we stand the strain? Are we willing to? Will it involve a return to wartime controls? Would not undue strain on us react unfavorably upon Europe and make a bad situation worse? These are some of the questions that have been debated.

There has been some reference to the possibility of a 'new isolationism,' growing out of a feeling that the very magnitude of the undertaking proves its futility; it is useless to go on trying to hold up with American dollars a situation which grows largely out of

[2] On 9 August the United States proposed to France 'an early conference' to discuss French views on the American and British plans to raise the level of industry in their zones, and on the output and control of the Ruhr coal mines.

Europe's continuing failures to straighten out its own political and economic affairs; further help from us will only mean further delay in Europe's coming to grips with its own problems; and for this we are not willing to burden further the American taxpayer or to resume wartime controls. It will be hard to say how much of this kind of sentiment there is until Congress reconvenes, in a session in which tax reduction will undoubtedly be one of the chief political issues. But it is clear that a convincing program of European self-help will be an essential condition of further American aid.

One possible danger in inviting sixteen European countries to study their needs is that each may see its own needs more clearly than the problem as a whole, with the result that the program, if it is to satisfy all, may be larger than is warranted. There may be a similar danger in our own procedure of appointing committees to study our resources to see how much we can help. We take pride in doing things in a large way. Some of our official statements immediately following Secretary Marshall's speech seemed to carry an emphasis on bigness; and probably such an emphasis would not be unwelcome to many in Europe. There have been suggestions that the nation that could devise and carry out the lend-lease program ought not to balk at a large program of postwar aid; and in the House of Commons in July Mr. Morrison was reported to have suggested resumption of lend-lease to help solve Britain's problem.

With this emphasis on size in the interest of Europe has gone an emphasis (by some Europeans and by some at home) on the need of a large-scale program in our own interest. With our gigantic powers of production, the argument runs, we cannot, without such a program, make good our promises to sustain high employment at home. Mr. Bevin has been reported to this effect, and the Russians from the start have pictured the Marshall Plan as a capitalistic dodge to keep our own economy off the rocks. This line of suggestion fits well into the Marxian thesis that capitalism has an inherent tendency toward over-production and under-consumption. The fact that our large exports have been an important factor in our postwar boom — and were after the last war — appears to give the argument special point at present. The question whether this country, or any highly industrialized capitalistic economy, can sustain itself at high employment without special stimuli (large military expenditures, public works, an export surplus) was certainly one of the most debated be-

tween the two wars; but few economists believe that we can attain
a condition of stable equilibrium in the world (and much that happened in the interwar period bears on this) by using the outside
world for leverage to sustain American employment. To pose the
present European problem in these terms is to challenge us to turn
our back on it and find the answer to our own problem of employment some other way, as in the end we must.

But for the present, at any rate, this emphasis on our need to
export to support employment is mistaken. For a free economy we
are exporting too much rather than too little; and with the large
home demands still unsatisfied, American foreign aid financed by
the taxpayer diverts to foreigners goods and services, and the money
to buy them, which would otherwise be used at home. Taking home
and foreign demands together, our present danger is one of over-
utilization rather than under-utilization of American resources. Mr.
Hoover has been quite right in saying we must not overstrain our
own resources if we really want to help. Our exports have been one
important cause of the rise of our price-level — a rise since June 1946
unprecedented in any equal peacetime period. The price rise has
greatly increased the cost of European imports and has thus been
an important factor in the dollar shortage. The British have said it
has reduced the value of our loan to them by about $1 billion. Above
all, we must avoid this kind of vicious circle. But should we do so by
resuming rationing and price controls or by limiting our aid? And
might we not again, as in the war, meet the strain in part by increasing output further, if we organized expressly for the task? It is around
questions like these that much of the debate has revolved.

But there has been also a quite different approach. As against
the view that European recovery will require a further large-scale
program of American financial aid, it has been suggested that the
dollar shortage — which is a way of putting the need for further
American aid — has been much exaggerated. Official figures show
that the outside world's holdings of gold and dollar balances are
still about $18 billion, which is higher than before the war; and to
these have been added estimates of some $10 billion of American
loans and grants authorized but still unutilized. Such figures, though
not inaccurate, give a wrong impression. Of our own contributions
still unused, nearly two-thirds represent our share of the capital of
the International Bank (only a small fraction of which has been

called up) and our quota in the Monetary Fund. How much use can be made of these institutions in this situation is an important but a problematical question, and I shall discuss it later. Of the remainder, a number of items authorized do not bear on the situation in Western Europe. In very large part also, the gold and dollar balances do not bear directly on the problem. Some large part, particularly in a time of world-wide inflation like the present, must be held immobilized as monetary reserves. Much of the rest is financing abnormally large exports to parts of the world outside of Europe, a fact that points to the need of retaining our export controls — as Congress so wisely did toward the end of the last session — and relieving the strain on our own economy by external rationing. The gold and dollar balances of the liberated countries of Western Europe have shrunk from $5.4 billion just before the war to $2.5 billion in March 1947. The acute situation in France I have already described. England's gold reserves constitute her last line of defense; if sterling is to play its role as a world currency — and this has been an objective in our postwar planning quite as much as in Britain's — their draining away will need to be watched with very anxious care.

There may nevertheless be a tendency to exaggerate the magnitude of the problem. We seem to swing between extremes. Undoubtedly, as Secretary Marshall has said, European reconstruction is going to take longer and prove harder than had been assumed — though why we should have expected an early recovery is hard to say, since after the last war it took until 1925 for European production to get back to the prewar level, and the Second World War was much bigger than the first. But it is far from true that in the past two years European recovery has made no headway. In much of Europe there is nothing radically wrong that the solution of certain key problems and key situations would not cure. Production in the Scandinavian countries is close to or above the prewar level, though there are some balance-of-payments difficulties (notably in Sweden) which arise mainly from the disturbed conditions elsewhere. Belgium has made a brilliant recovery based in part upon a drastic anti-inflationary monetary program. Britain, though certainly one of the main sore spots, has pushed its production to 10 to 20 per cent beyond the 1938 level. Holland, which also quickly instituted a monetary reform, has now raised its production to nearly 90 per cent of prewar, and her main troubles stem (as do so many others) from the big hole in Germany, and also from the conditions in Indonesia. In France the recovery has been to about 90 per cent of prewar production, and in Italy to 68 per cent; in both cases the main trouble appears to be monetary inflation, and until that is cured the acute balance-of-payments difficulties are likely to remain. About the rest of Europe one cannot say much; we do not know much about what goes on behind the iron curtain. But our Government has stated that neither Poland nor Hungary is in need of further relief, and there have been reports of marked industrial progress in Poland and Czechoslovakia. In southeastern Europe the bad economic and political conditions go back far beyond the last war, and quite apart from any attitude we may have toward the Russian satellites they can hardly be regarded as an important part of the immediate problem (or at any rate a part we can do much about). For Greece and Turkey we have already a program of assistance under way.

III

This brief survey will have served its purpose if it brings out the need for breaking the problem down into its parts. What are the specific situations and conditions the correction of which would set a European recovery in motion? In its general nature the present problem is not new, and perhaps what we need most of all is historical perspective. What did we do, or fail to do, after the First World War from which, looking back, we might get some guidance? We should consider not only the immediate postwar period but the whole experience between the wars. What we do now will affect international relations and the structure of world organization for a long time to come.

The first war produced profound maladjustments in the internal economies of the European countries and in their balances of payment. The United States was converted from a borrowing to a lending country. Germany's international position, by the loss of foreign assets, trade, and shipping, was affected in the same kind of way as Britain's after this war. Most of the European countries had international deficits due to shortages of food, raw materials and other goods, internal inflation and the loss of foreign assets; there was the same kind of 'dollar shortage' as at present, though on a smaller scale. England did not have a deficit but did suffer a loss of foreign markets and investments that marked the first undermining of her international creditor position, now dramatically completed by the second war.[3]

We had no plans for the transition from war to peace, beyond loans for relief, sales on credit of surplus war stocks, and governmental and bank credits to finance exports; after 1920 our Government withdrew from the financing of external aid and left the field to private lending. We refused to join the League of Nations or to sign the Versailles Peace Treaty. International developments in the 'twenties were dominated by the controversies over German reparation payments owed to our Allies and the war debts owed by them to us, and by the closely related large-scale outflow of American private capital. I shall not try to tell in detail the story of the reparation payments, the 'final' London Settlement of 1921, which broke down within a year and was followed by the French invasion of the Ruhr, hyperinflation in Germany and other parts of Europe, and the complete destruction of the German currency; the Dawes Plan of 1924 and the Young Plan of 1929; the final breakdown in the great depression; or the parallel story of our refusal to recognize the interdependence of the war debts and reparations or accept a feasible settlement, and the final abandonment of the question in the great depression, though we have not yet canceled our claims.

Granting the impossibility of compressing a decade into a few pages, we can find three outstanding lessons in the 'twenties. (1) Though food was supplied by relief organizations in the immediate postwar period, no international plan was developed to provide other goods, particularly raw materials, essential for European reconstruction. The problem was not faced as an international issue until the Brussels Conference of October 1922, when the Ter Meulen Plan for raw material credits was presented but failed to materialize. Countries were left to obtain raw materials and other needed goods out of their own financial resources and with their inter-

---

[3] An important thesis, held especially by those who think a multilateral trade world no longer feasible, is that the change in the position of Britain, around which nineteenth-century world trade was organized, began well before the first war, and that the wars and the experiences in between have merely hastened it. There is, I think, much truth in this view, but I do not accept the conclusion that multilateral trade is no longer feasible. See *Post-War Monetary Plans,* op. cit. Chap. 5.

national positions already acutely in deficit. Our exports, initially very large, underwent a severe decline. Wartime controls in Europe, internal and external, broke down, prices rose violently, the foreign exchanges collapsed, tax receipts declined while expenditures increased, the deficits being covered by government demands upon the central banks until government credit collapsed, and monetary inflation undermined not only the power to produce but the social and political fabric of the Continent. (2) The reparation payments and the war debts, superimposed upon the already unbalanced international position, not only greatly intensified the external maladjustments and the internal inflation but for years kept international policy persistently pointed in the wrong direction. (3) The outflow of American capital served as the great counterweight; but I think it must be concluded, as we look back today, that though our capital exports alleviated, and on the surface in the last half of the decade even seemed to have cured, Europe's difficulties, in the end they intensified the maladjustments and contributed greatly to the severity of the world depression of the 'thirties. But this is a complex subject, and what to conclude for present policy is not an easy task.

As I have indicated, reconstruction in Europe came too late. It did not get under way until inflation had run its course. Though the first of the League loans, which did so much for the smaller countries of central and southeastern Europe, went into effect in Austria in October 1922, German reconstruction was not attempted until 1924 (the Dawes Plan), England resumed the gold standard in 1925, the French budget was balanced and the franc stabilized in 1926–8, and the Polish stabilization came in 1927. These were all parts of the attempt to restore the gold standard, which had broken down in the war, and with the controls removed had given way after the war to international currency chaos and internal inflation. Whether this attempt to reconstruct the world as it had been was foredoomed to failure because a world organization of the gold-standard, multilateral-trade type was no longer workable, or whether the new collapse was due to the specific errors committed — the long delay, the overvaluation involved in restoring the prewar pound (Keynes's 'Economic Consequences of Mr. Churchill'), the undervaluation of the franc, the inclusion of reparation payments in the Dawes Plan, American protectionism, and the Smoot-Hawley tariff

— has been the world's most debated economic question ever since. It provides the key to much of the discussion of Bretton Woods and the International Trade Organization and its Charter.

The 'twenties were the big decade of American private international investment. It was our first experience and we did it badly. The optimism engendered by our long period of prosperity from 1922 to 1929, the high interest rates obtainable, the easy task of salesmanship distorted our vision and put the emphasis on the apparent profits rather than on productivity. The eventual losses have been an almost insurmountable deterrent to further private foreign investment ever since. The conclusion, however, that our capital exports were mistaken is easier to reach now than it was then. The restoration of the gold standard and balanced budgets and the large rebound in European production and trade that accompanied them in the last half of the 'twenties — and it was in that period that our capital exports were really large — were conditions calculated to invite investment, which in turn further stimulated production and trade. Between 1925 and 1929 the world production of primary products rose by 11 per cent, industrial production by about 23 per cent and the volume of world trade by about 20 per cent.

It is the occurrence of the great depression that makes the record look so bad — and the human propensity to rationalize history after the event. The question really raised is what caused the great depression, how much was it due to domestic developments within the United States (where it began and was most severe), and how much to international maladjustments that had been staved off but in the end were intensified by an extravagant wave of American foreign investment. This is a question that will probably never be settled, though I lean to the view that the causes were more domestic than foreign. It was apparent, however, even in the 'twenties that our capital exports to Germany were unduly large and in considerable part misdirected. It has been estimated that between 1924 and 1930 Germany borrowed from abroad, mainly from this country, about 30 billion marks. With these loans she was able to make her reparation payments under the Dawes Plan and to rationalize her industries and increase her capacity to pay. There was a body of respectable economic opinion which held that this was a logical way of solving the reparations problem so far as the German end of it was concerned, though it still left unsettled the questions whether other countries were really willing to receive the payments, whether Germany could make net remittances after the capital inflow had diminished, and perhaps above all (and this is a question which has entered into the present postwar discussion of German reparations) whether the rest of the world wanted to see Germany's economic power developed by this process. Between 1924 and 1930, by the aid of these loans, Germany not only built up her industries and paid reparations but increased her gold reserves, built up foreign balances and investments of almost 10 billion marks and, in addition, enjoyed a large surplus of imports despite the fact that she was paying reparations both in money and in kind. She also indulged in many extravagant expenditures at home. As the American capital inflow continued, it became increasingly short-term (roughly half of the whole was short-term), and, when finally the storm broke over Europe in 1931, it was the flight of short-term capital, first from Austria, then from Germany, and finally from London that precipitated the new collapse of the gold standard, drew three-quarters of a billion dollars of gold from our market in the five weeks following England's going off gold in September,[4] and led to a wave of hoarding gold, internally and externally, round the world which did not end until our bank holiday of February 1933. This was followed by our own experiment of going off gold and devaluating the dollar — a chapter which did not end until the Gold Reserve Act of 30 January 1934.

The great dividing line of the interwar period is the year 1931. Thereafter, the world increasingly turned its back on the gold standard and multilateral trade. The 'thirties were a period of greatly restricted international trade and investment. Neither really recovered from the blow of the depression. But the flight of short-term capital to this country continued, accompanied by an absorption of the world's gold on a scale much exceeding even the flight of short-term capital and gold of the early 'twenties. The first Roosevelt Administration was intensely nationalistic, at least in its early years, and must take its very large share of the blame for the failure of the World Monetary Conference of 1933, which was the last attempt,

[4] See 'The Crisis of the Gold Standard,' in *Post-War Monetary Plans,* op. cit. Chap. 16.

before the present, to stabilize world conditions of currency and trade by organized international co-operation on multilateral trade and currency lines.

The broad fact about the 'thirties was the turning away from multilateral trade and the search for internal stability and security even at the expense of international trade. We watched it go through its various phases, the leaning toward autarky, the depreciation of currencies that ended only in a vicious circle, the spread of restrictive trade and currency devices — bilateral clearing agreements, quotas and other direct import controls, exchange controls. One of the large issues in economic thinking is whether the events and the policies of the 'thirties, including our own, were inevitable against the earlier background, and whether — looking not merely at the depression and what may have caused it but at the whole sweep of change in world organization and relationships which many, especially in Europe, trace back even beyond the First World War — the meaning is that the nineteenth-century kind of world has disappeared, and we have been making the mistake repeatedly of vainly trying to set it up again. It is clear that in the beginning the whole movement was involuntary and defensive; it grew perforce out of the contraction of trade in the depression, the panic flights of short-term capital and, as the Hitler menace grew and war approached, out of political insecurity. But deeper-seated forces have also been suggested, such as a growing lack of balance in the world between agriculture and industry and the cumulative advantage of the United States in world trade, based on our comparative self-sufficiency, rapid technological progress, and the strong foreign demand for our consumer durable goods and capital goods.[5] It is perhaps these broader consider-

[5] See my paper, 'International Trade with Planned Economies: The ITO Charter,' in *Post-War Monetary Plans,* op. cit. Chap. 5. The imbalance between agriculture and industry has been especially emphasized by some foreign economists. They trace it back before the first war and emphasize its impairment of the complementary character of world trade characteristic of the nineteenth-century expansive phase; the rate of growth of population in Europe was declining; European investment had resulted in more primary production abroad than Europe could absorb. The first war (like the second) greatly expanded non-European agricultural output, and when European agriculture was revived in the 'twenties (and protected) the terms of trade turned increasingly against the agricultural countries. See, for example, H. W. Arndt, 'The Economic Lessons of the Nineteen-Thirties,' Oxford University Press, New York, 1944 (issued under the auspices of the Royal Institute of International Affairs),

ations that have given currency to the phrase 'chronic dollar shortage.'

One final circumstance to be mentioned is Secretary Hull's attempt to combat the tide by his trade treaties. The restrictive trade and currency practices of the 'thirties were frankly discriminatory. They represented an attempt to balance accounts between individual countries, a method which obviously gives much freer play than multilateral trade for protecting the internal economy against external strains, and is the logical counterpart of the movement toward internal economic planning. The Reciprocal Trade Agreements Act of 1934 was an attempt at compromise along lines now being carried forward in the discussions of the International Trade Organization and its Charter. As a step toward restoring multilateral trade, it sanctioned bilateral trade agreements based on the principle of non-discrimination, which was a reassertion of the most-favored-nation principle that had previously characterized our tariff policy.

As we look back over the interwar period, it seems clear that the generalization often made that the wave of nationalism following the war wrecked the peace needs elaboration. The chief mistake, which certainly was nationalistic, was our refusal to join the League of Nations, which Wilson hoped would overcome the imperfections of the peace treaty. Much of the bargaining among the European countries at the peace table was nationalistic and paved the way for our isolationism. But the failure to organize the transition from war to a normal state of peace was probably largely due to ignorance. The world had never had such a war and was slow to appreciate what conversion to peace involved. The attempts to collect reparations and war debts were understandable, and perhaps we had to go through those experiences to find out their economic consequences. The attempt at reconstruction, though much too late and involving many mistakes, was nevertheless, in its broad outline, the kind of attempt that most of us, at least in this country, would want to make again. The depression presents the most difficulty; I can only repeat that I think it was primarily of American domestic origin, though with many complicating international circumstances. It brought

---

and Sir Hubert D. Henderson, 'The International Economic Problem,' *Stamp Memorial Lecture,* Oxford University Press, London, 1946. For an analysis of England's changing position, which suggests that she must turn increasingly inward, see Sir Henry Clay, 'Britain's Declining Role in World Trade,' *Foreign Affairs,* April 1946.

down the whole house of cards, and the possibility of its recurrence is probably today the chief holdback round the world against the kind of world economic organization we should like to re-create. The real period of nationalism, so far as trade and currency are concerned, was the 'thirties, and, looking to the longer future, it raises the hardest questions that our postwar planning has to face.

IV

Looking at our present problems in the light of this background, we can see that in various ways the postwar record has been better. We have joined, and helped to create, the United Nations. We have given much time and thought to the creation of international institutions — the Monetary Fund, the International Bank, the International Trade Organization and its Charter — which look toward the restoration of multilateral trade and currency arrangements and the reduction of the restrictive trade and currency practices of the 'thirties. We have made the loan to Britain. We helped to organize UNRRA and made the largest contribution to it. The Export-Import Bank has loaned extensively to meet the needs of other countries for raw materials and other American goods. Our Government has provided some $10 billion in loans and $5 billion in gifts, and there is a considerable further amount authorized but unutilized; this year's [1947] budget already provides for some $4.5 billion of foreign expenditures. In addition, we have been engaged in international exploration of many questions — food, the atomic bomb, and many others.

In a number of respects, the world has embarked upon postwar reconstruction under better conditions than last time. As a point of departure, the restrictive trade and currency devices of the 'thirties, which were much strengthened during the war, have been an advantage rather than an evil. We have not had the wildly fluctuating foreign exchange rates. Exchange controls, nonconvertibility of currencies, direct import controls have been retained for the transition period, though profoundly modified in the single case of Britain by the Anglo-American Financial Agreement. The lesson of the perverse and often destructive movements of capital in the interwar period — especially the short-term balances — has been learned, and the Fund Agreement provides for the permanent retention of exchange control over capital transactions.

There will be no problem this time of Allied war debts owed to this country. Lend-lease, it was always recognized, was a glamorous name for outright grants, and the accounts have been settled (except for Russia), though we might well have thrown in the amounts remaining after the war instead of converting them into loans. But in England's case there is an accumulation of some $14 billion of external debt; in magnitude it is fully comparable with the reparation payments or the inter-Allied debts last time, and may well give rise to problems not dissimilar. As to reparations, the attempt to collect them has not been given up but has taken a new form which may avoid the transfer difficulties but raise others not less serious. Before, the main danger was that to develop Germany's capacity to pay reparations out of current output would make her too strong; now the danger is that the collection of reparations out of Germany's physical capital will make her too weak for the economic good of the rest of Europe, her own population, and ourselves so long as we have to go on paying the bill by relief expenditures in Germany.

In some respects we have made the same mistakes as before. We have submerged the concrete in the abstract, the short-run in the long-run. We have thought too much in terms of broad (and even doctrinaire) principles and not enough about the kind of world to which they would apply. We have been preoccupied with organizational forms and procedures which could operate successfully only when more normal conditions have been achieved. We have, in other words, failed again to appreciate the difficulties of the transition period or to provide an adequate program for dealing with them. We have not thought enough in terms of the key situations or conditions the correction of which would go far to produce a general recovery.

So far as conditions in western Europe are concerned, the decisions about Germany must supply the largest part of the answer to what is wrong. It was probably a mistake to take up the minor peace settlements before the major one, but it would probably have taken time anyway — the experience with Russia as it has unfolded, and the mounting pressure upon Germany's neighbors which has been the consequence of the protracted economic stagnation in Germany — to bring the issues to a head. I cannot attempt to describe the nature or the causes of the stalemate,[6] the Russian insistence on

[6] For excellent accounts see Mr. Hoover's Report No. 3 to the President on his economic mission to Austria and Germany, *The New York Times,* 18 March

reparations before unification, the French insistence on a settlement of Germany's western border and on international economic administration of the Ruhr before unification, the lack of balance between industry and agriculture created by the loss of territory to Poland and Russia, the failure to achieve any kind of integrated economy (though there is now joint administration of the American and British military zones) which has probably done more to impede recovery thus far than the plant removals on reparations account, the very low 'level of industry' formula agreed upon in March 1946 in fulfillment of the Potsdam Agreement, and the part played in it by the Morgenthau conception of the 'pastoral state.' Still less can I undertake to outline a program of correction, but it is clear that the solution cannot wait for the Marshall Plan, and it is heartening that Anglo-American discussions (to be followed apparently by discussions with France) are under way on the problem of Ruhr coal. Coal and transport appear to be the key problems in western Europe; their solution would go far to hasten general recovery.

For the rest of Europe, we must await the plans of the Committee for European Economic Co-operation. But there is a strong presumption, I think, that if the German problem is wisely handled, they should not, in Europe's own interest, involve very large-scale American financial aid. France, as I have indicated, has an acute balance-of-payments problem, and further loans will probably be needed by Holland, Italy, Austria, and others. One important question is how much the International Bank can help, and whether the risks will be of a kind that the Bank can undertake. Another is how much other European countries better situated (notably Switzerland) can help. But the main point, I think — and this a lesson from the interwar period — is that the difficulties cannot be solved merely or mainly by American dollars.

A basic difficulty is the widespread inflation. It has taken this time a new form, which has gained the name 'suppressed inflation' in contrast to the open inflation that ran through Europe in the 'twenties. It is most marked in Germany and England, the French and Italian inflations being something between this new kind and the old. It is a deficiency of goods and a superfluity of money — as

---

1947; and E. S. Mason, 'Has Our Policy in Germany Failed?' *Foreign Affairs*, July 1946.

inflation always is—but operating under direct controls over prices and quantities, with the result that excess purchasing power continuously seeks to find an outlet, which in turn requires further extensions of controls. With prices held down, stocks of goods are in a state of acute depletion, and labor and buying power are drawn off into employments using less vitally necessary stocks of goods or none at all. The labor unions exploit the shortage of labor in essential industries to extort more pay for less work, and at the same time the premium on leisure is maximized because money wages buy less. Farmers have no incentive to bring their goods to market, and, as Secretary Marshall said, the town-and-country basis of a healthy economy disappears. This is a harder kind of inflation to deal with than the old one, which did at any rate burn itself out; it is likely to be more prolonged and much more dangerous to democratic institutions. It could lead to a kind of creeping stagnation with no outcome except a revolutionary change in economic and political forms. It greatly intensifies the balance-of-payments deficits by reducing goods available for export and creating an acute need for imports. This is a problem with which the European countries themselves must deal. One good first step would be to extinguish or immobilize the money 'overhang' in the way Belgium and Holland did, or by some plan like (though I hope simpler than) the Colm-Dodge-Goldsmith Plan drawn up by our experts for Germany.

One further comment should be made on the task of the European committee. A situation like the present creates great pressure toward the integration of Europe within the territorial limits which Russia's attitude imposes. There has been talk of the Marshall Plan versus the Molotov Plan. In view of the predominantly agricultural character of eastern Europe and the concentration of industries in the west it is difficult to believe that the economic relationships will not in the end prevail. As Mr. Stassen has urged, the door must be left open. I am skeptical of anything so formalized as a western European economic bloc or a customs union, though there is much that the western European countries can do to lessen trade barriers between them, better integrate their interchange of goods and services, improve transportation and the mobility of labor. If Europe could make itself self-sufficient in fuel alone, as it used to be, that would be a great step forward and would go far to improve the balance-of-payments difficulties.

V

As Germany is the key to recovery on the Continent, so England presents the central problem so far as the restoration of multilateral trade and currency arrangements is concerned. I have referred already to the revolutionary change in Britain's international position wrought by the war. It seemed to me clear long before the war ended what this change would mean for the problem of postwar reconstruction, and I sought in my earlier articles [7] to give it priority over Bretton Woods or any other postwar question. In my view, we lost two years between the time the Keynes and White Plans were announced in April 1943, and the time the Anglo-American loan negotiations were begun in the last half of 1945, that might better have been devoted to the exploration of the British problem. Before we got to it, both our own and the British experts working on the Monetary Fund had been led to minimize the importance of a separate handling of the British problem and much of the spirit of wartime co-operation had been lost. The solution arrived at was, in my opinion, inadequate for the problem. We should have made a gift rather than a loan — perhaps at an earlier date we could have agreed, as I suggested, upon an extension of lend-lease for this special purpose. But the thinking in both countries had been led into other channels.

I will not attempt in the brief space remaining to analyze the British loan negotiations. Our chief fault was not in the loan itself — though the repayment with interest on top of the liquidation of Britain's external war debt constitutes a problem of which I cannot see the outcome — but in the conditions attached to the loan. I suspect they were due not only to the fear of Congressional disapproval of anything that did not look like a good commercial bargain, but to the feeling that we had been too lax in our treatment of convertibility of currencies and exchange controls at Bretton Woods, and saw an opportunity to use our power to promote our traditional doctrine of nondiscrimination at the expense of a borrower who had no choice but to accept our terms.

The rationalizations of the Financial Agreement and the predictions about the British and American balances of payment by both the American and the British negotiators, including Lord Keynes

[7] *Post-War Monetary Plans,* op. cit. chaps. 6, 8–9.

in his posthumous paper,[8] were much too optimistic. In part the disappointing result has been due to the British fuel crisis last winter and to the rise in the American price level. But it was apparent last fall that the rise in British exports, which had been pronounced since the fall of 1945, was tapering off. In part, the difficulties are Britain's own, an outgrowth of the 'suppressed inflation' I have described. There is a question, too, how much the failure to live up to the anticipated schedule of reduction of the British deficit may have been due to the internal program of nationalization and economic planning. But that this was a major cause seems dubious, except for such things as the large-scale building program and the stimulation of consumption by the food subsidies, both of which any other government would probably have felt forced to undertake. The fact is that the situation that has developed is such as to require a changed attitude not only by the government but by the whole country toward its way of life — and this by a country that has not yet got out of the war, though it was on the winning side.

The main trouble is that the external pressures and obligations are too great, and it is not clear how they are to be brought within Britain's capacity to bear. The largest item, I think, is the overseas expenditure, which in 1946 accounted for three-fourths of the total international deficit of £400 million.[9] Britain has reached the point where her foreign commitments, military and financial — including her equal sharing with us of expenditures in Germany, the size of her armed forces abroad (and at home) and other expenses — must be sharply cut. When that has been done, the maintenance of the home economy, with whatever export-import relation that may entail, is unavoidably her own problem, though it will surely require a further loan to cover the transition period.

It seems certain that Britain will require a freer hand in governing her international trade and currency relations. This is the point of her request for a new discussion of the convertibility and non-discrimination clauses of the loan agreement. It is clear now that these clauses were premature. Convertibility of sterling is desirable as soon as it is feasible, if sterling is to play its role as a world cur-

[8] 'The Balance of Payments of the United States,' *Economic Journal,* June 1946.

[9] 'National Income and Expenditure of the United Kingdom, 1938 to 1946,' Cmd. 7099, April 1947.

rency; and nondiscrimination is the right ultimate objective if we are to succeed in restoring a multilateral system of world trade. But applied prematurely they defeat their purpose. So far as can now be estimated, the drawings on the British loan in recent months much exceed the requirements of Britain's own international deficit; and it seems evident that convertibility has become a means of funneling a considerable part of the world's demand for dollars through London.[10] Nondiscrimination under present circumstances may become a weapon throttling international trade: if countries cannot buy from us they may not be permitted to buy from each other even though they have the money or the goods to buy with. The British complain, too, that nondiscrimination works one-sidedly; we feel free to resort to 'tied loans' but object to 'tied trade,' the matching of exports and imports between pairs of countries; we discriminate also in favor of our shipping — an industry that on grounds of comparative cost might better be left to other countries.

VI

It was not my purpose in this paper to present an American program. I have tried to draw some lessons from the developments after the two wars that might help us chart our course. We shall need to provide further financial aid, and as much as the conditions warrant. But the conclusion as I have drawn it is that American dollars should not be the main reliance. The condition of 'world dollar shortage' is not at present a general condition but a special one in specific countries. It is a consequence of failure thus far to develop adequate production (and to restrict home buying power). Our function should be to assist and alleviate the process, but with assurance that our aid is to be co-ordinated with self-help in a way that will avoid its merely postponing the adjustments that only the European countries themselves can carry through. I doubt the need

[10] On 13 August a new drawing of $150 million on the loan was announced, and on 20 August a further drawing of $150 million, reducing the amount remaining to $700 million. On the latter date the American and British Governments, by the publication of an exchange of letters between the Chancellor of the Exchequer and the Secretary of the Treasury, announced the suspension of free convertibility of sterling into dollars. On 21 August Britain gave notice that it would draw $300 million more on 25 and 29 August to cover the import commitments already made and would temporarily freeze the remainder of the loan ($400 million).

of internal rationing or the feasibility of a return to price control, though I believed in 1946 that a flexible price control, such as many favored, would have been better than the more rigid system the Administration insisted upon, and much better than the virtually complete absence of control which in the past fifteen months has resulted in the great rise of prices that has increased the cost to Europe of our exports. We can help keep prices down by rationing exports to the countries that need them less and whose demand for them has been strengthened by their abnormally large gold and dollar holdings (the counterpart of our own domestic wartime savings). Throughout the whole experience since 1918 runs the lesson that we must concentrate on the key situations and conditions, correction of which would promote a general recovery and the kind of world trade organization we are seeking to restore. If we do this intelligently, I think our exports and our export surplus will be less in future than they have been the past two years, and will be more effective.

As I said earlier, much of our effort has been directed toward long-run objectives, toward the devising of international trade and currency organizations which can function effectively only after more normal conditions have been restored by other means. This is true of the Monetary Fund and of ITO. Only the International Bank can be regarded as properly having transitional as well as long-run uses. In my *Foreign Affairs* paper in October 1944, I urged that the Bank's purposes be broadened to include stabilization (or general reconstruction) loans in addition to the 'specific projects' that the Bank's articles of agreement emphasized. This purpose was included by Congress in our Bretton Woods Agreements Act and accepted by the Bank; it was the basis of the loan of $250 million to France last May. The Bank should be used to the maximum possible in this situation, and also the Export-Import Bank, which now has about $1 billion of free funds. Though it would undoubtedly strain the logic of the Fund, and the present restriction of its loans to 'seasonal and cyclical' purposes, we should explore thoroughly the possibilities of using it. Whatever may have been the intention when the Fund was set up, there is something incongruous in the spectacle of an institution which now has about $3.2 billion of gold and dollars merely standing by.

On our trade and currency policy, a number of true but familiar things might be said. As a creditor country we must be willing not only to invest abroad but to import the goods our capital creates. But this is for the future; foreign production is now so low, relative to foreign needs, that our imports are limited by scarcity rather than unwillingness to import. More relevant to present problems is our attitude toward the ITO Charter and related currency questions. These are matters calling for tolerance and wise understanding of other countries' difficulties. We face the task of creating a workable system of trade and currency in a very mixed world, a system acceptable to both free and planned economies. It will have to be an evolutionary process. We must start from where we are and not try to impose some system ready made. To the extent that we put pressure on other nations to give up their present arrangements before we are prepared to offer better ones, we are likely to increase the cost to ourselves of reconstruction. For the transition period, and perhaps some time thereafter, our attitude toward bilateral agreements and discriminatory practices will have to take account of circumstances. The question to be asked should be whether they are likely to encourage a growth of trade or the opposite, rather than whether they violate the pure principles we seek to promote.

Above everything, the world is looking to us to maintain stability at home at a high level of output and employment. As I said earlier, it was the great depression of the 'thirties that caused other countries to turn their backs on multilateral trade and seek security in protective trade and currency devices. It is the fear of recurrence of depression here that constitutes today their main reservation against our trade and currency plans. But we are far from agreed among ourselves as to how domestic stability can be maintained, and the most relevant and hopeful aspect of the matter is that, looking beyond the present inflation and its correction, we seem to have a good prospect of sustained high production and employment for some time ahead. In any event, it does seem clear that the greatest contribution we can make toward preserving our kind of economic system, here and elsewhere in the world, will be through the maintenance of a stable and prosperous economy at home, coupled with a liberal and constructive trade and investment policy abroad.

5

The Task of Economic Recovery

MUCH has happened since I wrote last fall in these pages.[1]
Then the European Recovery Program was in its initial exploratory
stage. Following the completion of the Paris report of the sixteen-
nation Committee of European Economic Co-operation, of the Harriman, Krug, and Nourse Committee reports here at home, President Truman submitted to Congress a program of European aid
from which, after extensive hearings, emerged the Economic Co-
operation Act of 1948 (Title I of the Foreign Assistance Act) signed
by the President on 4 April. Mr. Paul Hoffman was appointed the
American Administrator, and Mr. Averell Harriman, the American
Special Representative in Europe. The program got under way at
approximately the 1 April deadline that had been set, with no real
break after the Interim Aid program which Congress had passed in
the special session last December.

This is a record of bipartisan co-operation in foreign policy in
which we may well take satisfaction. It was entirely understandable
that the debate in Congress should center upon the amount of
aid and the method of administration. Between 1 July 1945, and 31
December 1947, we had made to the Western European countries
loans and grants of nearly $12 billion, of which about $10 billion had
already been used up. When, on top of this, the Paris Committee —
after substantially slashing its first draft in conference with Mr.
Clayton — presented in September an estimate of $19.6 billion for the
next four years, it intensified the discussion which had been going
on ever since Secretary Marshall's speech in June. There were sharp
differences of opinion as to how much more European aid our econ-

Foreign Affairs, July 1948; *Post-War Monetary Plans* (Blackwell edition,
1949).
[1] See Chap. 4 above.

omy could stand without bringing on an inflation here that would defeat the program; whether dollars really were the cure for Europe's ills; and how we could make sure they would be spent effectively to promote recovery rather than merely to postpone the corrective measures which only the European countries themselves could undertake. The Harriman Committee reduced the estimated four-year cost to the Treasury to an amount which ranged from $12.5 billion to $17.2 billion depending upon whether more or less favorable assumptions were adopted; and the President in his message to Congress of 19 December proposed a $17 billion four-year program.

But it was quickly recognized that any figures beyond the first year were highly conjectural, and the debate centered upon the initial amount to be appropriated. The President asked for $6.8 billion for fifteen months, and the only change made by Congress, in response to Senator Vandenberg's suggestion, was to reduce it to $5.3 billion for twelve months from 1 April 1948, thus giving Congress an opportunity to debate the matter anew early next year in the light of the first year's experience. Whether this is enough for the first year is of course a matter of conjecture. It can be affected either way by many circumstances. But it has, I think, been generally accepted both here and in Europe as an adequate indication of our serious intentions, and at the same time it is not so large, when spread out over the sixteen countries and Western Germany, as to remove desirable pressure upon our Administrator and upon the European countries for making sure the funds are spent effectively. One great merit of the Act is the large measure of discretion left to the American Administrator. We are embarked upon an unprecedented program, involving diverse and to a large extent unforeseeable conditions in different countries, in which wise management will count for much more than detailed legislation. Meanwhile, the 'watch-dog' committee set up by the Act will give Congress ample opportunity to keep in touch.

My chief concern, as I watched the Economic Co-operation Act take shape, was that in our absorption in the size of the appropriation and the form of the American administration, we appeared to have lost sight of what I had understood, after the Secretary's speech, to be the essence of the Marshall Plan — the need of an integrated program of European co-operation and self-help, upon which American aid was to be contingent. Our experience after both wars had been that piecemeal aid to individual countries is of doubtful effectiveness; and it was from this kind of procedure, as I understood, that we sought to get away.

The report of the Committee of European Economic Co-operation last September, made in response to the Secretary's request, was an impressive document, considering the short time in which it was prepared; but despite much excellent analysis and much emphasis on the need of European co-operation, what mainly emerged from it was the statement of the amount of aid required from us. This was understandable, since we had asked for such an estimate. The method adopted by the Committee in estimating the amount of aid was to aggregate the international deficits of the sixteen countries over a four-year period. Though everyone who has attempted to make such estimates knows how much guessing is involved, there is probably no other way to reach a first approximation. In arriving at its estimates, the Committee tried to take account of the nature of the European problem as a whole and how much intra-European co-operation could be expected, including such difficult questions as the recovery of Western Germany and its future role in the European economy. The danger, nevertheless, in this approach is that it tends to put American aid on a bilateral basis.

An integrated plan of European co-operation could not, of course, be worked out in a few weeks or months, and the Committee emphasized the desirability of establishing a continuing organization. But apart from setting up a few committees or study groups to work on special problems, such as the possibilities of intra-European multilateral monetary clearance and customs unions, the Committee seemed almost to have disappeared from September until March, and the only organization functioning effectively was the United Nations Economic Commission for Europe in Geneva. This Commission includes some of the Eastern European countries that rejected the Marshall Plan, as well as those in the west which accepted it. It would be interesting to know whether this apparent lapse was due to action or inaction on our part or on the part of the Western European countries.

But whatever may have been going on backstage to retard Western European co-operation in the winter months, two events in March and April went far to restore the emphasis of the original Marshall Plan. On 17 March — perhaps in response to Mr. Bevin's speech in

January calling for Western European union — Britain, France, Belgium, the Netherlands and Luxembourg signed in Brussels a fifty-year Treaty, which provides for joint military defense against aggression and for co-ordination of efforts 'to create in Western Europe a firm basis for European economic recovery.' The Treaty sets up a permanent Consultative Council of the five Powers, and provides that they 'may, by agreement, invite any other state to accede'; at the same time it leaves untouched their obligations under the United Nations Charter. The fact that concurrently with the signing of this Treaty President Truman called upon Congress for expansion of our defense program as well as for speedy passage of the Economic Co-operation Act should serve notice that, unlike the situation of 1914 and 1939, there can now be no lack of certainty as to the consequences of further aggression in Europe.

On 15 March, the Committee of European Economic Co-operation was reconvened in Paris. It began its meeting with the adoption of a report which made an unfavorable impression upon American observers and confirmed the view that not much had been accomplished since the September report. Its keynote appeared to be that not much could be done, even by way of preparation, until our aid was forthcoming. Of the ten 'measures of co-operation' cited in the report, seven were the work of the Economic Commission for Europe in Geneva, which had been set up, and its program laid out, by the United Nations, well before the sixteen countries had held their first meeting in Paris the preceding summer. In agriculture, the co-operation cited had been accomplished by the Food and Agriculture Organization of the United Nations; and on manpower problems, apart from an inconclusive conference in Rome, progress had been entirely due to bilateral negotiations quite outside the sixteen-nation Committee. Of the customs union projects cited, the Benelux program, which long antedates the Marshall Plan, was the only one that had been actually adopted. A mixed commission has reported favorably on the prospects for a French-Italian customs union. Græco-Turkish and Scandinavian unions are still in the discussion stage.

The only measure to which the Committee could point as its own work was the Inter-European Monetary Compensation Agreement, for the clearing of trade balances of ten participating countries, acting through the Bank for International Settlements as agent; and the results of the first three monthly compensation operations had been so meager that the Committee concluded that the agreement could not be 'fully efficacious so long as the monetary crisis in Europe persists.' My view is that only dollar reserves supplied for the purpose would make it work, and it seems clear from the first twelve months' allocations of American aid which have now been tentatively made by the Administrator that dollars for this project will not be supplied. This is one of the many difficult questions we shall have to face. Intra-European clearance, if it could be realized, would be an important step toward the breakdown of the network of bilateral trade and payment agreements in which the European economy is now entangled. But it may be that it will come most effectively at a later stage when more progress has been made in developing production and restoring monetary stability in the European countries. This need not mean, however, that there may not be at least partial alternatives, through the use, for example, as Belgium has suggested, of the local currency deposits which will arise from our grants, for the financing of intra-European trade.[2] Another possibility would be a loan from the International Bank to serve as a clearings reserve, which would be entirely in line with the stabilization — as against the 'specific projects' — conception of the Bank's function.[3]

But though the Paris Conference began lamely it ended most constructively. Spurred on, no doubt, by the Brussels Treaty and by the passage of our Economic Co-operation Act, it adopted on 16 April a Convention setting up a permanent Organization for European Economic Co-operation, including the sixteen countries and the western zones of Germany, with headquarters in Paris. The Convention provides for a Council under the chairmanship of Premier Spaak of Belgium; for an Executive Committee of seven members, under the chairmanship of Sir Edmund Hall-Patch of Britain; a permanent Secretariat, with the French economist, Robert Marjolin, as Secretary-General; and a number of technical committees. The role that this European organization will play, in co-operation with our Administrator and our Special Representative in Europe, may well be the decisive factor in determining whether we shall have a truly inte-

[2] Since this was written, it has been reported that a proposal of this nature has been tentatively agreed upon by the finance ministers of the five Powers of the Brussels pact.

[3] For discussion of this important distinction, see my *Post-War Monetary Plans*, op. cit. Chap. 5, pp. 95–6.

grated plan of European recovery, or merely a series of loans and grants to the individual countries, based on their external deficits.

II

From this brief survey of how the means and the machinery of the European Recovery Program have been provided we turn to the task itself. It is begun under better conditions than seemed probable a year ago. Some of the sense of impending crisis has passed. As regards our own economy, it now seems clear that the program will not produce such inflationary pressures as were feared. In magnitude it represents a continuation rather than an expansion of our earlier postwar aid to Europe. Pressure upon us of world demand as a whole has somewhat abated, and our export surplus this year promises to be considerably less than last. We appear now to have a better balance of inflationary and deflationary forces than at any time since the war ended. It seems not improbable that the great growth of our national product since 1939, combined with the pronounced rise of prices that followed the breakdown of OPA and continued with intermittent interruptions to the end of last year, may by now have caught up with the wartime expansion of our money supply; we perhaps have more to fear from specific pressures upon goods in short supply than from over-all inflation. But even in this respect our situation has improved. The break in the grain markets in January and February was in response to the changed statistical outlook in agriculture, both here and in the world at large. No other single change would do more to lessen inflationary pressures in Europe, both internally and externally, or provide more favorable conditions for the first year of the Recovery Program, than the agricultural improvement that seems in prospect.

Meanwhile, we must take account of the fact that some new inflationary threats have appeared at home. Not the least is the third round of wage increases whose outcome, as I write, is still unclear. In addition, we have had the tax reduction and the new program of rearmament. As regards the last, as the President's Council of Economic Advisers pointed out in its April report, there has now been enough abatement of demand, including foreign, to permit us to absorb safely some expansion of military expenditures. It seems clear, too, that such expenditures will come mainly next year rather than this. If, by then, the combined pressures of postwar demand for consumption and capital goods that have been taxing our economy to capacity have somewhat eased off, and if the foreign situation is not more acute in its political aspect and shows the economic improvement that seems now not unlikely, the general effect here may be one of sustained high activity rather than more inflation. All in all, it now seems probable that we shall have a better balanced situation than in previous years, and that our immediate problem will be mainly one of guarding against bottlenecks, as, for example, in steel, that might require some method of compulsory allocation.

In Europe, also, the situation is becoming clearer, and seems in many ways more encouraging than a year ago. The complete absorption of Czechoslovakia by the Russians was a severe blow to our hopes for east-west co-operation, but in France and Italy the Communists' bid for power has been withstood. On economic conditions, much the most illuminating and comprehensive survey that has yet appeared is that published by the Economic Commission for Europe on 30 March. It shows that by the end of last year, for a group of fifteen European countries including Western Germany, industrial production had recovered to about 90 per cent of the 1938 level, and, excluding Germany, to about 105 per cent. This is a much more rapid recovery than after World War I, when the prewar level of output was not reached until 1925. From this and other sources it seems clear that the only countries in Western Europe where production is still seriously lagging are Italy, Austria, and Germany; and it continues to be true, as I emphasized in my paper last fall, that Germany, where production is still less than 40 per cent of prewar, constitutes the most serious drag on recovery in Europe.

From this evidence of improvement in Europe two most interesting questions arise. How, in so short a time, and before the Marshall Plan had even gone into effect, could so pronounced a change for the better, as compared with last summer's sense of crisis, have come about? And why, if recovery has been so much more rapid than after the first war, is such a large-scale, four-year plan of American aid required? The answers to these questions go far to indicate the nature of the postwar problem. It is necessary to recall that the depression in this country in 1920–21 gave a severe setback to European recovery and that the failure to provide a governmental program of American aid halted the recovery abroad. Also, Europe's inability to finance her raw material and other capital requirements contributed heavily to depression here when our export surplus collapsed in the second half of 1920. The progress that has been made since 1945, with American aid less co-ordinated but quite as large as that now planned, provides grounds for hoping that our present program may succeed, but not for concluding that it is unnecessary.

Important aspects of the European recovery thus far have been its irregularity and its limited character. It was really pronounced only up to the end of 1946, and was achieved in part through the depletion of available domestic stocks; when these had been drawn down to abnormally low levels, the expansion came to a halt and in some cases was reversed. Last year was mainly one of recession and subsequent leveling off in production. Among the retarding factors were the severity of the winter of 1946–7, the summer drought, the resulting food crisis, and the fuel shortage. But even apart from these, as after the first war, the shortage of industrial raw materials needed from abroad severely limited the further expansion of output. Over the whole situation hung the interrelated maladies of domestic inflation and external deficits; and it was the dramatic deterioration in these two fundamental factors in the last half of 1947 — punctuated by such events as the British convertibility crisis and the astonishingly rapid melting away of our loan to Britain, and by the runaway rise of prices in France and the threatened exhaustion within a few months of French gold and dollar reserves — that most decisively indicated the need of a large-scale, long-range program of American aid integrated with European co-operation and self-help.

This year the reports from Europe have been much more favorable, and leave little doubt that the recovery has been resumed on a substantial scale. In the first quarter, production in Great Britain, Norway, and Denmark was some 20 per cent above prewar, and some 10 per cent above in France, Sweden, Belgium, and the Netherlands; all had reached levels considerably higher than in 1947; but apart from Ruhr coal, production in Germany, Italy, Austria, and Greece was still seriously lagging. Basic in the resumption of recovery has been the much improved availability of coal, which normally furnishes about four-fifths of Europe's fuel supply. American interim aid and the mild winter helped build up stocks. Polish coal exports have steadily expanded. In Britain, the efforts to speed up coal mining are now meeting with substantial success; it now seems probable that the target of 211 million tons for this year which Britain gave to the Paris Conference last summer will be more than reached; and British coal exports are again becoming an important factor. The one bright spot in Germany is the marked expansion of coal output in the Ruhr. Surely one of the most hopeful signs of recovery in Europe is the prospect that Europe will soon again be self-sufficient in coal. Along with this has come substantial improvement in the output of steel and of nitrogen fertilizers, badly needed for the rehabilitation of European agriculture. In Britain the yearly rate of steel production in April exceeded 15 million tons, an all-time record, while in France, where steel output had been seriously lagging, the level has now reached that of 1938. Other important indications of European recovery are the rapid restoration of the transport system, and the steps that have been recently taken to relieve labor shortages by the shifting of Italian workers to France and Belgium, and of some displaced persons from Germany to Britain.

III

These signs of progress in Europe, and quite possibly of a better balanced situation here at home, are most encouraging. They indicate that, with wise management, we may by 1952 have got a long way toward our goal. But it will help our perspective, and guard against undue expectations, if we examine more closely the nature of the goal and what its accomplishment involves. The external deficit is the crux of the European problem. To find a solution of it has been the main object of our efforts. As stated in the Economic Co-operation Act, the objective is 'the achievement by the countries of Europe of a healthy economy independent of extraordinary outside assistance.'

But the subject is complex and has given rise to a great disparity of views, among economists as well as laymen. As so often in economics, the differences may be mainly in emphasis, but it is just such differences that determine policy. Undoubtedly to some extent the deficits in the balances of payment of the European countries are a consequence of the internal inflation, which raises the cost of exports and attracts imports; and this condition points to the need for correcting the internal inflation as the cure for the external deficit. This is the basis of the view that 'dollars cannot save Europe,' but may only postpone corrective measures. A view allied to this is that the European currencies are overvalued and that the cure of the external deficit is to let them depreciate to the point where the external value of the currency is brought into line with the internal price inflation. Within this general framework there have been numerous analyses which attempt to show with more precision what the inflationary pressures are and how they might be cured. Obviously, when demand exceeds supply at the existing price level — and that is what inflation is — the reasons must be excessive expenditure for private consumption, or for capital goods, or for the needs of government; and it is just as obvious that such expenditures absorb resources that might otherwise produce exports, and (if foreign loans or gifts can be found to finance them) invite imports to fill the gap between home production and expenditure. It is thus literally true that reducing home demand relative to home supply would remove the external deficit.

But many such analyses seem to me little better than exercises in arithmetic. Familiar prescriptions advise tightening the consumers' belts and balancing the governments' budgets. Another which has come in for special emphasis during the past year has been to reduce capital expenditures. This is the thesis of Roy Harrod, the English economist, whose book *Are These Hardships Necessary?* has commanded wide attention and run rapidly through two editions.[4] His answer, quite simply, is no; Britain has only to reduce her capital expenditures to reduce her foreign deficit. His arithmetic is impeccable. But any other reduction of home expenditure would give the same result, and one is led back to the economic question of what can actually be done, and what it is advisable to do, in the given situation.

Interwoven with such analysis, and a great storm center of debate, is the question of methods — whether to return to a free-market economy, bring the inflation out into the open, and cure it by general monetary and fiscal measures, or to continue with the direct controls (a heritage of the war) that have resulted in the 'repressed' inflation which threatens to paralyze the whole economy. This is a most tangled subject, and it is often difficult to separate objective analysis from philosophical predilection. We saw, in all countries, that free-market methods are not workable in a war economy. It was a question of the magnitude of the changes involved and of the adaptability of the economy to such changes. This is still the question in Europe,

---

[4] Roy Forbes Harrod, *Are These Hardships Necessary?* Rupert, Hart-Davis, London, 1947.

but with the important added facts that, first, the will to submit to direct controls is weakened in peace, except in a police state where the individual will does not count, and second, that the production-consumption objectives are not nearly so concentrated and clean cut as in a war economy.

But it comes down to a choice of evils. Open inflation, too, can be a most destructive process, as we saw after the first war. Moreover, the European countries are by no means wholly free to choose, and what we find in practically all of them is some combination of free-market methods and direct controls. In all there is a tight control over the balance of payments and a network of bilateral trade agreements. Internally, Belgium and the Netherlands, and more recently France and Italy, have been working away from direct controls and relying increasingly — and with considerable success — upon monetary and fiscal controls, though one might question whether anti-inflation is not being somewhat overdone in Italy. But in England the response to last summer's crisis has been in both directions. This year's new budget calls for a substantial surplus, imports of consumption goods have been further curtailed, and capital expenditures reduced; but also further direct steps have been taken to control labor mobility, and to stabilize prices, costs, and profits. There is, of course, much complaint that the economy does not function well, but how much of the blame to assign to the severity of the problem and how much to the defectiveness of methods is the difficult question. As regards production, and the ratio of exports to total output, Britain's record after all is among the best in Europe. But so serious is the balance-of-payments problem that, despite the improvement in output, British reserves are still substantially and rapidly diminishing.

This brings me back to the external deficit. If Europe's problem were only that of repairing war damage and reconverting to peace, it would still call for some external aid during the transition period; and inflation, whether open or repressed, could best be fought by a combination of such aid, to help restore production, and of internal measures to restrain demand. There would, I think, be a strong presumption that in the course of the transition period — though not as rapidly as in the United States, because in Europe the scarcities were more acute and productive capacity much less — direct controls should give way to free-market processes. But this is not at all the correct picture. There is nothing in economic history comparable with the structural change that has occurred in Europe's international position.

The pattern of international trade that developed in the nineteenth century has been entirely altered. We saw this only gradually after the war, and the Marshall Plan is the product of our better insight; but we shall probably be long in realizing its full implications. I have in my own thinking dropped the distinction between 'transition' and 'normal.' It is now three years since the war ended; the Recovery Program is to cover another four, and no one knows what the structure or the condition of the world economy will be then, except that it will conform to nothing that we heretofore have known as normal.

Before the war, Europe had a deficit in trade with the western world but a surplus with the east. Within Europe, trade rested upon a triangular relationship in which Germany sold on balance to the other countries, while England was a net importer from the Continent. Throughout the world, trade rested on multilateral relations, in which sales on balance to Europe were the characteristic feature. Underneath such arrangements lay Europe's income from foreign investments built up over a long period, and from shipping and other services. This is the structure that has now been swept away. As given in the ECE report, Europe's income from investment and services has declined from $2.1 billion in 1938 to a deficit of $0.6 billion in 1947. The British *Economic Survey for* 1948 compares a net surplus of receipts from non-trade items of $928,000,-000 in 1938 with a net deficit of $904,000,000 in 1947. But even such figures do not give the full magnitude of the change. With Germany partitioned, the adverse foreign balance of the western zones, at a prewar living standard, would be not less than $2 billion. To cover this by any other method than American relief would require a corresponding expansion of their exports. And to this must be added substantial allowances for the disruption of east-west European trade, and for the pronounced lagging of intra-European trade generally, which is a point particularly stressed in the ECE report.

IV

This is not a picture which suggests an early or an easy remedy. Though European recovery thus far has been encouraging, production will have to be carried very much beyond any previous level to achieve 'a healthy economy independent of extraordinary outside assistance.' For the new international structure, prewar benchmarks have no meaning. In the background of the problem lies the fact that there was evidence before the war that the structure of trade was changing in ways now so dramatically brought into the light. I tried in my earlier paper to trace the course of change, the resulting contraction of trade, and the decay of multilateral trade. Deep-seated in the whole process has been the growing predominance of the United States, resting on cumulative advantages of size and technological progress, and expressing itself in the so-much-discussed chronic dollar shortage.

What ultimate answer there may be for this disequilibrium in which trade runs persistently in our favor and against Europe — a disequilibrium now so greatly intensified by the war — one cannot foresee, but two parts of an approach to the answer do seem clear. We must think of the objective of the Marshall Plan in terms of reshaping the European economy and adjusting it to its changed world position, and of making the necessary adjustments in our own. We must also regard it as the beginning rather than the end of the adjustment process.

It is not my purpose here to discuss in detail the policies or procedures of the Recovery Program. Perhaps at this stage, from the outside, one can do little more than prepare the ground for such discussion. But some points must be emphasized. One that I mentioned earlier is that the task is one of clear thinking and good management. Another is the importance of seeing the problem as a whole, and getting Europe itself so to regard it. The permanent Organization of European Economic Co-operation is a long step forward, though valuable time was lost. I have not been much impressed by the 'study groups' or the thinking about European co-operation in terms of customs unions or some of the other 'measures of co-operation' which hold out little hope of reasonably short-term results. As the Benelux experiment indicates, a customs union (or even a low-tariff union) is at best a long-drawn-out process of negotiation, which then leads on to questions of co-ordination of fiscal and monetary policies, and implies more yielding of sovereignty than countries will accept save by a slow process. Such studies should continue, of course, but they seem to me quite secondary to the central task of analyzing the European economy as a whole and accepting the responsibility, in the first instance, for an integrated plan that sees beyond the immediate national interests of its members.

The OEEC should be the counterpart in Europe of our own Economic Co-operation Administration, with the individual European countries working through it rather than directly with ourselves. One of its chief tasks should be co-operation with our Administrator, through our Special Representative in Europe, in making decisions about the uses of the foreign currency deposits which are to be set aside by the participating countries in amounts equivalent to the dollar costs of goods supplied as grants-in-aid. Since these grants will be much the larger part of our aid (though the ratio of grants to loans will vary from country to country), the uses made of them will be a major determinant of the success of the whole program. The problem is complex and delicate, and could easily be a chief source of friction and confusion both at home and abroad. We have wisely left almost complete discretion to the Administrator, beyond a general statement that the purposes should be to promote production and trade and correct inflation. But with conditions so different in the various countries, it will be difficult to say in advance what the operations should be or how they should be timed; and the placing of initial responsibility upon the OEEC should not only result in a better integrated program, but go far to meet the charge that we are interfering in the internal affairs of individual countries.

One other point that must be emphasized is that the Recovery Program is primarily a program of investment, even though this will involve food as well as raw material, equipment, or other kinds of capital goods. It may well be true, as the Harriman Committee indicated and as Mr. Harrod contends for England, that European capital expenditures have been excessive. But this is relative. It is important to distinguish between capital outlays that increase output and productivity and those for housing or general welfare that do not contribute so directly; and it is important also to distinguish between longer- and shorter-run investment, with a presumption in favor of the latter. But it defeats the whole program to lose sight of the fact that Europe's most essential need is for capital expenditure. This would be true even though the task were merely that of postwar rehabilitation following wartime under-investment. But the picture which I have tried to draw of the structural change in Europe's international position can point to no other conclusion than that the way out, if Europe is to become independent of 'extraordinary outside assistance,' must be through the development of her export capacity and of home production in place of imports.

Another major aspect of the problem is to revive intra-European trade, and to break down, so far as may be, the obstacles to east-west trade. It would be a shortsighted policy to co-operate with Russia by playing her own game. The best way to meet it is to promote Western European production to the point where Eastern Europe cannot afford to forego the advantages of trade. There have been some indications from Geneva that Russia is not wholly impervious to this kind of persuasion, and the continued existence of the Economic Commission for Europe might well be the vehicle for such developments. Given continuance of the recovery such as now seems in prospect and enough evidence of determination to stand together militarily and politically, Western Europe, with the aid of the Recovery Program, might produce a changed attitude toward east-west trade. In view of the predominantly agricultural character of Eastern Europe, the concentration of industries in the west, and the need for outlets for industries in the in-between countries like Czechoslovakia and Poland, it is difficult to believe that the economic relationships will not in the end prevail. At any rate, short of supplying war goods, the better policy is to keep the door open.

The lagging of trade among the Western European countries seems to me pre-eminently a problem for the Organization of European Economic Co-operation. As I suggested earlier, it is partly a question of financing and of developing a clearings mechanism. But it is partly also a question of trade negotiations, which might be worked out through the OEEC into something approaching multilateral trade, as part of a program of co-ordination made possible by American aid in expanding output. For the present, this seems to me a more promising approach than our actually financing an intra-European clearings mechanism.

V

As I said earlier, the Recovery Program must be regarded as the beginning rather than the end. A new pattern of international trade must be developed, and with it a much more complex body of principles and procedures than applied to the old one. Though Americans are thinking about Europe now, the internal stability and external relations of our own economy present questions no less difficult. The object of the present program is to reduce Europe's external deficit by 1952 to a level that will obviate the need for extraordinary outside assistance. But in the new pattern, world trade will require American foreign investment as the balancing agent and the means of growth almost as surely as the pattern of the nineteenth century was evolved through European foreign investment. This seems the basic aspect of the structural change in international relations which, starting perhaps before the first war, was brought into full effect by the second.

What is meant by the goal of the Marshall Plan, therefore, is that, as we hope, the formal machinery of American administration of aid, mainly in the form of grants, can be terminated. But it would be a mistake to assume that by 1952 the European problem will be solved, or that we can foresee now what the further processes of adjustment will be. So far, since the war, we have had a condition of sellers' markets, and while this has not been an unmixed blessing for Europe because of the effects of inflation on the terms of trade, it has meant that exports have been limited by capacity to produce much more than by competitive costs. But besides the great changes in the underlying structure of world trade, there have been changes in tastes, in growth of secondary production in newer countries, and in productivity; and when the present abnormal demands for goods have abated, these changes may well have an important effect upon the trade position of the European countries. The restoration of European equilibrium will have to be a process of increasing productivity through capital investment, and perhaps also in part a process of turning inward, with home trade growing in relation to foreign trade. Some European economists favor this latter as the ultimate solution; but it is difficult to see how populations so dense as those in Europe can subsist on a reasonable living standard by turning inward. A more likely course would be the development of colonial areas and other relatively undeveloped parts of the world; but this suggests a long process.

As the creditor country in whatever new trade pattern is to be evolved, we should be prepared not only to invest abroad after 1952 — though increasingly in the form of private investment — but to import the goods our capital creates. Unfortunately, this is more than a question of reorienting our commercial policy, difficult though that is. Much more deeply, it is a question of correcting the disequilibrium arising from our cumulative productivity advantage, combined with abnormally strong demand for our consumer durable goods and capital goods. International trade theory in the nineteenth century took no account of such chronic maladjustments. The answer to this problem — or to England's problem, now that her trade position built up through generations has turned against her — does not readily suggest itself. No less a question is the maintenance of economic stability at home. It was our great depression of the 'thirties that caused other countries to turn their backs on multilateral trade and seek security in protective trade and currency devices. A recurrence is what Russia hopes for, and the rest of the world fears. One can thus find plenty to temper undue optimism as regards the longer future. But for the present things are not going badly, and the outlook for the Marshall Plan seems much better than a year ago.

6

Europe after 1952
The Long-Term Recovery Problem

LAST July in these pages I discussed the task of European re-covery.[1] We were then in the initial stage. The Economic Co-operation Act had been passed at the beginning of April. The far-flung organization of ECA had been set up, with its central office in Washington under Mr. Hoffman, its Paris office under Mr. Harriman, and its American delegations in the individual European countries covered by the Marshall Plan. Sir Oliver Franks's European Committee (CEEC), which at Secretary Marshall's invitation had made the original survey of the problem in Paris in the summer of 1947, had been followed in April by the permanent Organization for European Economic Co-operation, consisting of a Secretariat under Robert Marjolin, an Executive Committee under the chairmanship of Sir Edmund Hall-Patch, and a Council headed by Premier Spaak of Belgium.

It was a strenuous period, with everything needing to be done at once — the recruiting of personnel, the finding of quarters, the setting up of administrative procedures, the determination and allotment of the amounts and kinds of aid and sources of supply, first for the spring quarter of 1948 and then for the first full year, July–June 1948-9. From the start it was recognized that means must be found to revive trade within Western Europe itself, which was seriously lagging behind the recovery both of European production and of trade with the outside world; and, as one main approach to this problem, the European and American organizations devoted about four months to the difficult task of working out the Agreement for Intra-European Payments and Compensations, which was adopted last October. By

Foreign Affairs, April 1949.
[1] See Chap. 5 above.

then it was time to prepare the program for the second year, 1949–50, for presentation to Congress in February.

All this, quite apart from the immense detail involved in the day-to-day administration, suggests a most busy calendar for the first year of the recovery program. Yet it leaves out the year's most significant development. The Marshall Plan had been conceived from the beginning as a long-term program, combining self-help and mutual help on the part of the European countries, with the provision of aid on our part, with the objective, as stated in our Act, of making Western Europe independent of 'extraordinary outside assistance' by 1 July 1952. Mr. Hoffman, therefore, in July of last year called upon the European Organization to produce a master four-year plan for reaching this objective. The OEEC Secretariat promptly sent out a questionnaire to the nineteen European participants with a request that they prepare their individual four-year plans. In November and December these plans were presented to the Executive Committee by each country in turn and subjected to discussion by the others. Meanwhile, the Secretariat and the Executive Committee undertook an over-all analysis of the plans, which was approved and published by the Council on 30 December in the form of an 'Interim Report on the European Recovery Program.'

II

This report has been hailed by *The Economist* as 'one of the great economic texts of our generation.' It is not a 'master plan,' but a further step in the analysis of the problem in the light of the composite picture which emerges from the nineteen individual plans. It was to be expected that, at least on paper, the individual countries, faced with their solemn undertaking under the Marshall Plan to achieve viability in four years with our aid, would find a way to do so. But it was to be expected also that the plans, prepared separately, would when put together reveal incompatibilities. One thing that the summing up brings out is that the countries in the aggregate were counting on an intra-European surplus to pay part of their dollar deficit, and when this manifest impossibility is allowed for, they come out with a dollar deficit of $1.3 billion, a sterling area (outside Europe) surplus of $700 million, an almost even balance with the rest of the world (a $200 million deficit), and a net dollar deficit of $800 million. But this the OEEC, after a most thorough analysis, finds much too optimistic; and it concludes that, unless 'drastic changes in present policies' are made, Western Europe will in 1952–3 fall short of covering its planned imports from the outside world by $3 billion. This means that as compared with the current year, July–June 1948–9, when the amount of aid being provided is $4.875 billion, we shall by June 1952 have gone considerably less than halfway toward our objective, unless 'drastic changes in policies' are made.

This conclusion, if accepted as valid, will come as a shock to the American people, who have been assured that the Marshall Plan is a program of aid to end aid. It should also shake whatever complacency there may have been in Europe. But the report, though realistic, is not defeatist. A joint recovery program, as it points out, must be prepared in three stages: first the individual plans, second their examination in the present report, to isolate the problems and clarify the issues; and third the 'plans of action,' which, in association with ECA, the European Organization now proposes to undertake 'to resolve the serious problems that have emerged.'

Thus far, though substantial progress has been made in expanding European production, and some countries, notably Britain, have made definite headway in closing the gap in their external balance, there has been little co-ordinated attack upon the problem as a whole. The emphasis in Europe has been mostly on self-help rather than on mutual help; and here at home, except perhaps in Point Four of the President's inaugural address, our thinking seems not to have got much beyond the providing of aid on an *ad hoc,* year-to-year basis.

III

The important question, of course, is how good a case the report makes out for its conclusion. In work of this sort the margins of error are inevitably large. The national programs vary widely in quality and contain various sorts of estimates, many of them merely forecasts in areas of economic activity in which governments exert little positive control. The general outcome in 1952 will be much affected by conditions in the outside world. It must be recognized, too, that the external balance is a net figure; even the OEEC estimated dollar deficit is only 12 per cent of the planned imports, and about 7 per cent of total foreign transactions, export and import; and a very small fraction indeed of total Western European production, which is estimated for 1952 at $170 to $180 billion.

On the other hand, the report itself, though decidedly more pessimistic than the individual plans, contains, as I shall indicate later, some estimates that might be considered optimistic. But perhaps the most significant fact is that all three surveys that we have had of this problem — the CEEC report of September 1947, the Harriman Committee appraisal of that report, and now this one — have come out with a substantial dollar deficit still remaining in 1952. One of the things that interest me most about the present report, as compared with the initial Paris report, is that while in the earlier years the deficits are this time smaller — the Paris report estimated a deficit in 1948 of over $8 billion against an actual deficit of about $5 billion, and a 1949 deficit of about $6 billion against perhaps $4.5 billion actually — the estimated deficits for the later years are in this new survey larger than in the old one. For some time it has been my view that such an outcome might well be expected, and that the problem might increasingly present itself as an approach to a plateau, which might be fairly quickly reached, but which once reached might prove difficult to get beyond.

IV

Granted that the estimated dollar deficit after the Marshall Plan has ended may be subject to a considerable margin of error, what we are mainly concerned with is the nature of the problem, and the reasons why, after this more intensive analysis, the OEEC is led to conclude that the gap will be serious. I would not myself hazard a guess as to what the deficit may be in 1952, but I am much impressed with the stubbornness of the problem, which is not merely whether the deficit can be wiped out in 1952, but whether means can be found to prevent its reappearing.

There have developed in the literature two schools of thought that are traceable as far back as the controversies over German reparations after World War I. They might be called the national income approach and the balance-of-payments (or, as we then called it, the transfer) approach to the problem. The difference lies mainly in the emphasis placed on internal and external aspects. The old problem was how to (a) produce within Germany and (b) transfer to other countries substantial yearly amounts of reparation payments. This time the question is how to expand Western Europe's production sufficiently beyond the prewar level to enable it to pay with current goods and services for imports which formerly were received in payment of 'invisible' income representing the earnings from foreign investments, built up over generations, and from services. Western Europe's invisible income before the war was roughly $2 billion a year, whereas in 1947 there was a net deficit on invisible account of about $750 million. The actual trade deficit in 1947 was, of course, much larger than this shift of $2.75 billion in the invisible account, the difference representing in large part the wartime destruction and disruption of production and trade. But the loss of invisible income is the hard core of the problem. To overcome it involves much more than simple recovery from war.

This brings us back to the question of relative emphasis on internal and external factors. By emphasizing the expansibility of production and making optimistic assumptions about the external trade and payment adjustments expected to follow, the attainment of Western European viability by 1952 can be made to appear less difficult than the OEEC report suggests. The national programs call for an expansion of 30 per cent beyond prewar in industrial production, and 15 per cent in agriculture, for a combined total of $170 to $180 billion by 1952. Though the report estimates that actual production may fall short of this goal by 4 to 8 per cent, or by as much as $15 billion, it would still seem that, unless the external aspects of the problem are very difficult indeed, such an expansion of production should be adequate to overcome Western Europe's dollar deficit. Moreover, the expansion that has already been achieved is impressive. For the full year of 1948, industrial production, excluding Western Germany, was 14 per cent beyond 1938, and including Western Germany, about equal to 1938; whereas after World War I, production did not recover to the prewar level until 1925. Even in Western Germany there has been marked improvement since the currency reform last June, though it is yet too soon to say whether inflation has been permanently halted.

This improvement in production is encouraging. But its implications for the future are subject to important qualifications. European recovery since the end of the war has been irregular. There was pronounced expansion up to the end of 1946, followed by a serious setback in 1947 because of bad harvests, the drawing down of domestic stocks in the preceding expansion, the fuel shortage, and the need of raw materials from abroad. Over the whole situation hung the interrelated maladies of domestic inflation and external deficits which led to such events as the British convertibility crisis and the astonishingly rapid melting away of our loan, and to a runaway rise of prices in France and the threatened exhaustion within a few months of French gold and dollar reserves. But by the last quarter of 1947, the recovery had been resumed, and the most significant fact about 1948 appears to be that the level of output, though much above 1947 as a whole, has revealed a sidewise tendency, not much above the level reached at the end of 1947. As stated in a recent United Nations report, 'in many branches of industry production seemed to have reached the limits of available capacity and manpower.' [2] Even in England, an approach to a plateau seems to be indicated in the figures of production (though not as yet in exports) since the last quarter of 1947. In Italy there is substantial unemployment, and even Belgium, which was a leader in the earlier recovery, has been recently encountering difficulties, with reports of unemployment in certain industries.

Another important qualification, of course, is that European progress thus far has been accompanied, practically throughout the postwar period, by substantial American aid and affords by itself little indication of what the level of production will turn out to be when the aid is cut off. This leads to the investment aspect of the problem. The Western European countries have been quite right in recognizing that it is only by increasing their productive capacity and their productivity through investment that they can hope to overcome their external deficit. With the level of consumption some 20 per cent below prewar, there is surely not much further room for belt-tightening. On the contrary, it seems clear, for political as well as economic reasons, that the scale of living must be raised, at the same time that exports must be expanded relative to imports. The European Recovery Program, if it is to be anything other than a subsidy indefinitely

[2] *Major Economic Changes in* 1948. Columbia University Press, New York, 1949. This statement relates to the first nine months of 1948. An ECA report received since the above was written ('Recovery Guides,' February 1949) indicates new peaks in both production and trade in the last quarter of 1948, combined output in the OEEC countries (including Western Germany) being '13 per cent above the last quarter of 1947, and 5 per cent above the 1938 level.'

continued, must be directed toward investment. But an investment program for Western Europe presents difficult questions of timing, composition, and size. Most of the countries have investment programs amounting to 20 per cent or more of gross national product, a ratio that is high even as compared with that of the United States in boom years. These plans will need to be examined carefully in relation to such factors as their possible inflationary effects, the level of consumption implied, the monetary, fiscal and direct control policies the programs will require, and the relation of investment to the changes in international trade and payments which constitute the goal of the Recovery Program.

In breaking down the aggregates, there should be a strong presumption in favor of shorter-run as against longer-run investment, and in favor of capital outlays that contribute directly to increased output and productivity as against (within the tolerable limits) those for housing and general welfare which contribute only indirectly. The most essential consideration is that the investment programs should be properly geared into the foreign trade and payment changes contemplated in the four-year programs. As they now stand, the national programs include much uneconomic duplication, and seem in considerable degree directed toward achieving national self-sufficiency rather than an integrated expansion of production and trade for Western Europe as a whole. The timing in some of them also seems badly conceived, since they attempt to crowd into four years plans for mechanization of agriculture, for example, which might require ten or fifteen years. There is excessive emphasis on oil and oil refining, for a continent that can be self-sufficient in coal, and should so far as possible make do with what it has when it is under the necessity of holding imports to the essential minimum. There is a very large emphasis on textiles, traditionally a major European export, but one that historically has proved particularly vulnerable as other parts of the world have become industrialized. One of the most significant announcements made by OEEC officials since the publication of the report is that they now propose to examine these investment programs intensively in consultation with the European governments in an effort to obtain this year a better balanced and coordinated program.

One of the chief difficulties thus far has been the effect of investment on inflation. Investment expenditures increase money incomes without producing, until some time later, goods on which the incomes can be spent. Unless, therefore, increased investment is accompanied by increased saving, prices rise, pressure for wage increases follows, and there ensues the familiar inflationary spiral; or if attempts are made to hold down prices and wage rates by direct controls, the excess purchasing power generated by investment expenditures presses into less essential employments requiring ever-widening circles of control. Investment has been a major dilemma for most European countries. They cannot achieve external viability without it, but if its effects are inflationary they defeat the purpose by stimulating imports, reducing exports, and diverting to home consumption production and expenditure needed to reduce the foreign deficit. The cure is to take off the excess purchasing power through monetary and fiscal restrictive measures (supplemented in varying degree in different countries by direct controls),[3] and so far as these are not fully effective to cut back the investment programs. Following the British convertibility crisis in 1947, Sir Stafford Cripps found it necessary to use all of these methods, though still leaving British investment at 20 per cent of gross national product; and the success of the anti-inflationary policies has undoubtedly had much to do with Britain's marked progress over the past year and a half in overcoming her external deficit. The Bizone currency reform, though the final outcome is still uncertain, is having similar effects. Belgium's method has been to follow up her early, and strikingly successful, currency reform with a policy of keeping the gap between money and goods filled with consumption goods produced for home and foreign markets. But this policy not only collides with the need of other countries to restrict consumption — the 'austerity' policy — but is definitely short-run since it threatens to leave Belgium behind in the race for productivity and productive expansion which the logic of Europe's position makes imperative.

The most stubborn case of inflation has been that of France. Traditionally, the French economy has been the best balanced, as between industry and agriculture, in Western Europe, and France has today less of a problem of structural change in her balance of payments than most of the other major countries. Yet she is now receiving, directly and indirectly, the largest amount of ECA aid — more than a quarter

[3] There is not room for discussion of general versus direct controls, or 'open' versus 'repressed' inflation; see pp. 98–100.

of the whole — and Britain, which has the most difficult international problem (unless it be the Bizone) and the one of greatest consequence for world trade equilibrium, is now in effect sharing in the provision (or more precisely in the direction) of that aid under the Intra-European Payments Agreement. The main road to viability for France is through correction of inflation, and the chief question to be asked of the French program is whether the corrective measures outlined will be adequate and will be feasible. Until an answer is given, inflation constitutes a threat not only to viability for France but to the success of the entire ECA program. While it lasts, French imports will remain abnormally high and exports abnormally low; the flight of capital, both externally and into hoarding at home, will continue; and France will threaten to divert increasingly to herself ECA aid which should go to others. The French inflation presents a many-sided problem. One thing, if the statistics are right, it seems not to be is a scarcity inflation, which is always more difficult to correct. The increase in production, and particularly in agriculture since the bad harvest of 1947, has apparently kept pace with that of other countries. But bank credit has been too readily available, including borrowing from the Bank of France; taxes have been too low and tax evasion widespread; capital flight indicates a fundamental lack of confidence in the currency and in stability of the Government. The problem is more political than economic, and a strong government might, as once before, work a miracle overnight. The worst feature has been the outrunning of wage rates by prices; this is definitely an inflation at the expense of the poor. The solution must be to bring prices down, rather than put wages up; and until that happens, France may continue to be fertile soil for Communist-inspired unrest. There may, however, now be grounds for hoping that the French inflation has passed its worst phase.

V

Until inflation is overcome, we cannot get the true measure of Western Europe's external problem. But the relation runs both ways, and in varying degrees the pressures imposed upon the countries by their international position are a cause as well as an effect of the internal inflation. Even where inflation has been arrested, the expansibility of production is dependent upon finding foreign outlets for goods and foreign sources of supply. In 1938 imports were 13 per cent of national income for France, 20 per cent for the United Kingdom, 29 per cent for the Benelux countries, and 32 per cent for Norway, as against less than 5 per cent for the United States. In 1952, according to the national plans, 80 to 90 per cent of exports to the outside world will consist of manufactured goods; and on the import side raw materials and fuel supplies will constitute 55 per cent, and food 38 per cent. One of the greatest difficulties for such countries is that the close interdependence of imports and exports imposes severe limitations upon the possibilities of reshaping the structure of trade, and hence the internal economy. It is from this point of view that the reducibility of Western Europe's dollar deficit presents its more stubborn aspect; and it is in this light that the loss of invisible income is most serious. In 1938, 65 per cent of Western Europe's imports were financed by exports to the outside world, 30 per cent by invisible earnings, and 5 per cent by reserves, borrowing and gifts; in 1947, these proportions had changed to exports 38 per cent and use of reserves, borrowing, and gifts 62 per cent, with a net deficit of 4.8 per cent in invisible earnings. According to the national plans for 1952–3, exports and invisible earnings are expected to expand to a point where they could pay for 94 per cent of the imports from the outside world.

How this is to be attempted, and with what prospects of success, is the central theme of the OEEC report. As I said earlier, some of the report's own assumptions may be optimistic. Though not without some questioning, it takes over from the individual reports a conversion of a deficit of $750 million on invisible account in 1947 into a net surplus of $1.3 billion in 1952. This is to consist wholly of income from services (with income from investment showing a net deficit of $200 million), which would mean more than doubling the income from services in 1938. Generous allowances are made for the growth of tourist expenditures, immigrants' remittances, shipping earnings, and 'other items' ($555 million), which appear principally to be earnings from oil properties and to derive mainly from the British plan. This expected change in the invisible account must be emphasized, because, though the figures are not large as related to total foreign trade, they are large in relation to the net dollar deficit. A change of $2 billion, such as is here indicated, is more than twice the size of the net dollar deficit shown in the individual plans, and two-thirds as large as the deficit estimated in the OEEC report. To the extent that the loss of the invisible earnings can be thus restored directly, the need of changing the structure and pattern of Western Europe's trade is reduced, quite out of proportion to the total magnitude of trade. This should surely be one main line of attack on Western Europe's problem; and it raises serious questions — for example, about shipping and oil — as to how American policies and actions are involved, in ways that go beyond merely charging the taxpayer for ECA dollars, if we really want to see a viable Europe.

But it is only after allowing for this favorable change in invisible income that the OEEC report makes its estimate of a net dollar deficit of $3 billion in 1952. This is based on an analysis of the trade changes envisaged in the individual plans. The focal points of the problem are the behavior over the next three years of the United States balance of payments in relation to that of Western Europe, and the behavior of both toward the outside world. These relations, together with any change in the proportions of intra- and extra-Western European trade, embrace all possible alternatives. As to intra-Western European trade, the plans reveal that the volume, which in 1947 was about 60 per cent of the 1938 level, is expected to recover by 1952–3 only to the 1938 level. This at first sight seems surprising. There is a presumption that an area which has lost its means of obtaining an excess of imports (the invisible income) from the outside world would feel compelled to provide a larger proportion of its needs from within. Yet the fact that thus far this trade has lagged so badly is perhaps the most striking proof that the loss of invisible income is the hard core of the European problem. Formerly the pattern of intra-European trade rested on a German export surplus to the others and a large surplus of imports (some half billion dollars) by Britain from the Continent; but this triangle rested in turn upon Western Europe's — and particularly Britain's — invisible income from overseas. With the loss of the latter, the whole internal structure has collapsed. Now Britain is a net exporter to the Continent — though only our ECA dollars makes this possible — and in her four-year plan she is counting on a moderate export surplus with Western Europe after 1952, while the plans of the other countries reveal that they are counting on getting back their export surplus with Britain, on about the prewar scale. Meanwhile, with the German economy so drastically altered by partition, and with a compelling urge throughout Western Europe toward austerity, which works heavily against luxury goods previously so important in intra-European trade, there are strong arguments for the view that Western Europe must be more, rather than less, dependent on its trade with the outside world than she was before the war. The figures, moreover, are large. To regain the 1938 level of intra-Western European imports by 1952 will mean that these imports must be increased by $3 billion, or about 50 per cent, over their level in 1947. No other trade change in a single area contemplated by the plans approaches this in size, excepting only the planned contraction of imports from the United States, which is the other main horn of the dilemma. Though there is not space for discussion, it seems clear that one thing badly needed for recovery of intra-Western European trade is revision of the Payments Plan, which as it now functions provides the wrong incentives. Bad performance by a country (in the sense of failing to expand exports to the other participants) is rewarded by that country's getting in effect a larger share of ECA dollars, through the operation of the scheme of 'drawing rights' and 'contributions,' and good performance is penalized. Perhaps the most feasible objective for the next few years with respect to intra-Western European trade, and the one promising the most expansion of trade, would be to aim at more balanced trade within the area, reducing the present substantial debtor-creditor positions.

VI

Though one of the main tasks for Europe this year, in appraising and co-ordinating its national programs, must be to see to what extent and in what ways intra-European trade can be developed, the solution of the dollar deficit problem must be mainly sought through expansion of Western Europe's exports to the outside world, and through a shift in the sources from which it draws its imports. The national programs call for imports from outside the area in 1952–3 about equal in volume to those in 1938, and very slightly larger than in 1947; but within this aggregate Britain is planning a drastic reduction, to 78 per cent of 1938 (she has got imports down already to about 82 per cent), and most of the others are planning increases — France 7 per cent beyond 1938, Western Germany 14 per cent, Italy 37 per cent. Granted that real income is higher in Britain than on the Continent, and that her ability to make direct controls effective is superior, it does seem questionable for the Continental countries to put the whole burden of achieving viability upon the expansibility of exports.

Britain began that way, but after the convertibility crisis of 1947 when our loan ran out, she had to tighten import controls further, cut consumption further, and supply a larger fraction of it out of home production. Britain is planning a 50 per cent expansion in agriculture over prewar, France 25 per cent, and the others, in the aggregate, no change. More food from within, less of nonessential or less essential imports (I have mentioned oil), in these and other ways there should be some room for reducing imports even though, as I said earlier, the scale of living on the Continent must be raised above its present dangerous level.

Yet the main solution must be sought through expanding exports and shifting the sources of imports. The national plans call for an expansion of exports to the world outside Western Europe by one-third beyond 1938. But in 1947 such exports were only about two-thirds of 1938, so that what is involved is virtually doubling the 1947 exports by 1952; this would be an increase of $5.1 billion over 1947, and $2.65 billion over 1938. In what markets could such a volume of goods be sold, and where, except here, could the necessary materials and food supplies be found? It is after asking these questions and examining the data and the conditions area by area throughout the world that the OEEC report concludes that the plans are unduly optimistic. It concludes that, unless the policies of the Western European countries are 'radically changed,' it is unlikely that total exports to the outside world will greatly exceed the 1938 level. The individual plans call for exports in 1952–3 of $10.6 billion; this the report reduces to $8.5 billion, which would be only 7 per cent above 1938 but 57 per cent above 1947.[4] A further very interesting conclusion is that even a 'radical change' in policies (what is meant I will consider later) would not, in OEEC's opinion, increase exports by more than $1 billion or $1.5 billion and would thus still leave a substantial dollar deficit in 1952.

It is the area analysis that is the high point of the OEEC report. The two chief questions are how to shift Western European imports away from the United States, and how to find markets for exports. Before the war, less than a third of Western Europe's imports came from North and Central America, as against about 60 per cent in 1947. Imports from the rest of the world in 1947 were down $3.6

[4] Thirty-seven per cent over the level planned in the 1948–9 program.

billion from 1938,[5] and those from North and Central America were up $3.2 billion. The national programs propose to swing the composition back to something like that of 1938, to cut the imports from North and Central America by nearly half, a cut of $3.5 billion, and make this up by expansion of imports from the rest of the world. To do this, and at the same time find markets for an increased volume of exports, the plans strike out boldly in every direction. By 1952, exports to North and Central America are to be increased by nearly half over 1938 (more than double 1947) and exports to South America almost doubled (165 per cent over 1947); exports to the sterling area are to be increased by two-thirds, exports from Eastern Europe are to be increased to 80 per cent of 1938 (almost treble the volume of 1947), and those to the Far East are to be expanded to beyond the prewar level.

The export targets to the areas outside North America constitute the main grounds for pessimism in the OEEC report. With the chaotic conditions in the Far East not much can be counted on there. About South America, the facts are that imports have expanded by 75 per cent over 1938, and will probably have to contract, now that the South American countries are running out of gold and dollars. Practically all of the increase in imports has been from us; to reach the export target set in the OEEC national plans ($1 billion over 1938, and $1.25 billion over 1947) would require a 'reduction of at least one-half in the United States market in South America in 1947.' Prospects for expansion of exports to the sterling area are not encouraging. This is the only area in which Western Europe's exports have already recovered to the prewar level; she has 70 per cent of the market there for manufactures. But South Africa is now in trouble, through the fall in the purchasing power of gold, and must restrict her imports. India has a program for industrialization, involving restriction of competing imports. Australia's and New Zealand's ability to import has been stimulated by high prices for their agricultural exports, but now the tide is turning. A further increase of a billion dollars, such as the plans call for, in Western Europe's exports to the sterling area by 1952 does not seem likely.

[5] The breakdown of the decline in 1947 compared with 1938 is: sterling area (outside Europe) $900 million, Eastern Europe $2.1 billion, other countries (China, Japan, parts of the Middle East, Spain) $700 million.

It may well be that the most promising area, apart from exports to us, is in the east-west European trade. Before the war, Western Europe's exports to Eastern Europe amounted to $2.5 billion. The collapse of this trade after the war represents one of the most damaging gaps in the whole trade structure. But, as I said in my paper last year, it may be fully as damaging to the east as to the west. Since then, there have been a number of signs that point in that direction. In 1948, there was a substantial revival of east-west trade. British trade, in particular, is now higher in money terms than in 1938, and about two-thirds of it in volume; and British determination to develop it further is evidenced by the recent Anglo-Polish five-year trade agreement. What is now mainly lacking to restore east-west trade to the prewar level is the participation of Western Germany and Russia, with the former — so far as the trade comparison with prewar is concerned — being much the more important. The Bizone four-year plan calls for a rise in exports to and imports from Eastern Europe of half a billion dollars each. Ambitious though this is for so short a period, it has a solid basis in the prewar exchange of German manufactures (including capital goods) against Eastern European food and raw materials; and it deserves the most careful consideration by the Economic Commission for Europe in Geneva, which includes representatives of both eastern and western countries. That Commission is now engaged, apparently with general consent, upon a systematic survey of export-import requirements by each group from the other. Such a study, if it results in action by the governments, could be an important supplement to the work of OEEC in Paris. The OEEC countries, according to the national programs, are planning to import $2.3 billion of goods from Eastern Europe in 1952-3 (17 per cent of their total imports) and to export $2 billion (19 per cent of their total exports). Next to the relations with ourselves, nothing would go farther to create a viable Europe than the success of these plans for east-west trade.

VII

The main problem, however, lies in the direct trade with us. Western Europe's exports to North and Central America in 1947 amounted to only $1 billion, against imports from this area of more than $7 billion. We provided 60 per cent of Western Europe's imports but took only 20 per cent of her exports. Her total imports were about equal in volume to those of 1938, but her total exports were only about two-thirds of 1938. These figures give the main explanation of the dollar deficit, and the magnitude of the problem involved in trying to remove it with our ECA program by 1952. If the program is to succeed, the imports from us will have to be cut back at least to the prewar volume, a cut of some $3.5 billion, or financed by some other means than ECA dollars. It would seem, too, that exports to us would have to increase by about as much, if the figures of the OEEC report are to be accepted. No other way of removing the $3 billion net deficit which the report estimates for 1952 is suggested by it; nor would any other alternative carry much conviction in the light of the analysis of the whole problem as I have reviewed it.

As between cutting imports from us and expanding exports to us, it seems correct to say that, if ECA aid is cut off in 1952, the former is more certain than the latter. It cannot of course be merely assumed that our export program will end, since it is the result of economic and political (and military) compulsions which may in some degree be continuing after 1952. It cannot be overlooked that the whole program is based on the conception of a tolerable living standard, which it is in our interest as well as Europe's to maintain. But it has up to now been our national intention, firmly and repeatedly expressed, to cut the program off on schedule; and I am merely indicating that if we do, there will be more certainty of our exports to Europe declining drastically than of Europe's exports to us rising in anything like the same volume. One is struck in reading the national plans, and even the OEEC report, by how little real confidence there seems to be in the expansibility of Europe's exports to this country. Though the national plans call for an expansion of exports of $5 billion between 1947 and 1952, which would mean doubling them, they expect to get only one billion of this increase in our market; and though the OEEC report writes down the other export targets, and quite rightly says that the large potential market is here, it does not hazard any figure beyond saying that 'if enough vigor is applied, the estimates might be exceeded.' Even the very decided improvement in Britain's trade position in the last eighteen months (which has led to Sir Stafford Cripps's recent statement that Britain is already almost viable, except that she cannot use her non-dollar surplus to cover her dollar deficit) has not included any substantial increase of exports to us. Our total imports in 1948 were about 50 per cent higher than in 1938 and appreciably higher than in the good year 1937. But imports from Western Europe have not recovered even to the low 1938 level, and the share of Western Europe in our imports has fallen from 23 per cent in 1937 to about 13 per cent in 1948.

This pronounced dragging of Europe's exports to us may be due to various causes. No doubt in part it indicates the need for greater initiative, more attention to trade organization and distribution, greater emphasis on the market research. It suggests, too, the desirability of examining our tariff, with specific reference to the Marshall Plan. Much has been said in recent years about how our tariff has been liberalized since the middle 'thirties, by the reciprocal trade agreements, the rise of prices which has reduced the burden of the specific duties, and the further steps we have taken in connection with the ITO negotiations. But I suspect that our tariff still accords effective protection in just the range of goods in which Western Europe might otherwise compete; and beyond the actual protection, there is the potential, which comes to view in discussions, for example, of the effects of Swiss competition on our watch industry, or of British competition on New England woolens. The British now speak hopefully of our market for their small cars, but two answers that I have had from persons in our automobile industry are: first, that the market is only temporary and reflects the scarcity of American new cars, and, second, that if, however, there is a market, we will go after it.

A much larger question is whether the dollar is not now undervalued in relation to European currencies. This would help to explain why Western Europe's exports have done so much better in the sterling area, and even in South America, than here. Undoubtedly the references in the OEEC report to the need for 'radical changes' in policy if Western European exports are to expand substantially mean precisely this; and this clearly is the meaning of the recent announcement by OEEC, since its report was published, that analysis of the problem of 'stabilization of currencies' will be one of the major matters on its agenda this year. So long as a condition of sellers' markets existed after the war, the European countries were more concerned with avoiding increased cost of imports — so much needed for recovery and reconstruction — than with stimulating exports, which in the world at large were mainly limited by short supply rather than by cost. But with the present indications of change toward buyers' markets the case for currency depreciation has become much stronger, though, if the experience after the first war is any guide, there is a presumption that internal inflation must first be brought under control. I agree with the conclusion, which one can readily read between the lines of the OEEC report, that there should now be a thorough examination covering the whole field of currency relations. This is a task for the International Monetary Fund as well as for the OEEC. It should include the whole question of discrimination, through direct balance-of-payments control as well as exchange-rate adjustments. This is too technical a subject for discussion here. One important aspect is whether it should be directed against the United States or in favor of Western Europe, which are not necessarily the same thing. One effect of the growing scarcity of dollars throughout the world is the incentive it provides for other nations to make reciprocal trade arrangements which bypass us. There have recently been reports, for example, of discrimination in Latin-American countries against our cars and certain other goods and in favor of British, and against American oil-refining equipment in favor of European, even though this may involve serious delay. Such arrangements we can of course deplore, in the name of multilateral trade, but so long as such a pronounced bias of world trade in our favor persists, we ought not to stand in the way of measures which may help to correct it.

VIII

In the background of the whole European trade problem, however, and much the most discouraging aspect of it, is the prewar trend. I have spoken of Western Europe's wartime loss of foreign assets and earnings as the core of her present difficulty. The war, however, merely hastened and completed the great change in regional relations which had been going on since well before the first war. The great expansion of world trade in the nineteenth century was based upon the exchange of Europe's manufactures for food and raw materials from the widening world outside; but since the 1870's, the world outside Europe has become increasingly industrialized. Between 1870 and 1913 world production of manufactures increased fourfold, and between 1913 and 1939 it doubled, but world trade in manufactures has been a decreasing fraction; in the 1870's, one-third entered into international trade, in 1913 one-fifth, in 1938 one-tenth.

Meanwhile, the United States, with its great land area, its diversified resources, its rapid technological progress, has developed a rounded economy, on a high level of productivity and real income, to a degree never previously witnessed. It now produces more than 40 per cent of the world's manufactures, but still relies predominantly on home supplies of food and raw materials. Over the last hundred years, its foreign trade has declined from about 10 per cent to less than 5 per cent of its national income, compared with percentages of 10 to 30 or higher for the Western European countries. Between the 1870's and the last war, imports of manufactures dropped from about 38 per cent of our imports to less than one-quarter, while manufactures grew from one-seventh to about one-half of our total exports. In the process, the United States has looked increasingly to the non-European world for imports, largely in direct exchange for exports, and the share of Europe in our trade has undergone a continuing decline. The effect of the war has been to accentuate this shift, with the result that since the war the United States has been getting not only the bulk of its food and raw material imports from outside Europe but also a substantially larger part than previously of its manufactured imports, while the proportion of manufactures to total imports has diminished further.

This is the much discussed 'chronic dollar shortage.' One kind of solution of it might be found in American self-sufficiency, which might suggest that, once Europe was restored with our aid, trade would thereafter develop between Europe and the other parts of the world, leaving us comparatively in a backwater, but one which we could endure more readily than others. But, for the short run, this seems most unlikely since it is just the ground I have been covering in the analysis above. And, in the longer run, it seems even more improbable since the tendency for three-quarters of a century has been just the opposite. We have increasingly become a better market for the products of the younger countries and in the process have tended to push European manufactures out of their markets as well as our own. What the historical development suggests is that it is Western Europe that is in danger of being left in the backwater.

Exchange-rate adjustments, coupled with direct foreign trade controls, and combined into a policy of discrimination aimed at us, may, together with the ECA program, supply a short-run answer for the problem of Western European viability. But what the longer run answer is to be does not readily suggest itself. Basically, the cure is productivity, and to this the ECA program must be directed, but it seems optimistic indeed to suppose that that kind of solution can be found in four years. Moreover, it must be borne in mind that the problem is one in comparative productivity. Our own economy cannot be expected to stand still, and there is much in the history of international trade to suggest that a productivity advantage, once achieved, is cumulative, and thrives even on the measures that, under static conditions, might be expected to offset it. Thus, in the nineteenth century, England's foreign investment increased her own productivity fully as much as that of the countries where her investments were made. Foreign investment is a dynamic process which operates on both ends. This has to be borne in mind when we speak, though still rather vaguely despite Mr. Truman's fourth point, about foreign investment and the export of know-how, as being the logical accompaniment or follow-up policy for the Marshall Plan. Its most likely direction would be to the less developed parts of the world, rather than to Western Europe, in search — on the nineteenth-century analogy — of raw materials. We speak hopefully, now, as a possible solution of the chronic dollar shortage, of our growing need for petroleum, copper, and other materials, though postwar growth of such imports has been, at least in part, the result of wartime shortages. Though for some products, such as rubber and silk, the war has probably reduced our dependence on imports, it does seem probable that in the longer run we shall become more dependent on other countries for raw materials, and that our trade will take on increasingly the character of European nineteenth-century trade, an exchange of manufactures for raw materials and even foods. But it is not clear that a flow of capital from us, fostering this process, would greatly benefit Europe, except as, in an expanding world, there might be some room for all to benefit. One holdback that European countries seem to have on direct American investment there is that, unless accompanied by substantial increases in productivity, it would further burden their external balance. The experiences of the interwar period with its problems of blocked currencies growing out of private investment have not been forgotten.

IX

In concluding this paper, I am only more impressed with the gravity of the problem. The OEEC report has prepared the ground for a more intensive discussion of issues and plans of action. It will involve the work of many minds and the weighing of many interests. The announcements by OEEC, since its report, show the direction of thinking in Europe. Besides currency readjustment and co-ordination of the investment programs — certainly two major facets of the problem — they have emphasized further exploration of the development of Western Europe's overseas territories, an important, but not I think a major short-run, factor, and perhaps somewhat on a par with our own thinking, still vague, about foreign investment as a follow-up on ECA. One suggestion, I think by us, which seems to me of major significance, is that OEEC should take the initial responsibility for the use of the counterpart funds in local currency, which the Western European countries must deposit in amounts equal to our ECA grants, with a view to achieving a better co-ordinated policy, as regards their relation both to inflation and to investment. Heretofore, these funds have been handled by our local ECA delegations directly with the individual governments. The most significant developments have been the appointment of a steering committee, or super-board, for OEEC, to be composed of representatives of cabinet rank, and the announcement that OEEC has formally decided to stay in existence after 1952. This, too, I believe, has been, at least in part, the result of ECA suggestion. Another development has been to 'extend the understanding of the European public' by authorizing Secretary-General Marjolin to give more frequent information to the press.

One of the basic questions, I believe, in attempts to co-ordinate European plans for investment and trade relates to the kind of production and trade that Europe should be trying to develop. Heretofore she has to a large extent specialized in the lighter manufactures and in fine quality products, and to the extent possible these should be continued. There could be much lost motion involved in throwing out of work crafts and skills acquired over generations, and this is often forgotten when we speak of ambitious plans of integrating Europe on the American pattern, industrially and agriculturally. But this war, like others previously, has given a fresh impetus to industrial development in other parts of the world, and typically it is the imports of lighter manufactures which are restricted by such countries in favor of imports of capital (and consumer durable) goods which they need for development (and greater satisfaction) but have no near-by prospect of producing for themselves. It is interesting that the Economic Commission for Europe in March 1948 emphasized capital goods exports, and in a subsequent report on east-west trade emphasized the need of the Eastern European countries for capital goods from the west.

Particularly important are the questions for ourselves. As I indicated earlier, about oil and shipping, there are questions involved in the Marshall Plan that go beyond merely charging the taxpayer. One of our chief dangers is the development of a vested interest (and quite possibly a serious economic dependence) in our exports. They have been so large and have gone on now for a decade. Large foreign sales of agricultural products, and of many industrial products, are obvious alternatives to reducing prices at home, and it is no secret that the jockeying for allotments in the annual ECA programs is by no means confined to the European recipient countries — or even to private business interests here. Such questions have an obvious political tinge. With the filling up of domestic deferred demands we can expect this kind of interest to increase, particularly if we should come to feel — what yet seems to me unwarranted — that we are sliding into depression. On the import side, it remains to be seen how much our traditional attitude toward commercial policy has changed, or rather whether it has changed enough. How, for example, will the American public react to the conclusion that, following our ECA contributions of, say, some $15 billion, which come after earlier substantial postwar grants and loans, an essential part of the solution of Europe's imbalance will be exchange-rate and other adjustments intended to discriminate against us, even though the 'discrimination' merely means putting us back in relation to others to where we were before, and is for the general good?

These are some of the questions which we should face, not in 1952, but now. Some others, such as the effects of the military expenditures that will be involved in the North Atlantic Pact, I feel quite incompetent to discuss, except to say the obvious — that they much increase the complexity of the problem. Sticking strictly to the ECA program, there is one aspect that permits me to end on a more cheerful note.

I have said little about conditions in particular countries; the effect of the Marshall Plan has been to make us think in terms of Western Europe as a whole. But earlier, I had in many of my papers attached special importance to the plight of Britain, as the key to the problem of restoring postwar international trade equilibrium. Up to a year and a half ago, Britain's position looked by all odds the blackest, excepting only Germany. Now the British are able to announce that they are approaching viability, though not in dollars. Their four-year plan carries conviction that it will succeed, thought quite probably, as some of the Continental countries insist, in part at their expense — in the same sense that our progress has been at Europe's expense. A correction of the French inflation would be another long step forward.

Having watched Britain's performance, I should like to believe other miracles are possible, including even Western Europe's achievement of viability. This will require hard work all round and an impelling sense of pressure. Until the full results of such a policy are seen, I think we would do well to stick firmly to our schedule. British advice, and I think OEEC advice, is to put zero aid opposite the date 1 July 1952, but with full realization of the 'radical changes' in policy which this implies.

7

The British Crisis
A Problem in Economic Statesmanship

FROM the beginning, European recovery has presented a mixed picture. Last year the main ground for encouragement was the marked expansion of production, and the main worry — so far as internal conditions were concerned — was inflation. This year production has expanded further, and the peak of postwar inflation has been passed. In France the change came with dramatic suddenness early in the year, and since then the evidence of further progress has been continuous. In Western Germany there had been fear that the marked change produced by the currency reform of June 1948 would be only temporary and that inflation would break out again. But this danger has not materialized, and one of the outstanding developments of 1949 has been the recovery of German production, which before the currency reform had been less than 50 per cent of prewar and is now rapidly approaching the prewar level.

There is thus continuing evidence of substantial progress. Yet probably at no time since the recovery program began has there been more disposition to question the outcome, or to insist that drastic changes in policies are essential for success. In an article in this review last spring, I referred to the two schools of thought which existed, one emphasizing the internal aspects of the problem, the other the external.[1] This debate still goes on.

According to the one view, now that production has been expanded and inflation corrected, we are much closer to achieving the internal conditions which will inevitably result in the disappearance of the external deficit. This view holds that if we have as yet made no great

Foreign Affairs, October 1949.
[1] See Chap. 6 above.

headway with regard to the deficit, it is because the processes of internal change have not gone far enough, and in particular because in England, despite Sir Stafford Cripps's severe budgetary changes of last year, disinflation is being frustrated by nationalization, increased social welfare expenditures, excessive taxation, the continuance of direct controls, and the unwillingness or inability of the Labour Government to apply the necessary pressures on labor and business to bring down export costs.

The other view accepts practically all of this reasoning but insists that the problem is more difficult than such an analysis implies. Western Europe has suffered a great structural change in its international position. The east-west wall, the partition of Germany, the chaotic conditions in the Far East have combined to increase very greatly its dependence on the dollar area. At the same time, the loss of income from overseas investment and from services has greatly impaired Western Europe's ability to meet its long-standing trade deficit with North America. Thus the prewar pattern of trade, both within Europe and between it and the outside world, has been destroyed. The most serious aspect of the problem is that it is not merely the result of changes in this war but the culmination of a process of change which goes back to before the First World War. The restoration of production and the correction of inflation, though essential first steps, are not enough to correct this structural maladjustment. The ultimate solution must lie somewhere between increased productivity on the one hand and decreased real income on the other; but many puzzling questions arise — both long-run and short-run in character — as to how best to seek a tolerable and sustainable equilibrium. It was on these grounds that I suggested that recovery might take the form of an approach to a plateau, which might be fairly quickly reached but difficult to get beyond; and it was on similar grounds that the OEEC Interim Report last December concluded that by 1952 the dollar deficit of Western Europe might still be some $3 billion unless 'drastic changes in policy' are made.

II

Certainly the disturbing developments this year have been with the external aspects of the problem. Of these, much the most serious for the outcome of the recovery program is the new British reserve crisis. Sir Stafford Cripps's announcement on 6 July revealed that

Britain's reserve had dropped by $260 million in the second quarter, and was almost $400 million under the $2 billion which she has regarded, since the convertibility crisis of 1947, as marking the danger point for her. The causes for the drop included a direct increase in Britain's own dollar gap, a loss of dollar earnings by the other members of the sterling area, and acceleration of the slow drain of gold to Belgium and Switzerland. The report by Cripps was followed by a meeting in London with Secretary Snyder and Finance Minister Abbott of Canada, and later by a meeting of Commonwealth finance ministers. The announcement that Britain would cut dollar imports by 25 per cent was followed by similar statements by other sterling area countries. But these are regarded as stop-gap measures. The whole problem is to be surveyed at a conference scheduled to open in Washington about the time these lines appear in print.

After the first war, Britain's policy was dominated by the fear of loss of reserves. The gold standard which she restored in 1924, following the period of currency disorder and inflation which engulfed Europe, broke down in 1931; and ever since it has been referred to as a 'strait jacket' to which she would never return. The devaluation of 1931, which she did her utmost to avoid, turned out most beneficially. Quite contrary to orthodox theory, it was followed by a fall of prices elsewhere rather than by a rise in British prices. This favorable turn in the terms of trade improved Britain's trade position and undoubtedly played a large role in the rise in productivity as well as output which she experienced in the 'thirties.

The external strains of the 'twenties, the ensuing great depression, and the release from both through the devaluation made a deep mark on British economic thinking. With the development of Keynesian 'closed economy' economics, primary emphasis was increasingly placed on internal full-employment policy, which was to be kept free from external interference by the use of exchange-rate adjustments. But the gains proved short-lived. The sterling devaluation was part of a chain reaction that included devaluation of the dollar in 1933–4 and did not end until there had been further devaluations of the French and Belgium francs (the process in the case of those two countries had begun a decade earlier). Indeed, there is no evidence that the vicious circle would have ended but for the war and the direct controls, both external and internal, that came with it. Meanwhile Britain and many other countries had in the later 'thirties turned increasingly toward bilateral trade and exchange controls as the effective methods of relieving external strains. Despite all her efforts, Britain was by 1938 compelled to liquidate a small portion of her overseas assets to bring her international account into balance.

It is against this background that British postwar experience must be reviewed. With the profound change in her external balance wrought by the war (hastening and completing a process long under way), British policy has again been dominated by the fear of loss of reserves, but under conditions even more desperate than before. At the same time there has persisted the desire for complete autonomy at home, in the interest now not merely of full employment, but of the realization of the social welfare state. British policy since the war has been a mixture of those two opposing aims. The British and we in America were alike slow to appreciate the external problem. One of my complaints during the Monetary Fund negotiations was that for two years, when we had the advantage of close wartime co-operation, they diverted attention from the rehabilitation of the British position [2] as the basic prerequisite for achieving world equilibrium and restoring the network of multilateral trade and payments. The abrupt termination of lend-lease after the war revealed the full gravity of the problem and precipitated the Anglo-American loan negotiation. The credit of $3.75 billion granted in July 1946 was intended to cover a five-year period during which Britain's external deficit could be overcome and a surplus created for interest and amortization payments; but within little more than a year virtually all of it had been used up. The loan melted away with astonishing rapidity after the pound, in accordance with the agreement, was made convertible in July 1947. This failure, together with rising inflation on the Continent and the growing threat of Communism, led to the Marshall Plan. And now again, in little more than a year after the Plan's adoption, we are confronted with a British crisis.

This, in broad outline, is how the average American taxpayer may now view the matter, not unfairly. But the picture when properly filled in is less black. Britain has in fact made great progress with her external deficit. Before this new crisis arose, she had reduced her

---

[2] Keynes's clearing union, of some $30 billion or more, was a heroic conception, which he doubtless hoped would serve all purposes. Though I thought it technically superior to the Fund, as a monetary mechanism, there was never a reasonable expectation that we would underwrite it.

imports to about 80 per cent of prewar and expanded her exports to 50 per cent more than prewar. At the end of last year, she was able to declare that she had achieved over-all viability in her international accounts, except that her surpluses elsewhere could not be used to cover her dollar deficit. Even when thus qualified, this is an astonishing performance. To appraise it objectively, we must take account of the inherent difficulty of manipulating the balance of payments of a country whose exports are so dependent on its needs for outside materials and food. This is the condition that confronts Western Europe generally, and the condition that in the 'twenties made the German reparations 'transfer problem,' as we then called it, so intractable. That Britain — in such circumstances, and in a world still in great disorder — should have been able to fill up the gap in her external balance caused by the loss of overseas assets and income which she had acquired over generations is an achievement greatly to her credit. This remains true whatever may remain to be said by way of qualification. Certainly it could not have been accomplished without the most severe austerity, quite unlike anything one finds in most parts of Western Europe.

III

Much was being said, however, even before this new crisis arose, by way of qualification and even disparagement, both here and on the Continent; and the crisis is bringing some fundamental issues to a head. When I visited Europe last fall, Britain was clearly the spearhead of the recovery, but her methods were regarded on the Continent (except in the Scandinavian countries) with suspicion and distaste. There were complaints that British austerity was depriving some of the Continental countries of their formerly rich English market for less essential goods. Underneath much of the criticism lay the ideological conflict between, on the one hand, direct controls and planning as practised by Britain and the Scandinavian countries, and, on the other, the policy followed by some of the Continental countries looking toward freer internal markets and reliance on general monetary and fiscal controls. In many quarters, too, as in the United States, there was hostility to Socialism and the welfare state. This year, with inflation passing, the Continent is presenting a more convincing picture of recovery. In some cases, there even is substantial improvement in foreign trade. As a result, as I found on my trip this summer, it is felt that earlier suspicions about British methods and British progress are being confirmed; and the animosity that was engendered over the payments agreement has done much to sharpen the criticism. There has been much the same kind of re-action in America, and much complaint that American dollars are going to underwrite British socialistic experiments rather than to close the dollar gap.

Britain's internal policies since the war have undergone many changes, and at times have called forth praise and at other times severe criticism from the British themselves. For a country in Britain's position, the decision to retain direct controls (certainly externally, and to a large extent internally) was unavoidable; and the debate on this score has been mainly over whether the internal decontrol, which has already been considerable, might not have gone faster than it has. I agreed with much of the criticism by British economists in 1947 about the repressed inflation and the 'empty economy' which was resulting from undue reliance on direct controls as against those of a monetary and fiscal nature. But the discussion seemed to pro-vide a more convincing proof of the need of more effective monetary and fiscal measures than it did of the possibility of dispensing with the direct controls. There is much truth in the view that it was when Cripps moved over from the Board of Trade to the Treasury, fol-lowing the convertibility crisis, that Britain really began to make headway with her external problem, and that the reason for this was largely his budgetary attack on the inflation. The change which he wrought in his 1948 budget from a deficit to a substantial surplus has had few parallels in postwar history.

Yet it is probably the budget, more than any other aspect of British internal policy, that is now being criticized, both within Britain and from outside; for it is here that the conflict between the social welfare state and the balance of payments comes most sharply into focus. There is little evidence as yet that nationalization in itself has been holding back production and productivity (though the steel industry might present a clearer case). But there is general complaint that the budget is too high, on both sides. One can question how much this is a matter of social philosophy and how much the effect of war, which in Britain was unusually destructive and severe. Doubtless it is made up of both. But the question arises of how much social wel-fare a country so beset from without can afford. The answer cannot be given merely by progressively more severe doses of austerity. This is negative, and if carried too far is self-defeating.[3] Despite some attempts to cut them back, British social expenditures — for housing, education, social security, health — have shown a strong upward trend. For a time it was possible to dissipate and disguise the effect of these by reducing military and overseas expenditures (partly at the expense of the United States). But if one counts in public investment, local and national, there is today a serious question how much budgetary surplus still remains. Meanwhile taxes, always essentially restrictive, have been raised so high, on both individual and business incomes, as to dry up saving and destroy incentives among workers, producers, and investors. This is a process by which any gains in productivity, whether resulting from Marshall Plan aid or otherwise, are put in constant danger of being swallowed up in expenditures that do not contribute to productive effort. How far this process has gone, I must leave to English economists better acquainted with the intricacies of the British budget and national income accounts to determine. It provides an interesting commentary on the wave of discussion that sprang up, both here and in Britain, some years ago of why a large budget was better than a small one, and how a budget could never be too large, since a government has no propensity to save. In postwar Britain, the excess saving thesis (part of the 'closed economy' analysis) must have increasingly a far-off sound.

Without doubt, another major British difficulty has been over-full employment. We suffered from it in America, too, before the present recession. In our kind of system, efficiency requires freedom of direction of resources, which in turn requires some slack. In a planned and controlled society this is regarded as waste. But the moot question is whether fuller employment, beyond some point, does not mean lower productivity and real income. Though full employment has become the declared objective of public policy in Britain, and also here and in some other countries, the economists have yet to produce a workable concept. Up to now, however, it is doubtful how much the over-full employment in Britain has been the result of conscious policy. Like the United States and much of the rest of the world, Britain has been in a boom; and the effects of it have been intensified there by the fact that, added to all the war-created shortages at home,

---

[3] This is just as true of internal austerity as Cripps has admitted that it is with respect to his new import cuts.

there has been the overriding pressure to equate the foreign balance. Even the Marshall Plan, in so far as it has led to over-ambitious investment programs to raise productivity in the future, may be lowering it in the present. This has been the nature of Britain's dilemma.

IV

The new crisis, as I have said, should bring these issues to a head. Whatever else the conference in Washington may produce, no program for stopping Britain's loss of reserves and correcting her dollar deficit will carry conviction unless the right foundation in British internal policy is laid. But to suppose that this alone could solve the external problem would be, I think, a profound oversimplification. We are brought back to the two schools of thought I mentioned earlier, and the relative importance of internal and external factors. The hard core of the problem is the conjuncture of a great structural change in the international position of Europe — particularly of Britain — and of a growing predominance in the world of a relatively self-contained, but highly unstable, United States.

This is not a new problem, though it has been greatly intensified by the war. It provides, I think, the main explanation of the decay of the multilateral trade and payments system during the interwar period. The difficulties it presents are both short-run and long-run. The long-run aspects I discussed in the article already cited, emphasizing particularly the secular tendency toward a widening gap in productivity as between this country and Europe.[4] But the present crisis is more immediately related to the short-run aspects. American booms and depressions have an intensified effect abroad. This explains the persistent attempts made by some countries in the course of the ITO discussions to get a guarantee of American stability as the price of their adherence to a multilateral system; and is a large part of the explanation of the numerous 'escape clauses' to which we were obliged

---

[4] There is not room in the present article for further discussion. The ECE's *Economic Survey of Europe in* 1948 (Geneva: 1949) has since made the same point. The problem, however, needs further statistical analysis. For a good beginning, see L. Rostás, *Comparative Productivity in British and American Industry,* National Institute of Economic and Social Research, Cambridge, England, 1949. Since the war, the gain in United States productivity has been slight; but it has always come irregularly, and the present depression will probably increase it substantially. After the depression of 1920–21, there was an advance of 10 per cent a year in American productivity for two successive years.

to consent before any agreement on the ITO charter could be reached. Our present depression is not large, by comparison with depressions of the past, and for us it will probably prove salutary. Yet — whatever the other considerations — it is certainly the main immediate cause of the present British crisis. It has depressed not only Britain's direct exports to us, but even more importantly the exports to us of primary products from the other sterling area countries the dollar earnings of which go to build up Britain's reserve. This in turn reacts on British exports to those countries; and it will be surprising if it does not also affect Continental exports round the whole circle.

The point to emphasize is that this is not a matter for mutual reproach, but a serious dilemma. As I have said, by past standards our depression has not been large, and it seems an unreasonable counsel of perfection to ask us to do a great deal better; but it does threaten to have large effects elsewhere. Perhaps the main hope lies in the prospect that it may have passed its worst phase, so far as inventory liquidation and the fall in the prices of primary products are concerned. If so, however, the problem will be postponed rather than solved. In a world of such unequal parts, the maintenance of a mutually advantageous balance is at best precarious, and one cannot dismiss, as merely wilful, attempts to avoid the effects of our instability through proposals for price stabilization of primary products (we have that problem at home), or even the making of bilateral trade bargains involving known quantities and prices. If multilateral trade is to be restored in such a world, it will have to be by some far more sophisticated, and much more gradual, process than we have been willing to contemplate.

Britain stands in a peculiar, indeed a unique, relation to this problem. Leaving the United States aside, she is still the greatest trading nation; it is her balance-of-payments position that has been most profoundly changed; and it is her trade relations and policies that have the greatest influence on the whole pattern and technique of trade and payment. Nothing better illustrates the complexities of the problem than the striking fact that Britain in recent years has been not only a leader in the development of bilateral trade, but also the chief organizer of multilateral trade and payment arrangements. Besides developing the sterling area, with a common reserve and the pooling of dollar earnings, she has also been steadily developing the system of sterling transferable accounts in Europe and other parts of the world. The fact that sterling was being widely used as a clearing currency was a major reason for the convertibility crisis of 1947; and even today, though sterling is not convertible into dollars, its use as a clearing currency is a major reason for Britain's precarious reserve position. This fact is the reason why this is a crisis for the sterling area rather than Britain alone. It is the reason also why Belgium, which was one of the chief sources of pressure on sterling in 1947, has ever since been a chief source of drain on British gold reserves. Though Britain's own trade with Belgium is roughly in balance, Belgium's trade with the sterling area, and particularly the fact that her Congo trade and earnings are paid via sterling,[5] have been causing a gold drain on Britain of more than $100 million a year — a fact which, of course, had much to do with Britain's attitude toward the revision of the intra-European payments plan.

V

One of the largest questions raised by the British crisis is whether a general reorientation of the recovery program is not now needed. The Marshall Plan has served admirably to restore Western European production to above its prewar level, and it has thereby been a potent force in overcoming inflation and warding off Communism. But we face now the even more difficult task of restoring equilibrium in trade. As the present crisis indicates, this is not merely a Western European problem but a world problem, with the question of an adjustment between the sterling area and the dollar area one of the most basic issues.

In Europe there is a growing disposition to ask whether the recovery program has not lost a sense of direction. The 'master plan' approach, the 'integration of Europe,' and even the lesser objective of mutual help through the co-ordination of investment have very markedly lost ground. The creation of the Consultative Group of Ministers and the eight-point program which resulted from it last March have not given the impetus intended. There is a feeling that, so far as the trade problem is concerned, we this year have been largely marking time; and perhaps nothing could prove it better than the inordinate amount of effort devoted to so minor a segment of the problem as the intra-European payments plan. There also is a disposition to question the effectiveness of the technique of the

[5] Belgium, unlike Britain, did not lose her foreign assets.

Marshall Plan for this second phase. It is a plan to provide goods, under American supervision and control, the allotments to be based on the dollar deficits. Many feel that for the task of trade adjustment this technique provides the wrong incentives, creating in the United States an interest in disposal of surpluses at the taxpayers' expense, and in Europe too much emphasis on investment programs (often insufficiently thought through) and too little emphasis on current production and costs. The effect, it is asserted, is to delay rather than hasten the closing of the dollar gap.

The program as now organized imposes a crushing burden of administration. The screening of the yearly programs of the nineteen recipient countries, first in Europe and then in Washington; the delays and uncertainties involved in our practice of first 'legislating' and then 'appropriating,' the time which officials must devote to expounding and defending the programs — all this means, almost inevitably, that more fundamental analysis and policy making regarding the ultimate goal get smothered by the sheer day-to-day burden of 'processing the dollars.' The preparation of the 1949–50 program began last October; the appropriation for it is, as I write, two months late; and not until the appropriation is made can the individual country allotments (and the drawing rights in the payments plan) be finally determined. In these circumstances, some critics feel that the programing and the screening can be little more than an elaborate pretense.

Interest is therefore shifting to the problems of the individual countries and to key situations. On the technical side, the thinking is more in terms of reserves, exchange rates, and trade policies than the programing of goods. And, as I have said, there is a shift in interest toward the trade problem in the world as a whole rather than the specific ECA program. Britain and the sterling area, and their relation to the dollar area, lie in the very center of the wider problem.

VI

The Washington conference can hardly be more than the beginning of an attack upon this wider problem. The dilemma posed by Britain and the sterling area is that of a world within a world — or, as it has come to be called, the problem of the two worlds. It is also called, by those who are hopeful that adjustment between the two areas will eventually be reached, the problem of the halfway house.

At the onset of the present crisis, both hopes and fears were expressed that the sterling area would collapse. Some Americans and Europeans have regarded the sterling area with suspicion, as Britain's attempt to develop, with ECA aid, a trading empire, behind a wall of discriminatory trade practices, wherein she and her group can live free from the pressures of American efficiency and low costs. We might not necessarily object (the argument continues) to this attempt by the British to create a higher-cost but more planned and secure world of their own, however distasteful it would be on ideological grounds, if we did not have to feed dollars into it continuously at our taxpayers' expense.

But this view is oversimplified and does much less than justice to the postwar achievement of Britain and the sterling area. Measured by the amount by which they have reduced their dollar deficit, their performance has been better than that of Western Europe as a whole. Measured by advances in productivity, or by the rise in export prices since before the war, their performance is also better. As to the suspicion that the ultimate objective is a world apart, our policy of course should always be to see that such an objective does not materialize, at least at our expense. But in my view there is little basis for the fear; and instead of indulging in it we would do better to study the circumstances that have governed Britain's policy and seek through co-operation with her and the other sterling countries to create the conditions which would help to make the two worlds one. The sterling area arrangement, if the gap between it and the dollar area can be bridged and a stable balance reached, offers the best prospect today of achieving a viable pattern of world trade to replace that shattered by the war.

Though Cripps has resolutely rejected it, devaluation of sterling is the most obvious and the most discussed manner of attacking the problem directly. The wave of talk about it last spring undoubtedly contributed to the loss of British reserves. Much could be accomplished without devaluation, and what it would itself accomplish is much more uncertain than a simple analysis in terms of purchasing power parities and comparative costs would suggest. One major argument against devaluation is the internal inflationary effect. In 1931 this danger was slight because Britain, like the world generally, was in a state of depression, with unemployed resources. This fact, combined with the circumstance that she was a large and then unrestricted import market, caused external prices to fall rather than British prices to rise as a result of the devaluation. But now both circumstances are reversed. Britain still suffers from over-full employment and low real income, and her imports are already so restricted that the possibility that she can again push the economic burden of sterling devaluation onto other countries seems remote. This means not only that the corrective effect of the devaluation on the external balance would have to come, this time, almost purely from the export side, but that much sterner measures would have to be taken to prevent the devaluation from being dissipated by an internal wage-price spiral.

Another danger (as we saw in the interwar period) is of setting off an external spiral in the form of a vicious circle of currency depreciations feeding on itself. There has been much interest in 'floating' rates of exchange. Before the war, I favored a high degree of autonomy and flexibility in the exchange rates of the smaller countries; and one of the most persistent criticisms of the International Monetary Fund has been that its articles of agreement unduly limit such flexibility. But I have long insisted that the case for the key currencies — the dollar and the pound — is different. They should remain firm, or subject to change only as a rare resort. Indeed, there never has been a good case for devaluing the dollar, and our devaluation of 1933–4 (and also our role in the Monetary Conference of 1933) has, in my view, been a major cause of the international trade disorders and the breakdown of the multilateral system. The difficulty with devaluing sterling now is that, despite the great body of literature on the subject, no one knows *how much* to devalue, or whether the new rate could be held. Another major difficulty is the uncertainty as to the effect of sterling devaluation on the other sterling area countries, which would undoubtedly follow Britain's lead. In the period between the wars we had much experience with the effect of currency devaluations on exports of primary products subject to inelastic demand; the increase in quantity exported may be more than offset, we found, by the fall in price. Britain benefited by this fact in 1931, and was able to stage a recovery — and temporarily an improvement of her international position — on cheap imports. But in the present case, with the dollar earnings of the sterling area pooled, the effect of devaluation might be to increase, rather than to relieve, the drain on British reserves. This could be an additional reason, along with the desire for protection against the effects of an American depression, for the British to advocate commodity stabilization agreements.

One badly needed adjustment in the British position, whether devaluation is to be undertaken or not, is an effective disposition of the wartime sterling balances. The disturbing effect of these was recognized during the Anglo-American loan negotiations, but no satisfactory solution of the problem was then found. They were a contributing factor in the convertibility crisis of 1947, and they have continued ever since to distort Britain's trade and threaten the stability of the pound. They explain the 'cheap sterling' rates which result from the willingness of some wartime creditors to dispose of their sterling balances through roundabout operations circumventing the British exchange controls. So long as these balances remain, they will be a persistent source of pressure on sterling, even if it is devalued; and they might well give rise to claims for repayment at the present rate, adding to the problem created by the fact that some $2.5 billion of sterling balances are already subject to a guaranteed rate.

But there is another, and even more important, aspect. Last year the repayment of sterling liabilities amounted to $844 million, a sum not much smaller than the net amount received by Britain from ECA. Such payments take the form of 'unrequited exports' which divert British resources needed to reduce the dollar deficit. Together with British capital exports to the sterling area, they explain the paradox of Britain's having become viable over-all by the end of last year, at the same time that she still had a large dollar deficit. They mean, in effect, that ECA aid is funneled through the British economy to outside recipients, and are an important part of the explanation why the expansion of British exports since the war has been so much toward the sterling area and so little, in comparison, toward the dollar area. If this abnormal basis of trading were removed, either British exports would be more nearly matched by imports from outside the dollar area, reducing her need to import from us, or resources would be released for expanding exports to the dollar area and exerting the necessary pressures to reduce costs and develop an effective trading organization for this purpose. In present circumstances, however, the pressures are in the opposite direction; and until these balances are disposed of in some way, and this cause for the distortion of the trade pattern removed, there can be no assurance that devaluation would be definitive, or that it would accomplish its purpose of correcting the dollar deficit.

VII

With these qualifications in mind, and laying a large emphasis on the correlative actions to which they point, I have been inclining to the view (as an increasing number of English economists seem to do) that sterling devaluation, at some stage, will be a necessary part of the process of adjusting the imbalance between the sterling and the dollar areas, and, rightly handled, could contribute importantly to all-round trade adjustment. It would probably lead the way to an all-round adjustment of exchange rates, and this might overcome, at least temporarily, the bias in world trade that expresses itself in the universal dollar shortage. The fact is that the dollar needs to be appreciated; and this seems the most practicable way of doing it. The best defense against another vicious circle of depreciations would be for the dollar this time to stand firm. And the best answer to the question of how to make a new sterling rate carry conviction of permanence would be for the United States to help support it. Indeed, it seems clear that if we advise devaluation we should take a definite obligation to co-operate in making it effective. This might well prove a reason why, in the end, both sides would wish to move slowly, and make sure that everything possible was being done on other lines; and that is, I think, the right approach. The need for American co-operation in making sterling devaluation a success leads to the thought, already referred to, that American aid in the form of reserves might now be more effective than the continuance of ECA aid in its present form. This suggestion would undoubtedly encounter the objection that it is a return to the technique which fared so badly in 1947. But the underlying conditions regarding production and inflation are now much more favorable, and the results might be much better.

American co-operation will also be required in other ways, with or without devaluation. Besides the commodity stabilization proposals already mentioned, there have been a number of other suggestions worth exploring. An immediately effective way to offset the effects of our depression on the primary products of the sterling area would be for us to stockpile them. Another suggestion, widely discussed in Europe, is an all-round increase in the price of gold. Doubling the price of gold would restore its prewar relationship to the price of other commodities and would stimulate gold production, which has fallen by 40 per cent since 1940. It also would greatly increase the size of existing gold reserves. Such a change in the price of gold, it is argued in Europe, might relieve the general dollar shortage by as much as $1 billion a year. Britain and the sterling area would particularly benefit. But such a proposal would undoubtedly encounter strong American resistance. To raise the price of gold would not be to correct the imbalance so much as to ease the effects of it temporarily; and from our standpoint it would be all too reminiscent of the gold inflows of the interwar period and their monetary and banking repercussions. Nevertheless, in times like these, even such a proposal deserves careful study.

But none of these measures — including even devaluation — gets at the real causes of imbalance. They lie deeper — in the impact of our economy on the world, our relative self-containment, our short-run instability, and our long-run tendency to outstrip others in productivity. According to historical precedent, the solution may ultimately be found in American capital export — and the export of technology and skill, in accordance with President Truman's 'Point Four' — not so much to Europe as to less-developed areas, which might then become better markets for European goods as well as ours. But this is more the task of a generation than of a four-year program. In the meantime, I think we shall have to accept some form of compromise between the multilaterally organized kind of world we formerly had, in which currencies were convertible, and the bilaterally organized and controlled system which has been threatening to supplant it. As the ITO negotiations indicated, this is a kind of pioneering into the unknown, making large demands for concessions and tolerance on both sides.

One kind of contribution we could make would be a candid exploration of our tariff and of our customs administration; these, I think, are still effective over the range of goods in which Britain and Western Europe might compete in our own market. Another is a relaxation of our attitude toward discrimination. Our doctrine of nondiscrimination, like the most-favored-nation principle from which it grew, has become more a device for retaining our advantages in trade than for restoring balanced trade. The OEEC Council has recently adopted a proposal, introduced by the British, for placing as much intra-European trade as possible on the basis of open general licenses. This seems a more effective approach toward getting better balanced and freer trade in Western Europe than is offered by the intra-European payments plan. Ironically, however, it must first be cleared with the United States, since it violates the nondiscrimination clause of the Anglo-American loan agreement.

There is, finally, as we all of course recognize, the difficult problem of stabilizing our own American economy. All countries which are heavily dependent on foreign trade find external strains a chief handicap in maintaining stability at home. Though we are much less affected in this respect than most, we are never wholly exempt from the urge to keep out imports or to expand exports in order to preserve domestic equilibrium at a high rate of employment. If we really want to achieve a world balance by some other means than the expenditure of our taxpayers' money, we have a special responsibility to strive to preserve stability at home in ways that help rather than hinder the attainment of a functioning world economy.

8

The Marshall Plan Halfway

We are now close to the halfway mark of the Marshall Plan. Last year, though the yearly program of aid was submitted to Congress in February, the process of first 'legislating' and then 'appropriating' for it was not completed until October, some three months after the program's fiscal year began. This year, this process has begun in an atmosphere of 'disappointment,' to cite Mr. Hoffman's phrase widely echoed in our press, over Western Europe's failure to make a stronger response to ECA's request, presented to the OEEC Council last 31 October, for a program of 'integration' to solve the dollar deficit and make Western Europe independent of 'extraordinary outside assistance' by 1 July 1952.

Adequate perspective is more than ever necessary. We may be in danger of swinging from undue optimism to undue pessimism, and in the latter mood of insisting on unduly simplified solutions. The year 1948, the first year of the Recovery Program, was marked by a spectacular rebound from the chaotic conditions of 1947 which had prompted Secretary Marshall's Cambridge speech that launched the program. This rebound was widely heralded in this country as evidence of the program's success. It should be remembered that it was the European Organization, in its first Interim Report, that first officially called attention to the fact that the recovery in 1948 merely brought us to the hard core of the problem of the dollar deficit. The Report predicted that, unless 'drastic changes in policy' were made, Western Europe's dollar deficit would still be some $3 billion in 1952.

The first effects of the Report were excellent. The rather shallow optimism that had prevailed, in Western Europe as well as here, disappeared. The Report called for a Plan of Action. On 17 February

Foreign Affairs, April 1950. The manuscript had to be cut by about one-fourth, and I am here presenting the complete paper.

1949, the OEEC Council adopted a set of principles which were made the basis of a plan of action, announced on 8 March by the newly created Consultative Group of Ministers. This seemed a brave start, but as the year wore on there was a growing impression of a lack of sense of direction. One reason for the change was undoubtedly the prolonged negotiation over the revision of the European Payments Agreement, which revealed difficulties and differences of a kind that are now coming forward again in connection with the proposed European Payments Union. These I shall discuss in a later section. Another was the British reserve crisis and the general setback to exports, not only from Britain and the sterling area but from Western Europe, that accompanied it. A third reason was the growing feeling that the Consultative Group of Ministers was not providing the vigorous leadership that had been hoped for from it; and along with this, there developed doubts about the adequacy of the plan of action. It was against this background that Mr. Hoffman, on 31 October, made his request to the OEEC Council that it should present a record of progress thus far made and a program of integration which might carry conviction to Congress in its consideration this year of the future of the Marshall Plan. Mr. Hoffman asked also for the appointment of a strong political leader, or 'co-ordinator,' who could resolve differences and expedite the program.

II

The response made to Mr. Hoffman's request is the OEEC's Second Report, adopted by the Council on 31 January, after meetings in Paris of the Consultative Group of Ministers with Mr. Hoffman, Mr. Harriman, and their chief aides.

The new report is in many ways encouraging. Despite the setback to trade last year, mainly in response to our recession, it seems now clearer than a year ago that what one might call the inherent logic of the Recovery Program is finding expression in the character and the time order of events. ECA aid, combined with Western Europe's own efforts, has greatly stimulated industrial production and has also, though to a much less degree, raised the level of real income. At present, even including Western Germany which had been lagging badly prior to the currency reform of June 1948, industrial production is 15 per cent above the level of 1938, and excluding Western Germany, about 30 per cent. This represents a doubling of industrial production since the low point of the postwar period and contrasts most favorably with the experience after the First World War, when the prewar level was not regained until 1925. This expansive effect of the program on production was the main fact apparent a year ago. There were understandable grounds for fear that this progress might not be continued, or only at a much slower rate, after the initial rebound. But this fear has not materialized, and the record of continuing progress in production in 1949 is impressive and reassuring.

The most encouraging development in 1949 was the passing of the peak of inflation. A strong drive for internal financial stability had been the first point on the March 1949 Plan of Action. While inflation persisted the effects of external aid were in constant danger of being dissipated by rising prices — or under conditions of 'repressed' inflation of being drawn off into less essential production — with the result that imports would be encouraged and exports discouraged, thus defeating the Recovery Program. Basically, the conquest of inflation has been made possible by the expansion of production and the removal of scarcities, in which the Recovery Program has played a major role, and by the adoption of the restrictive fiscal and monetary policies, which the rise of production has made possible.

How effective the attainment of internal financial stability has been, not only in promoting a further expansion in production and real income but also in reducing the external deficit, can be illustrated from the experiences of many of the participating countries, including the early monetary reform in Belgium, the British budget of 1948, the Italian deflationary measures, the German monetary reform of June 1948, and the passing of the peak of inflation in France in the early part of 1949. In each case, there was an improvement not only internally but in the foreign trade position. One of the most striking cases is that of France, which had previously had a deficit with almost every country, and had been regarded as one of the major obstacles to European recovery. But in the past year, since inflation has been halted, France has doubled her exports to the sterling area, increased her total exports by 80 per cent, and is now approaching over-all viability.

To this encouraging record, however, some qualification must be made. There is still no firm assurance that the battle against inflation has been permanently won. Britain's experience in 1949, and her announced program of further budgetary cuts, provides one illustration; and the relation of wage policy to political changes in France provides another. The wave of devaluations of currencies following the devaluation of sterling is requiring renewed vigilance in every country to safeguard against the external effects being dissipated by renewed inflation.

III

Two other points in the Plan of Action of March 1949 dealt with investment and the co-ordination of investment. The Recovery Program must be viewed primarily as a program of investment. Under the formula of 'self-help, mutual help, and external aid,' it was designed to support not only investment programs in the individual countries but also an integration of these programs that would ensure against tendencies toward autarky in the individual countries and would promote a well-balanced expansion of production and consumption and a rise of productivity in Western Europe as a whole.

The experience of the past two years has shown that the problem is beset with many difficulties. One of these has been the danger of overemphasis upon investment as against current output. The recognition of the great gap to be bridged between European and American productivity has had the effect, in itself understandable and even laudable, of inducing most of the participating countries to plan ambitious investment programs involving severe sacrifice of current consumption to future output and productivity. These programs have in many cases exceeded, as a percentage of gross national product, investment during boom years in the United States, where, owing to the much higher level of real income, a large volume of investment is much more tolerable. It must be recognized, also, that the technique of the Marshall Plan itself, directed as it is toward the programing of aid with a view to insuring that the aid shall be in the form of the most essential goods, has reinforced this tendency.

One problem has been that unduly large or imperfectly planned programs of investment might have the effect — taking into account existing scarcities and the low level of real income — of aggravating inflation, increasing the external deficit, and thereby defeating the basic purpose of the Recovery Program. Difficulties of this sort, inherent in the very nature of the task, have given rise to considerable controversy among economists and have presented some hard problems within OEEC, where it has at times seemed apparent that some countries, by emphasizing investment less than others, were achieving current advantages in production and trade (though at a risk to their future trade), and others, by emphasizing investment too much, were not only risking inflation but diverting to themselves ECA aid that would otherwise have gone to others. It is, therefore, reassuring, as we look back over the past two years, to find that, despite the difficulties, the investment programs have on the whole been sufficiently well conceived and administered so that the dangers of inflationary effects seem now much reduced, while the over-all result has been the marked expansion of production already mentioned and also a substantial increase in productivity, the full effects of which should become more apparent later.

Much less can be claimed for the international integration of investment. The first Interim Report called attention to the fact that the national four-year plans (presented in response to Mr. Hoffman's request of July 1948 for a 'master plan' emphasized self-help rather than mutual help, and revealed much wasteful duplication of investment. The Report called upon the participating countries to give special attention in 1949 to the co-ordination of investment, and this request was repeated in the Plan of Action of the Consultative Group of Ministers. In the second Report, there is presented a survey of the past year's experience. From this survey it must quite frankly be concluded that the past year, as regards co-ordination of investment, has been a year of exploration rather than achievement.

This exploration has revealed that, quite apart from such a fundamental question as to how much centralization of authority is needed, as against dependence on voluntary co-operation among the participating countries, the subject matter itself presents numerous complexities. One is the basic question of method, as between reliance on planning and on free market forces; and how to integrate investment as between countries where investment is planned and controlled and countries where it is not. Except for the simpler cases, like electric power where all-round expansion on a co-ordinated basis is obviously desirable, there are the uncertainties in forecasting aggregate demand and in locating production in the right places, having in mind that little work has yet been done, even on a theoretical level, on problems of location. There is the cartel problem, and the danger that private interests will undo what governments have planned. There is the very troublesome question of what relative

weight to put on current comparative costs and on future development — a question which has run through the whole history of international trade and finance and was never more important than today.
There are the questions of the desirable speed and scope of change,
of how fast and how far to go, questions which for old and settled
communities like those of Western Europe present far greater hazards
than for less-developed areas.

IV

I have dwelt on the co-ordination of investment not only to reveal
the difficulties encountered but also to indicate that the 'integration'
approach to the solution of Western Europe's dollar deficit should
not be regarded as new or as stemming exclusively from Mr. Hoffman's request of last October. From the beginning, it has been present
under various names and forms. The analytical structure of the original CEEC Report of 1947, which made the first survey of the problem, ran in terms of production, disinflation, co-operation, and
elimination of the dollar deficit. This same analytical scheme was
apparent in the first Interim Report, with co-operation taking the
dual form of integration of investment and the freeing of intra-
European trade and payment. What can be said to have happened
since October is an increased emphasis on integration and an increased emphasis on liberalization of trade and payment as the way
to achieve it, though the new Interim Report calls also for further
study and action within the related field of co-ordination of investment.

Following the 1947 Report, a Working Party was organized to
develop a system of intra-European clearing, to be operated by the
Bank for International Settlements. From this beginning, there
developed eventually the Intra-European Payments Agreement
adopted in October 1948 and renewed in revised form on 1 July 1949.[1]
When these discussions began, trade among the OEEC countries
had sunk to only 60 per cent of the 1938 level. It has now nearly recovered to the prewar level. Without doubt, this recovery, which has

[1] See my note on the revision of the Intra-European Payments Agreement,
Foreign Affairs, October 1949, pp. 153–5. I have not included this note in the
present volume, since the Payments Agreement was superseded by the European
Payments Union as of 1 July 1950, and the discussion now seems out of date.

occurred despite the general retention heretofore of bilateral trade and payments agreements, has been due primarily to the expansion of production, the removal of scarcities, and the overcoming of inflation. But the system of drawing rights and conditional aid, designed to enable the participating countries to obtain essential imports from each other, was undoubtedly also instrumental. It was recognized from the outset, however, that as a means of freeing trade and achieving balanced intra-European trade, the present kind of payments agreement has serious defects and could be regarded as no more than a temporary device. In the revision last year, attention was directed toward making the plan more flexible, and introducing competition among the participating countries by means of automatically transferable drawing rights. But in the final agreement reached, only 25 per cent of the drawing rights were made transferable. Moreover, the marked changes in the trade balances that have occurred since the revised plan was adopted have quite upset the estimates on which the drawing rights were based.

One of the outstanding features of 1949 was the striking tendency for intra-European trade balances to level off. France, for example, which previously had had a deficit with almost every other country, has since 1 July not had to use any of her drawing rights against the United Kingdom or Belgium. Belgium, whose intra-European surpluses had been about twice her dollar deficit, now has a much reduced surplus, if not an actual deficit. The United Kingdom, which previously had been a net exporter to the Continent, has become during the past year a moderate net importer from the other participating countries.

It may be premature to try to appraise the significance of this movement toward trade equilibrium within Western Europe. In part, it seems to be due to the realignment of currencies and to the events preceding and following sterling devaluation. But it seems also to have a deeper significance. The British change, for example, may well be part of the development of a trade pattern, growing out of her achievement this past year of over-all external viability, even though her dollar deficit persists. In the case of France, the change in trade position runs strikingly parallel to the overcoming of inflation early in 1949; and here, too, it may well be related to the fact that France has been approaching external viability over-all. Though we must wait for further evidence, the movement toward trade equilibrium within Western Europe seems to provide the most promising indication that has yet appeared of the development of a trade pattern that has a foundation in the logic of the changes in international relationships wrought by the war.

By destroying the pattern of trade between Europe and the outside world — particularly the earnings from overseas investment and services, along with a general impairment of trade with such areas as Eastern Europe and the Far East — the war not only greatly intensified the dollar-shortage problem but by that very fact swept away the basis on which the characteristic prewar pattern of intra-European surpluses and deficits had long rested. There was thus created a strong presumption that the trade of the Western European countries among themselves should move toward a position of even balance, except as that position might be modified by such movements of capital and credit as they might be able to sustain among themselves.

V

It is now greatly to be hoped that this movement toward equilibrium of trade and payments within Western Europe can be strengthened and consolidated. To achieve this result is undoubtedly one of the main purposes of the new measures for which Mr. Hoffman has been contending. The success already achieved now makes feasible a much more comprehensive attack on trade and payments barriers than was previously possible, and this in turn should increase Western Europe's ability to cope with its trade problems overseas.

The movement to liberalize trade had its beginnings last year as an outgrowth of the negotiations for the revision of the Payments Agreement. Proposals were made, and some actual steps taken, by a number of the participating countries; and the OEEC Council adopted a resolution calling on the participating countries to report by October how far they were prepared to put their intra-European trade on the basis of open general licenses rather than on the basis of bilateral agreements. This movement was greatly strengthened by Mr. Hoffman's statement to the Council on 31 October. In the new Interim Report, all the participants have undertaken to place a minimum of 50 per cent of their privately traded intra-European imports on this basis.

This, however, should be but a beginning. It is a fair presumption that in the present enlarged and better balanced state of intra-

European trade a liberalization of trade by 50 per cent would not produce any serious disturbance of trade or employment and would not seriously increase the competition which domestic producers would have to face. It is indeed for just this latter reason that the liberalization should be pursued much more vigorously in 1950. The movement will miss its main objective if it does not produce competition that is severe enough to promote productivity, serve as a guide to new investment and co-ordination of investment, and direct the further expansion of production and trade into the right channels for overcoming Western Europe's dollar deficit.

How fast the pace of trade liberalization will be from its present point is still uncertain. ECA has pressed for virtually complete liberalization by the end of 1950. The French have proposed an increase to 60 per cent by 1 July, provided the proposed Payments Union is by then in operation, and to 75 per cent by the end of the year. It has been said that these figures are well within the scope of British intentions, but that a number of other countries regard them as excessive. It should be noted, too, that hard currency countries, such as Belgium, are still excluded from the trade liberalization proposals by others, including Britain. One of the present uncertainties is how far the restraint on freeing intra-European trade stems from genuine balance-of-payment difficulties and how far from a desire to protect vested interests. It must be recognized that a too rapid pace of change might produce a serious setback in production, trade, and employment, and that this hazard is much greater in old and settled communities than it would be in less-developed areas. Even this caution, however, must be tempered by the fact that the period of external aid is limited, and results not achieved now may be much more difficult, if not impossible, to achieve later on.

VI

To achieve complete freedom of intra-European trade would require free transferability of currencies. Following Mr. Hoffman's statement of 31 October, ECA presented a proposal, in the hope that it would provide a basis for a statement of principles and the main outlines of a plan that could be incorporated in the new OEEC Report, which would then soon be followed up by the actual creation of a European Payments Union. At first there seemed to be general assent, at least as to the basic objective. But as the discussions continued, and the implications became clearer, important questions were raised, particularly by Great Britain. There was also a last-minute revelation that our own Government was not of one mind. The result was that in the OEEC meeting of 31 January, no plan for a Payments Union was adopted, and the whole matter is left for further study by the experts, without commitment.[2]

The basic purpose of the proposed Union is to set up a pool, consisting in part of gold or dollars and in part of credit facilities provided by the Union. Payments among the members would be effected through the Union, the payments taking the form partly of credits ('clearing units' transferable on the books of the Union) and partly of gold or dollars — the latter on an ascending scale for debtors and a descending scale for creditors, so as to bring pressure on both to work toward an even balance in their aggregate intra-European trade. A Board of Management would be created, with powers designed to facilitate this process. To set the Union going, ECA would provide a fund of 'free dollars,' to be withheld from the 'basic aid' allocated among the participating countries.

Many of the questions raised are to me reminiscent of old Bretton Woods discussions. Is the new Union to be merely the lender of last resort, or is it intended to supplant existing means of international payment? One of the chief objectives is to include within the area of liberalized trade and payment not only the Western European countries and their overseas territories but also Britain and the sterling area. From the standpoint of 'integration,' this seems to me a much more desirable objective than the narrower one of creating an intra-European area of freer trade and payment. But it does raise serious questions as to how the new multilateral payments system is to be related to the sterling system. The British have contended that if this can be done at all it can be only through assigning to the Union the more limited function of lender of last resort; and they have said that any more extended use of the Union would involve the freezing of all sterling area, and also transferable sterling, accounts. The British contention is that if the sterling system and the Union were in operation simultaneously, both would tend to work lop-

[2] The Payments Union was adopted in October 1950, effective from 1 July 1950, for a two-year period. For further discussion see below Chap. 9, pp. 177-9.

sidedly. For sterling holders would pay their deficits in sterling as at present, while Britain would be required to pay her European deficits in clearing units and to lose gold or dollars to the Union.

Another question that has been raised, and one that should be of special interest to us, is whether it is possible to operate any kind of gold or dollar settlement system in Europe so long as there is a dollar shortage. To put the question differently, could the Union be any stronger than the dollars we put into it? A temporary answer could be found through the provision of dollars by ECA for the next two years. But the proposed Union is intended to be a permanent mechanism, and the implication cannot be avoided that it is based on the assumption of Western Europe's achieving viability in dollars by 1952. A related question is whether, should this not prove to be the case, the United States is prepared to provide more dollars after 1952, or, as an alternative, to accept discrimination. A further question, that has been raised in this country as well as in Europe, is how the new Union and its Board of Management would be related to the International Monetary Fund.

VII

I do not regard these questions as insoluble, but they do indicate that time must be allowed for more thoroughgoing analysis than the payments problem has thus far received. Of necessity, some new arrangement must be made to supplant that expiring 1 July; and it should benefit greatly from the current discussions. One desirable criterion should be to build on what we have; and this, I believe, should involve a thorough survey of what can be done to rehabilitate sterling, which is already serving as the basis of the most extensive multilateral trading system that now exists. This would require, as one prime essential, a solution of the problem of the wartime sterling balances, which was put on the agenda for further work growing out of the Washington conference last September of the United States, Britain, and Canada.[3] Indeed, a solution of this problem is also mentioned as essential in the proposed European Payments Union.

As to the Payments Union, I should lean toward the lender-of-last-resort function. With ECA aid, the gold or dollar settlement feature could, I think, be made workable and would serve a desirable purpose

[3] See Chap. 7 above.

for the next two years; but the longer future is conjectural. This may be a good reason for continuing to regard European payments arrangements as temporary and experimental and for leaning toward more limited, rather than ambitious, and quite possibly hazardous, conceptions. What does seem particularly desirable is some intra-European credit arrangement which would permit the countries to think in terms of their aggregate European trade position (including their sterling area position), rather than in terms of bilateral trade balancing, and which would give time for corrective action without threatening immediate and substantial loss of reserves. One of the most critical difficulties in Europe today is that the war and the initial postwar confusion have stripped reserves to the danger point, so that the countries cannot ride out even minor international trade disturbances. This is one reason why I have favored increasingly over the past year a change in the technique of ECA aid, with less emphasis on programing and more on provision of reserves. Such a change would accord with the fact that now that the groundwork in production and internal financial stability has been laid, we need a more flexible approach to the problems of trade adjustment that remain.

VIII

In problems of this character, there is a kind of cause and effect dilemma. More liberal trade and payments arrangements would undoubtedly improve Western Europe's ability to overcome her external deficit. But we must bear in mind that it was the dollar shortage that produced the trade and payments restrictions even before the war, and has intensified them since the war. It is the threat of a continuing deficit after 1952 that now makes the Western European countries cautious about throwing off their trade restrictions and entering into payments arrangements which quite possibly after 1952 they would not be able to maintain. It is this kind of dilemma, also, that raises questions about intra-European co-operation, or integration, and the forms that it might take.

It is therefore essential to have as clear a view as we can of the possible future pattern of trade. The recent emphasis on integration in terms of analogy with the United States and its 'one big market' has suggested to some minds that Western Europe is being advised to solve its external problem by developing trade within itself. Seen in this way, the analogy would be quite misleading. Western Europe can perhaps to some extent reduce its overseas dependence, and OEEC plans, as outlined in the new Report, do call particularly for an expansion of agricultural production, which still has not reached the prewar level for the area as a whole. But we must bear in mind that the level of real income is still some 10 per cent below prewar; and whether it can be raised to a reasonable standard by a process of Western Europe's turning inward upon itself seems to me highly dubious. Basically, we have the problem of a small land area, with unbalanced resources, which in the past has had to look increasingly to the outside world, both for supplies and for markets, and in the process has developed a population density about four times that of the United States. American integration — through westward expansion into virgin territory within a single country — has involved not only the development of a great internal free market but a lessening dependence on the outside world. In the fundamental respect therefore of relative dependence on internal and external markets, it would surely be misleading for Western Europe to use the American economy as its model, though more could be said for it if Western and Eastern Europe were combined.

Moreover, our kind of integration, if applied in Europe, would involve a time schedule and a scope that reach far beyond the ECA program. Many of the questions raised by it are obviously political as well as economic. Indeed, this would be true even of the proposed Payments Union and the trade liberalization program if they were pushed to their logical limits; and this point has been stressed particularly in connection with the proposed Board of Management and its powers. As I pointed out earlier, this is also one of the main limiting factors on European co-ordination of investment. For really thoroughgoing integration on the American model, even if it were otherwise desirable or feasible, the main question raised would be whether political union would not have to precede economic integration.

IX

It is recognized, however, that the analogy with the American kind of integration is imperfect, and, so far as I know, there is no reference to it in the new Report. What undoubtedly was mainly intended was that a better integration of European production and trade would stimulate efficiency and might reduce the gap between American and

European productivity. The question of comparative productivity as between countries is a complex one. It involves not only comparisons of physical output per man hour, but comparative wages and other costs. Economists in some European countries do not concede that the comparison has been unfavorable since 1938; and for the postwar years at least, it is not clear that this country, with its rapidly rising wage costs and its emphasis on quantitative expansion more than on qualitative improvement of plant and equipment, has been outstripping or, possibly, even keeping pace with some of the European countries. It is not clear, either, whether the main difficulty, at least for some of the larger European countries, is the question of size of industries, having regard to their overseas as well as their domestic markets.

But, taking a longer view, I have felt that one of the main causes of world imbalance has been, and is likely to continue to be, our tendency to outstrip other countries in productivity. Often in the past our progress has come irregularly and has been associated with depressions, though not depressions long enough or deep enough to have cumulative destructive effects like the Great Depression of 1929–33. After the 1920–21 depression, American productivity increased 10 per cent a year for two successive years. One question for ourselves is whether our economy is still capable of that kind of progress. But one point to emphasize is that, under dynamic conditions, the growth of comparative productivities has to be regarded as a race; and the American economy cannot be expected to stand still while Europe is endeavoring to catch up. Certainly the burden of proof lies on those who question this conclusion; and, among other things, what they have to explain away is the succession of devaluations of currencies that has occurred since the First World War.

X

Essential as it is to raise European productivity, it seems to me unlikely that the dollar deficit can be eliminated primarily by direct exports to this country. It is important to bear in mind the relative magnitudes of trade and the historical trends. Even in 1938, the dollar area took only one-seventh of Western Europe's exports, while supplying one-fourth of her imports; and before that there had been a long history of a worsening imbalance in the direct trade between the two areas. Between 1938 and 1947, Western Europe's imports from the dollar area doubled, while exports dropped about 40 per cent. The crux of Western Europe's dollar problem is found in these facts, which accounted for a gap of about $6 billion on trade account, and including invisible items, of about $6.9 billion, in 1947, when the Marshall Plan was first conceived. Including capital transactions and the trade of the OEEC dependent overseas territories, the total gold and dollar deficit was $8.5 billion.

For the year ending 1 July 1950, the gold and dollar deficit of the OEEC countries with the United States and Canada is estimated in the Report at $4.4 billion; and the principal changes, compared with 1947, are a contraction of about $2.4 billion in imports from this area and an expansion of only $204 million in Western Europe's exports to the area.[4] The national programs for 1950-2 show for the whole period of 1947 to 1 July 1952 an estimated decrease of imports from the United States and Canada of $3.6 billion, and a rise in exports of $665 million. When these changes have been achieved, Western Europe's imports from this area will be $3.2 billion, and her exports to it $1.5 billion.

These figures, taken in relation to Western Europe's balance of payments as a whole, show clearly that the main solution is being sought through a contraction of imports from the dollar area accompanied by an expansion of exports to other parts of the world. For the whole period from 1947 to 1 July 1952, imports are expected to expand by $700 million (despite the contraction of $3.6 billion from the dollar area) and exports are expected to expand by $5.5 billion, of which only $665 million represents an expansion to the United States and Canada. Exports to this area will be less than 10 per cent of total Western European exports. Yet the increase in these exports compared with 1947 will be about 80 per cent. The contraction of imports from this area will be about 53 per cent. We shall be supplying Western Europe with nearly as large an amount of imports as in 1938, but they will represent only one-sixth of her total imports.

XI

These figures seem to me to give a more realistic view of the possible future pattern of trade than is implied in the emphasis on

[4] The poor showing in exports to us was due in part to our recession last year; the figures are $833 million in 1947, $1218 million in 1948, and $1037 million in 1949-50.

the dollar export drive, important as that is. They have important implications for trade policy. The chief one is that multilateral trade, not only within Europe, but even more in overseas trade, is the right objective. Europe must be able to use her trade surpluses elsewhere to cover her trade deficit with the dollar area. This implies, equally, that the ultimate goal must be convertibility of currencies, not only within Western Europe but throughout the world. Experience has already shown that the dollar deficit is proving more intractable than the over-all external deficit. Britain has been viable over-all for the past year but has not been able to use her surpluses elsewhere to meet her deficit with us. France is now approaching a similar condition. For the aggregate of the OEEC countries, this tendency is revealed in the summary of the national programs, which indicate an expected gold and dollar deficit in 1951–2 of $2.3 billion, though the over-all deficit is expected to be $1.5 billion, indicating that the OEEC countries expect to have a substantial surplus with the non-dollar world. The problem is thus becoming increasingly one of how to put the parts together to achieve a stable world equilibrium. It is quite clear that this objective will not be reached by 1952. The new OEEC Report is less pessimistic than the earlier one. It accepts the dollar deficit of $2.3 billion in 1951–2, indicated by the national programs, and concludes that the deficit will be further reduced by 1952–3. It indicates that the Western European countries are as firmly resolved as the United States that the program should end on schedule on 1 July 1952, though pointing out that there will still be special problems in a few countries, such as Western Germany, Austria, and Greece. This does not mean, however, that the problem of the dollar deficit will not remain. The termination of the ECA program on schedule should differentiate between the countries that have structural international trade problems still unsolved and the countries that do not, or whose difficulties stem from those of others. But the main effect, I think, will be to broaden the area of consideration of the problem of imbalance, focusing attention on the fact that it is a world problem and not merely a Western European problem. Indeed, there is growing awareness both here and in Europe of the need for a broader attack which should not wait for the ECA program to end.

The broader problem is to work out a sustainable pattern of world trade. This is a problem quite as much for us as for Western Europe, the sterling area, and other parts of the world. Its largest aspect, indeed, is the growing preponderance in the world of the American economy, its comparative self-containment, its long-run tendency to outstrip others in productivity, and its short-run instability, which, as was indicated last year, produces effects abroad quite out of proportion to the internal effects. About the future of American policy there are many uncertainties. Though the American tariff has been greatly liberalized since the mid-'thirties, and the United States has taken the lead in the ITO and GATT negotiations, many of the American duties are still prohibitive over the range of goods in which Western Europe might compete, and there is still a real question as to how much the American people have ceased to be protection-minded where it counts. The ITO Charter has not yet been accepted by Congress, and there have been recent indications of formidable opposition being organized against it. Between the desire of industrial and labor groups to keep out imports and the desire of farmers and industrialists to retain their war-swollen foreign markets as vents for surplus, even at the expense of the taxpayers — and the urge, common to all countries, to use the foreign balance as a stabilizer of home production and employment at high levels — there will undoubtedly be severe political tensions in the United States, the outcome of which it would be hazardous to predict.

The approach to Western European viability which I have suggested puts the main emphasis on reduction of imports from the United States and expansion of Western European trade with the non-dollar world, and a second, but still very important, emphasis on expansion of Western European exports to the United States and Canada. These changes, together with some expansion of intra-European relative to extra-European trade (to the extent that this is feasible consistently with raising real income to a reasonable level), seem to me to be the main lines of solution suggested by the relative magnitudes of trade and by the historical trends. This solution, however, presents various difficulties. It implies discrimination against American exports. Indeed, such discrimination is already implicit in the new measures for liberalization of trade and payments; and even though this is regarded as a means to an end, and the main emphasis is put on the rise in productivity, there is involved the acceptance, probably for some time to come, of a definite reorientation of American trade policy. This is not so much a matter of an actual change, as it is a matter of recognition of the change. The change was already involved in the 25 per cent cut of imports from the dollar area by Britain and the sterling area last summer, which must have been reviewed and approved at the Washington conference last September. Nevertheless, the working out of the implications of this change, in a spirit of co-operation rather than conflict, and with a view to expanding world trade, will doubtless present many difficulties. The most important questions should be whether this discrimination could be regarded as temporary or whether it would tend to crystallize into a permanent division into 'two worlds,' which would run counter to the professions, European as well as American, that the object of the Recovery Program is to restore a multilateral, nondiscriminatory trade world.

XII

The historical answer to unbalanced trade and productivity has been international investment. One of the most significant announcements in the new OEEC Report is that the Organization now proposes to undertake a study of foreign investment, which should cover economic as well as technical aspects. The interest in President Truman's Point Four indicates that American thinking is turning in the same direction. The problem now presented, however, is quite unprecedented, and the analogy with nineteenth-century experience could be misleading. Basically, what the world now requires is a flow of American capital accompanied by a flow of European exports to other parts of the world. Such a development is not only unprecedented historically, but presents new and complex theoretical problems. It is not a question of 'tied loans' but of an organic relation between the flow of capital and of goods. The danger is a further strengthening of trade ties between the United States and the less-developed parts of the world, leaving Western Europe in a backwater. From this point of view, it would seem advisable for Western Europe to co-operate as fully as possible with her own resources in international investment, as Britain has been doing in the sterling area.

As regards American investment, it seems unlikely that the main reliance could be put on private foreign investment, at least without substantial guarantees. A part of our puzzle has been that, while the role we should play in the world is that of a creditor country, the conditions are often more favorable for investment here, not only for Americans but also for others. The history of the interwar period is full of perverse and unstable capital movements which disturbed rather than restored international equilibrium. The kind of development program now needed would require planning, whether or not we like that word, because it would not be at all certain otherwise how the parts might fit together. It would require that attention be directed to key spots where aid either in the form of investments or of grants would relieve European difficulties — for example, the problem of the sterling war balances in the Middle and the Far East. It should give attention to military and political, as well as economic, considerations. It raises questions, for example, of our relation to such conferences as that recently held in Colombo by the British Commonwealths to explore the problems of Southeast Asia. One agency that could do effective work in this field, particularly after the ECA program has ended, is the Bank for International Reconstruction and Development. But there will also be a need for American governmental investment, and probably also for American grants of aid. But the annual amounts, I think, would not need to be large compared with those of the present ECA program. However, progress of this character will probably be slow, and most of the thinking about it probably lies ahead of us. I do not expect an early solution of the problem of world imbalance. But that is all the more reason, if this conclusion is right, why we should begin now, rather than wait for 1952. The hopeful aspect of the Western European problem is that it may by 1952 be 'manageable,' to quote the language of the new Report, without an organized program of 'extraordinary outside assistance.'

9

End of the Marshall Plan

IN April 1950 I discussed in these pages 'The Marshall Plan Half-way.' At that time the United States looked forward to completion of the European recovery program by mid-1952, as provided by the Economic Co-operation Act of April 1948. But in June 1950 came Korea. Since then we have been in a process of transition to the Mutual Security Program. Instead of the Marshall Plan, we now have a three-pronged program combining economic aid, now called 'defense support,' administered since last January by the Mutual Security Agency as successor to ECA; military aid under the Department of Defense; and Point Four (Technical Co-operation Administration) under the State Department. Averell Harriman as Director for Mutual Security has had the role of over-all co-ordinator of these activities.

In these circumstances we cannot attach the same significance as previously to the date mid-1952. Instead of providing the definitive cure for international imbalance, at least so far as Western Europe and its dollar gap are concerned, the Marshall Plan has become one more transitional experience in the increasingly complicated world situation that has been unfolding ever since the war. We can now only speculate whether, but for Korea and the rearmament program, the goal of independence from 'extraordinary outside assistance' might have been reached by mid-1952. Actually, as contemplated in our budget for the fiscal year beginning 1 July 1952, assistance to Europe will be much greater than in any year of the Marshall Plan, and foreign aid as a whole (except as modified by Congress) will be $7.9 billion, as against total Marshall Plan expenditures since April 1948 of $12 billion. It is, however, important for many reasons to try to appraise at this time this whole experience. How much progress has Europe really made? Has the setback in Western Europe's external balance that has occurred this past year, and which the OEEC report of last November called 'ominous,' been wholly due to temporary forces brought on by the Korean war and the rearmament program, or are there other forces suggesting deeper-seated maladjustments? Since the end of the Second World War, there have been sharply divided schools of thought as to the nature of Europe's economic difficulties.

The passing of ECA last 1 January was the occasion for much appraising of the Marshall Plan results. One of the most interesting statements was ECA's final press release. The positive achievements cited form a most impressive record, without parallel in history. After World War I it took seven years to regain the prewar level of production in Western Europe. At the end of 1951 industrial production was 41 per cent above prewar, 64 per cent above 1947, and well beyond the target originally set for 1952. Agricultural production was 9 per cent above prewar and 24 per cent above 1947. Gross national product — the total sum of Western Europe's production of goods and services — had risen 25 per cent in real terms in less than four years and was 15 per cent above prewar. The transportation system has been rehabilitated. Electrical output has doubled over prewar. Steel production has doubled since 1947 (and is one-fifth above prewar), giving a total production last year of 60 million tons as compared with 35 million produced by Russia and her satellites. Refined petroleum products have quadrupled over prewar.

In agricultural products the gains are less striking but substantial. Cereal production and bread grains have about regained their prewar level, and the output of potatoes, sugar, meat, milk, and oils is well above the targets set, and in every case except meat (where the prewar level was regained last year) substantially above prewar. The great disappointment has been in coal production, which is still somewhat behind the prewar output and about 20 per cent short of the goal set for 1951; of the one billion dollars for economic aid to Europe in our budget for the past fiscal year, about two-thirds represented payments for imports of American coal.

I have always regarded the Marshall Plan as primarily an investment program, whose purpose was not merely to restore war damage but to increase production and productivity to the point where Europe might hope to balance its international accounts without further external aid. A parallel objective was to increase real income, which had fallen below the limits of tolerance, and thus to raise consumption and to provide internal savings which could take over the burden of investment as external aid was tapered off. On these fundamental aims the Marshall Plan must now be regarded as an interrupted experiment, or at least one made vastly more complex by the need of rearming. It is always difficult to make comparisons of the level of consumption at different periods in a changing world, and this is especially true in a comparison of prewar and postwar levels, since wars often produce significant changes in the pattern of consumption, and allowances have to be made for such things as continuance of rent controls and food subsidies. The OEEC conclusion in its last annual report, June 1951, was that in 1950 per capita consumption in Western Europe as a whole was still somewhat below prewar, though this was mainly due to the low consumption levels still existing in Austria, Germany, Greece, Italy, and Turkey; in most other countries it was somewhat above prewar. How to improve — and above all to prevent a renewed decline of — Western Europe's real income will surely have to be a major consideration in the planning of the defense program if the progress that has been achieved by the Marshall Plan in warding off Communism from within is to be preserved.

When we turn to the investment aspect of the recovery program, the results achieved in the past four years are most impressive. As the OEEC report just mentioned indicates, as our aid has tapered off from year to year, in accordance with the Plan, the increase in investment financed out of domestic saving has been more rapid than the decline of external aid. 'There have been few periods in history when so high a proportion of resources has been freely devoted to investment in such unpromising conditions and with such impressive results. It may be estimated that in 1950 real per capita gross investment (i.e. measured at constant prices) was more than 10 per cent greater than in 1938. In terms of net investment the increase was much greater and probably amounted to about 40 per cent.'

II

In the light of this record it comes with something of a shock to find that in 1951 Western Europe's external trade deficit was about

$4.5 billion,[1] a deficit that was exceeded within the Marshall Plan period only by that of the first year, 1948, when the deficit was $5.4 billion. This is what the OEEC report called 'ominous.' Since the chief aim of the Plan was to remove the external deficit, must we conclude that we have come full circle, and are now back more or less at the point from which we started? Has nothing much, after all, been accomplished about the hoped-for freedom from 'extraordinary outside assistance?' And how could this happen in the face of such an impressive record of economic upbuilding as we have described?

The first, and the main, explanation is that this has been the effect of the Korean war and of the rearmament program that has come in its train. But a fact that may be even more significant in its implications for the longer run is the extraordinary violence of this effect. It appears to reveal once more the precarious nature of Western Europe's international position, and sets us wondering, as often before in my own case, as to whether — even apart from such major disturbances as Korea and rearmament — we are on the way toward a really durable and dependable solution.

To get light on such a question we must look back at the behavior of Western European trade since the war, and especially since the Marshall Plan began. Sir Oliver Franks's exploratory committee,[2] created in 1947 in response to Secretary Marshall's request for a program of self-help, mutual help and external aid, presented a four-point analysis: expansion of output along with general economic rehabilitation, internal financial stability (overcoming inflation), economic co-operation among the participating countries (through OEEC), and, finally, as the end result, the wiping out of the external deficit. Skipping for the time being from the first point to the last, and looking first at the volume of trade, the results are encouraging. Western Europe's foreign trade has not only recovered strongly from the year of collapse, 1947, but both overseas and within Europe it had by 1950 exceeded in volume that of 1938. Despite the setback in the external deficit in 1951, the growth

---

[1] This figure is based on January–September 1951 at annual rates of trade. See Economic Commission for Europe, *Economic Survey of Europe in 1951*, Geneva, 1952, p. 69.

[2] Committee of European Economic Co-operation, *General Report*, Department of State, Washington, D.C., September 1947.

in volume of trade has apparently continued; overseas exports in 1951 increased by $2.2 billion over 1950, and intra-European exports by $1.5 billion (at constant 1949 prices).[3] The general conclusion seems to be that though export trade for Western Europe as a whole has not fully kept pace with production, and has not yet attained the target set forth in the national four-year plans presented in 1948 (which was a one-third increase by 1952 over 1938), the production program and other measures taken under the Marshall Plan have had an effect on trade that provides strong support for the exploratory committee's analysis and expectations. It should be recalled, too, that these results have been accomplished with only about half as much external aid as the committee estimated would be needed.

When we come, however, to the balance of trade and payments, as distinguished from the volume of trade, the facts are much harder to appraise. They show erratic fluctuations even before Korea, and it is to this fact and its implications that I wish later to return. When we come to Korea itself and the defense program we find not only that they were mainly responsible for the 'ominous' widening of the gap in 1951 but also for the astonishingly good showing made in 1950. These violent changes are traceable both in Western Europe's balance of payments and in our own. Western Europe's trade deficit fell from $3.5 billion in 1949 to $2 billion in 1950; and when account is taken of invisible earnings, which far exceeded the exploratory committee's expectations, the current account balance of payments of the OEEC countries fell from $2.4 billion in 1949 to $846 million in 1950. The annual figures really conceal the full measure of the improvement, since there was an actual surplus on current account of $87 million in the second half of 1950. It is not to be wondered at that the OEEC report of June 1951 contains at times a note almost of exultation — was the problem solved! But one finds here and there also notes of warning and references to signs of impending change. By November 1951 we get a very different document, whose main theme is the 'ominous' widening of the deficit.[4]

We find the counterpart of these changes in our own balance of pay-

[3] ECE Survey, op. cit. p. 69; based on January–September 1951 at annual rates of trade.

[4] OEEC, *European Economic Co-operation*, Paris, November 1951.

ments. In 1947, the critical year before the Marshall Plan began, we had the huge excess of exports of $9.9 billion, and, including invisibles, a total export surplus of goods and services of $11.5 billion. In that year Western Europe's gold and dollar deficit was $8.5 billion dollars. In the first two years of the Marshall Plan our surplus was reduced by roughly half. Then came the abrupt decline in 1950 to a surplus of $1.4 billion on trade account, and $2.2 billion including services. Again, the yearly figures conceal the magnitude of the change, for in the third quarter of 1950 our current account surplus virtually vanished, and on trade alone we had a deficit for the first time in thirteen years. Here again, we can appreciate why the Europeans hoped the problem had been solved. But by the fourth quarter of 1950 the gap was widening. For the year 1951 as a whole we had an export surplus of goods and services of $5 billion and in the fourth quarter the surplus advanced to an annual rate of $7.5 billion, the highest rate since the British devaluation in September 1949.

III

We have thus a mixed result. Western Europe is much stronger than five years ago. Production and trade have expanded strikingly. But the external deficit, though almost overcome in 1950, has again opened up alarmingly. Though we may discount the deterioration as due to Korea and rearmament, we must discount the great improvement that preceded it as also due to these developments.

As I said earlier, it is the violence of these changes in the past two years that should give us chief concern. They represent a repetition, in an exaggerated form, of earlier experience. Since the war there have been recurrent drains on Western Europe's gold and dollar reserves. They have fallen into a biennial pattern, with a reserve crisis in every second year — 1947, 1949, 1951. They have forced drastic remedial measures — in 1947, abrupt termination of Britain's attempt at convertibility and nondiscrimination; in 1948, interim aid for France, the Marshall Plan, Cripps's austerity budget; in 1949, currency devaluations and severe direct import cuts. The renewed drain of British reserves since June 1951, reducing reserves by more than half and bringing them again almost to the pre-devaluation minimum, and the equally acute drain of French reserves, have again been followed by drastic import cuts and other measures.

These disturbances are sometimes called short run. They are short run only in the sense that they recur frequently. Their persistent recurrence suggests that they are symptomatic of deeper-seated difficulties. Since the end of World War I, the world has been troubled by maldistribution of gold reserves and a persistent bias toward gold absorption by this country. In the interwar period gold drains forced recurrent waves of currency devaluations and in the end led to direct exchange and trade controls and a marked deterioration of multilateral trade. This was all in the background before World War II greatly intensified the problem. With reserves now much smaller than before the war in relation to price levels and the volume of trade, there is a fundamental lack of confidence in the ability of countries to maintain stable currencies. Even minor swings in the trade position are magnified by fear and speculation — flights of capital, black markets, delays and accelerations of payments and of receipts by exporters and importers. When knowledge of thinness of reserves is coupled with knowledge that currency devaluations can be and have frequently been forced, the stage is set for recurrent crises such as we have seen; and the evidence seems to be that not even direct controls can stifle them, though necessity forces further resort to such controls on each new occasion. The problem of Western Europe is not merely to solve the dollar gap, difficult and uncertain as that question is, but in addition to build up reserves to an adequate level, and to do this in the face of the strong bias toward gold absorption by this country which has persisted ever since 1914. It was hardly to be expected that the Marshall Plan by itself could achieve such a result, even apart from Korea and rearmament.

The Western European countries are heavily dependent upon foreign trade. Basically, their trade is an exchange of their manufactured goods for raw materials and food. Thus exports are closely tied to imports, and, though foreign trade may expand with home production, there is little leeway in which to bring about favorable changes in the balance of trade. This was a major problem with the German reparation payments in the 'twenties, and it is the kind of problem that is often overlooked when people talk about the expansibility of production as a cure for trade imbalance. Throughout the Marshall Plan period the availability of supplies, particularly of raw materials, was a constant worry. In each of the biennial swings in the trade balance that I have mentioned, one can readily trace the fluctuations in the stocks of raw materials on hand. The good showing made by Britain in 1946 under the Anglo-American loan was largely an expression of the running down of stocks which resulted from curbing imports and stimulating exports, and this process has been repeated ever since, accentuating the swings in the trade balance.

A related factor has been the pronounced swings in the terms of trade. How important these can be was indicated by the official British statement that the adverse change in the terms of trade in 1951 cost Britain more than the increase in her defense expenditures. The kinds of goods that Europe buys are subject to much wider price swings than the kinds of goods she sells. The first effect of the Korean war was a sharp rise in raw material prices, in many cases by severalfold. This rise affected first our own trade position and later that of Western Europe. It largely accounts for the big upswing in Europe's position in 1950 and the marked downturn in 1951. We had a pronounced expansion of imports in 1950. Through government stockpiling and business inventory accumulation in this country at high prices Europe enjoyed for a time a double benefit. Our purchases of raw materials, particularly from the sterling area countries, whose dollar earnings, through the sterling area dollar pool, go to swell Britain's reserves, had much to do with the rise in Britain's reserves from $1.4 billion, just prior to sterling devaluation in September 1949, to $3.8 billion by June 1951. At the same time Europe's own exports to both the dollar and the non-dollar world flourished, imports were held down, stocks of goods were drawn down, and before the string had run out the results were highly impressive.

But in 1951 came the inevitable reversal. Western Europe found itself forced to replenish stocks at import prices much above those before Korea. The rise of import prices not only caused a sharply adverse change in the terms of trade but brought on a new outburst of inflationary pressure, after inflation had been held well in check for a considerable period, despite even the currency devaluations of September 1949. From June 1950 to the end of 1951 the wholesale price level rose 28 per cent in Britain and 47 per cent in France. In the case of Britain, at least, which is farther along with rearmament than the Continental countries, the competition of the defense program with the export industries for home and foreign resources began to make itself sharply felt, to the point where the Churchill Government conceded that the defense program would have to be spread over a longer period of time.

The reference earlier to the sterling area indicates the importance for Western Europe of triangular trade. One of the things that became apparent, even in our own official thinking (ECA), as the Marshall Plan progressed, was that Europe's exports to us were too small to provide the main cure for the dollar deficit. Granted that the drive for exports to the United States should be strongly pushed, the main problem was to shift the source of Europe's supply away from us to third countries, and to expand Europe's exports primarily to such countries. Such a pattern of trade, to be self-sustaining, would mean a surplus of exports to the non-dollar world, a surplus of exports by the latter to this country, and a European surplus of imports from us, to be financed in this manner. In such a pattern of trade the effect of swings in the terms of trade is complex. If our imports from the raw-material-producing countries rise in volume and in price, Western European exports to such countries are likely to rise in volume and in price, and this change, coupled with some increase in Western European direct exports to us, can have highly favorable effects.

But against this is the fact that Western Europe in its own buying of raw materials is adversely affected. What will come out of such changes depends upon the circumstances of the particular case. As I have said, Western Europe benefited in 1950, and suffered heavily in 1951, from the changes in the terms of trade. A further factor is that when the terms of trade move against the raw-material-producing countries, as they did after the price rise passed its peak, Europe is apt to lose in volume of exports to such countries, but to find her terms of trade improving through the fall of raw material import prices. Since the third quarter of 1951, Britain's terms of trade have been gradually improving, and this change has been reflected this year in the reduction of the drain on Britain's reserves. But this may not be the end of the road either, for as the position of the raw material countries worsens they come under pressure to cut their imports not only from us but from Europe. Thus since the meeting of the Commonwealth Finance Ministers in London last January we have seen the emergence of a new sterling area policy, in which the sterling area countries reserve the right to cut imports even against Britain herself. Considering that the essence of the sterling area has been the freedom of trade and capital movements within the area, and the maintenance in consequence of the largest area of fully multilateral trade which still remains, such a policy may have significant implications for the future.

The rise and the fall of raw material prices and the consequent violent swings in the terms of trade and in the volume of trade are strikingly illustrated by the behavior of wool, rubber, and tin since Korea. Chiefly because of the phenomenal rise in the prices of these three commodities, export receipts from the United States and Western European countries by the countries producing them (primarily the sterling area) totaled $1.5 billion more during the twelve months from mid-1950 to mid-1951 than during the six months preceding Korea, at an annual rate; and then, in the third quarter of 1951, fell by an amount equivalent to $1.1 billion a year.[5] Such erratic swings (and one could amplify by taking more commodities) act as a two-edged sword for some European countries, particularly the United Kingdom; Britain has continuously been whipsawed by fluctuations in the terms of trade, which when favorable for her are unfavorable for the outer sterling area, and vice versa. The complexity of her task as banker for the sterling area under such conditions will, I think, raise serious questions for the future unless, through the development of more effective policies for the area as a whole, some correction of these violent fluctuations can be achieved. In recent years confidence in the future of the sterling area has waxed and waned with each recurrent swing, and the time seems to have passed when the area can be expected to survive on such an informal and almost organizationless basis as in the past.

IV

The point to emphasize, as I said earlier, is that these disturbances in trade and payments, while intensified since Korea, are in no sense new. This is only the last in a series of such crises. It is a striking

[5] ECE, *Economic Survey of Europe in 1951*, p. 12.

fact, for example, that when British reserves were drained so heavily in 1949 and sterling devaluation was forced on an unwilling Cabinet, Britain's own trade was not out of balance — she had had for some time an over-all balance except that she could not use her surpluses elsewhere to cover her dollar deficit — and Britain was not seriously experiencing inflation. It was mainly the drain resulting from trade deficits in the outer sterling area that caused the crisis. And it was mainly an abrupt decline in American imports from the raw-material sterling area countries that produced these trade deficits.

This fact illustrates a further cause of world trade maladjustment. What was for us a very minor business recession was greatly magnified in its external effects. Our imports constitute a small fraction of our gross national product — in most years under 5 per cent — but they are sensitive to changes in our level of output and employment. It is estimated in the last United Nations' special report that an American recession of the magnitude of 1937-8, when our employment fell by 4 per cent and our merchandise imports by 36 per cent, would, if it occurred today, reduce the dollar income of the outside world by 10 billion dollars.[6] And yet, historically, a fall in employment of 4 per cent would hardly be called a major depression. It is easy to understand by comparison what disastrous effects our Great Depression of the early 'thirties had on world trade, and why in the discussions of the ITO Charter (which in the end this country turned down) other countries insisted on some kind of guarantee of stability in the United States and on escape clauses if American instability threatened to drain off their reserves.

How seriously this problem of the effects of these short-run fluctuations in our imports is regarded is shown by the United Nations' special report prepared by a group of international experts, including two American economists, in 1949.[7] The report proposed that a country whose imports fell off because of a domestic recession should supply an equivalent amount of its currency, through the International Monetary Fund, to the countries whose exports had declined in consequence. I have elsewhere criticized this proposal as being an arithmetic rather than an economic solution of the prob-

[6] United Nations, *Measures for International Economic Stability,* New York, 1951.

[7] United Nations, *National and International Measures for Full Employment,* Lake Success, 1949.

lem, and one which no country could be expected to accept in such a generalized, mechanical form without examining the circumstances of the particular case.[8]

The formula was obviously aimed at the United States, and at the meeting of the Economic and Social Council in Geneva in July–August 1950, our representative stated that the United States Government 'was not prepared' to enter into any commitment 'automatically to provide indefinite amounts of public funds over long periods.' The subject, however, was not entirely dropped, and last year a second group of experts was appointed to consider the problem further. There is not space to discuss their suggestions, but the main one is that the International Monetary Fund should address itself to this problem. There has been growing criticism, even within the Fund itself, of its inactivity — until the recent Australian credit the Fund has been virtually inactive for two years — and we should welcome the recent signs of a new orientation of its policies. In my discussions of the Fund in 1943-4, I was skeptical of its usefulness under the conditions likely to obtain after the war.[9] But the fact is that it does have unutilized gold and dollar resources of over $2 billion which could, I think, help substantially to bolster the reserve position of countries in periods of strain. The United Nations' report also discusses the swings in the terms of trade resulting from price fluctuations of primary products and recommends a new examination of the possibilities of international commodity agreements as a means of reducing such fluctuations.[10]

V

The impact of the United States on the outside world is the basic international economic problem. The short-run disturbances I have discussed are symptomatic of deeper-seated maladjustments arising out of long-run cumulative changes in the relative positions of the trading countries. The great size of the United States, its large home market, its diversified resources, its comparative self-sufficiency, its high productivity, and rapid technological progress have introduced a tendency away from, rather than toward, equilibrium in world trade. Until this tendency can be removed, dealing with

[8] See Chap. 2, pp. 41-2.
[9] See *Post-War Monetary Plans,* op. cit. chaps. 6–11 inclusive.
[10] See United Nations, op. cit. 1951.

the short-run disturbances, important though that is, can at best have only palliative effects. The basic question about the Marshall Plan is how much it has contributed toward a solution of this imbalance. The great virtue of the Marshall Plan conception was that it did look toward a fundamental solution through intra-European integration. The urge for integration has been present under some form or name ever since the Plan began in 1948. I have already discussed the strong emphasis on investment to improve European productivity. It was recognized, however, that national investment plans, supported by external aid, were only a beginning and that the objective should be intra-European co-ordination of investment.[11] But though the OEEC did much exploratory work, it had no power of action, and the discussion bogged down on the question of whether political union must precede integration of investment, production, and trade, or whether economic integration for special purposes would promote the merging of sovereignty.

The Marshall Plan, though it did not of itself achieve co-ordination of investment in Western Europe, did much to promote what is now being called the functional approach to the problem, and the new turn of events since Korea has furthered this approach. The program for liberalization of trade, the European Payments Union, the Schuman Plan, the European Defense Community, and the proposals for integrating agriculture and co-ordinating transport are all promising steps in this direction. In the unsettled conditions of October 1949, when there were strong grounds for doubt about how the Marshall Plan would turn out, Paul Hoffman made his plea for a program of integration as the only way of raising European productivity toward our level and thus of solving the basic imbalance. The only immediate step that proved feasible was the liberalization of trade and payments. In the second half of the Marshall Plan, this program played the leading role. Liberalization of trade was carried up to 75 per cent of goods privately traded and a 'common list' of freely traded goods was developed. International payment was multilateralized among the OEEC countries through the establishment of the European Payments Union on 1 July 1950.

The Payments Union has been hailed as the major achievement of the Marshall Plan toward intra-European co-operation. Certainly

[11] For a discussion of the difficulties involved in co-ordination of investment, see Chap. 8.

it has succeeded better than its critics anticipated, and the OEEC countries have this year decided to continue it beyond the tentative date of mid-1952 originally set. The Payments Union, however, cannot by itself be regarded as anything more than an initial step toward integration, and even the continued existence of the Union cannot yet be taken for granted. Though it has weathered many difficulties, notably the German deficit position in 1950–51, and has, in that case particularly, demonstrated effective powers of management, the Union is winding up its experimental two-year period with some fundamental questions on which further light will be needed.

One is whether the success of the Union will require feeding more dollars into it. The Union now has almost intact its dollar reserve of $350 million granted by the ECA at the time of its creation (as of 1 May, the reserve was only $25 million below that original amount). But this statement conceals the fact that nearly a half billion dollars of Marshall aid has in indirect ways been utilized, and in addition economic aid was still being given to the individual countries. There is thus left open the question of how the Union will fare now that the Marshall Plan has ended. Our Government has turned a deaf ear to the repeated demands by many Europeans that it furnish from $200 million to $250 million to strengthen the Union's dollar reserves for the rearmament period, and from current reports this decision has been accepted and further dollar aid has not been made a condition of the continuance of the Union.

Another vexing question is what to do about intractable creditor positions, notably that of Belgium, whose credits in the Union now far exceed the original quota and have been threatening to exhaust the Union's reserves. This year Belgium's receipt of gold and dollars from the Union has been cut below the sum to which she was entitled, and the solution now being worked on as I write (if Belgium will accept it, her alternative being presumably withdrawal from the Union) is refunding of the excess credit. But such a solution would be only temporary and does not solve the problem of the intractable creditor position. Belgium has had a persistent export surplus to the other Western European countries ever since the war, which appears to rest in part at least upon the fact that, with the liberal trade policies she has been pursuing, she tends to buy on balance from the United States and to recoup her dollar deficit by means of her European surpluses. In considerable part, the goods imported from us become the basis of Belgium's exports to OEEC countries. This is a striking illustration of how dependent the success of the Payments Union is upon discrimination against the dollar area. A gap in the wall, as in Belgium's case, represents a drain of dollars not from Belgium alone but from the OEEC countries as a whole. Thus we are brought back to the question whether Western Europe (or any other part of the world subject to persistent dollar drain) has any alternative other than to try either to protect itself by direct discriminatory controls aimed at cutting imports from the dollar area or to build up its productivity (and thus its exports) to the point where the dollar shortage problem ceases to exist. This is the fundamental problem not only for the OEEC countries and the Payments Union but also for the sterling area and the sterling dollar pool.

The most discouraging feature of postwar experience is that we have not yet been able to find a solution to the problem of trade deficits which does not involve cuts in imports through direct controls. Even the German case I referred to earlier, which has been much cited as an illustration of what can be accomplished by monetary and fiscal measures, did involve direct import cuts, and, as I have indicated, Britain and the sterling area countries have felt themselves forced to resort to these cuts not only against us but against each other. Moreover, in its recent reserve crisis Britain's import cuts were directed against the OEEC countries to overcome her trade deficits with them and her loss of gold and dollars to the Payments Union. France pursued a similar course, and both France and Britain cut back their trade liberalization program to 60 per cent.

VI

Clearly what is needed in Europe is integration in some more fundamental sense than merely a monetary clearing union or a program of trade liberalization. That is why many are now looking forward to the Schuman Plan and to the European Defense Community, in the hope of achieving an integration in terms of production, distribution, and co-ordinated investment. The Schuman Plan Treaty was signed a year ago by France, Germany, Belgium, Luxembourg, Netherlands, and Italy, and the process of ratification is virtually completed. Unless something goes radically wrong in Western Europe, it should not be long before the Plan comes fully into force. When that happens, there will be created one single market for European coal and steel, a market which in terms of population will be about as large as ours. All tariff barriers and quantitative controls between the six countries of the community, as well as all discriminatory and restrictive practices, will be eliminated with respect to coal and steel, and coal and steel cartels will be outlawed.

This is a bright vision. Jean Monnet, its principal author, has hailed it, and also the Pleven Plan for a European Army (European Defense Community) which, organizationally, is drawn up on similar lines, 'as the first institutions . . . of a United States of Europe.' The Schuman Plan has encountered many difficulties and doubtless there will be more. Despite the elaborate organizational machinery, there will be room for play of national interests. Already there has been comment on the jockeying for position among the member nations and of pressure on the Steel Committee of OEEC to sanction increases of output in advance of the institution of the Plan, so that the countries will be in more favorable position for consideration of quotas after the Plan has gone into effect. Of basic importance in the Plan is the co-ordination of investment, the goal which, as I have indicated, has all along been sought under the Marshall Plan but without concrete results. If the Plan cannot eliminate high cost production and develop a really competitive market, it will fail of its purpose, and Europe will probably be facing again the problems of inefficient distribution of steel and coal capacity and the cartel practices that follow in their train. Though a transition period is provided for, in which countries will be compensated for elimination of high cost production (as in the case of Belgian coal), it will undoubtedly be easier to co-ordinate investment without undue national pressures through expansion of output. This raises in some minds the possibility of excess capacity. Germany had such a problem between the two wars and found an outlet in armament. In view, however, of the fact that the standard of living in Europe is still very low and that the OEEC has announced a new program calling for a 25 per cent increase in gross national product by 1956, it seems premature to worry unduly about excess steel capacity, and there is surely no such problem for coal, which has been so badly lagging. If a Western European economy at all comparable with ours in productive capacity and productivity is to be created, Western Europe will have to think in much larger terms than heretofore.

VII

This year economic conditions in Europe seem somewhat better. The anti-inflationary measures taken by the Pinay Government have been well received by the French people. Perhaps the main effects have been psychological and political, but the budgetary situation has improved, price increases have been checked, and, as I write, a large internal loan designed to draw out gold from hoarding is in prospect; the external drain has been checked and France's position in the Payments Union has improved. In Britain the Conservative Government has introduced important budgetary changes, has partly removed the food subsidies, and has taken steps to promote labor efficiency and reduce the pressure for wage advances by putting income tax on an incentive basis. The drain of dollar reserves has been substantially reduced, but, as of the end of April, the much hoped for counterswing had not yet occurred. Both France and England have increased the bank rate. The Bank of England discount rate has twice been increased, to a level of 4 per cent, after having remained unchanged (except for a two-month period in 1939 at the outbreak of the war) at 2 per cent from 1932 to last November. In Europe, particularly during the second half of the Marshall Plan, there has been a general renaissance of central bank control. The Bank of England's actions were among the last in a succession that has spread pretty much throughout Western Europe.[12] A growing number of economists feel that this reversion to monetary orthodoxy, if backed up by adequate fiscal policies, may point the way toward a more effective control of inflation.

But one must suspend judgment on whether progress is being made toward overcoming the biennial pattern of recurring crises and recoveries. Since the end of the war, each upswing after the crisis has followed a fairly definite pattern. The measures taken to stem the crisis begin to have some effect. The forces of fear and speculation pressing on the currency overreach themselves. Confidence be-

[12] In this country also there are promising signs of a revival of general monetary control, particularly the Treasury-Federal Reserve accord of March 1951.

gins to grow that the worst has been seen for the time being, flights from the currency subside and are followed by some backflow. But none of this means necessarily that there is confidence that a durable solution has been found. Western Europe's foreign trade problem is only part of that existing in the world as a whole. As I have indicated, throughout the Marshall Plan period the availability of supplies was a constant worry. The great increase of industrial production here and in Western Europe, in Canada, and in some other countries is making imperative an accelerated development of primary products. Industrial production in the world as a whole since 1938 has increased by some 50 per cent, while the output of raw materials has at most increased by 10 per cent. Some experts have estimated that, apart from the United States, the world's food production is now lower than before the war, and even the gain in raw materials is questionable if we take out a few large items, such as petroleum and aluminum.

This brings us back to the discussion of the terms of trade. For perhaps three-quarters of a century the problem had been whether the industrial countries could absorb the food and raw materials which they had been instrumental in developing in other countries, on terms of trade tolerable to the latter. Now there appear to be signs that the imbalance is swinging the other way, not merely in the short-run sense of Korea and rearmament but for the longer run. The absorption of metals is an outstanding example, and it is due not only to the great growth of investment in capital goods industries but to the growth of the consumer durable goods industries. American consumption of such products as automobiles, refrigerators, washing machines, and vacuum cleaners has doubled and trebled since before the war. Meanwhile, there are sharply divergent views as to the purposes of international investment or grants of aid. The less developed countries, with their recently-won sovereignty and their growing social welfare consciousness, often do not welcome the nineteenth-century kind of foreign investment, which they regard as 'exploitation,' a process of extraction at low cost of what the industrial countries wanted, while doing little or nothing toward creating a better rounded economy and a better scale of living.

Thus, the urge for industrialization in the underdeveloped countries collides with the world need for primary production. How to

reconcile this conflict and achieve a better balance of production
and trade in the world as a whole is the great problem for the future.
One of its most important aspects is the question of what part the
European countries should play in it. If they do not participate, they
run the danger of being forced into a backwater through the growth
of direct trade between this country and the less-developed countries. Probably what has held the sterling area together more than
anything else has been the free flow of capital throughout the area.
Even under the Marshall Plan, American aid was in effect merely
siphoned through the British economy to the sterling area countries
in the form of 'unrequited exports.' Now this strain on the British
economy will be accentuated by the rearmament program, and
there will be similar problems for France and Belgium with respect
to their overseas territories. I can only conclude that the problem
of how to reach a stable world economic balance will long be with
us and will require thinking and planning in new areas of economic
policy where we are as yet merely in the pioneering stage. The Point
Four program and the Colombo Plan, though proceeding slowly, are
at least indications that we are beginning to perceive the nature of
the problem.

Immediately upon us are the problems of rearmament. The latest
OEEC report contains a warning that there may be a new inflationary outburst in Europe next fall or winter, and one of the most
debated questions here at home has been whether the sidewise movement which we have had since the spring of 1951 will be followed
by renewed inflationary pressure as our defense program gets into
full stride. Many, both in Europe and here, have warned that a program too big or too rapid would not only lead to renewed inflation
but would open up a serious danger of deflation when the build-up
is completed and the replacement phase of the program is reached.
In Britain, as I have said, the need of stretching out the military
program has already been officially conceded, and for some time
past the time-schedule of our own program has also been undergoing a process of stretching out. On the Continent, except for the
heavy burden on France in Indo-China, the defense program is still
in its early stages. Meanwhile, there is complaint in Europe that our
aid, both military and economic, has been seriously lagging. There
have also been complaints this year, including formal protests to
our State Department by Italy and Britain and actual tariff retaliation

by Belgium, that our tariff practices belie our preachments about freer trade. There is nothing new in this. One of our chief problems is, and long has been, with ourselves. We cannot hope to achieve freer trade in a better balanced world if we do not live up to it ourselves.

Part III

Earlier Papers

10

Free Enterprise and Full Employment

I AGREED to take part in this symposium with considerable misgiving, and did so on the understanding that I should not be expected to present an economic program for the postwar period but could discuss some of the basic ideas and issues involved. The fundamental problem is how to achieve a high, stable, and growing level of production, income, and employment. It is a problem not primarily of the transition from war to peace but of the long-run operation of our economy under normal peacetime conditions.

The problem has domestic and international aspects so intertwined that there is little point in trying to say which is the more important. As the literature developed in the interwar period, there was much emphasis upon the conflict that appeared to be involved — for example, in the discussion of the gold standard — between internal and external economic stability. The development of monetary, and later of fiscal, policy was largely on lines of the 'closed economy' analysis and away from the ideal of an internationally interdependent world which had characterized nineteenth-century economics. This still seems to me one of the basic issues. But there is probably by now a large measure of agreement on the following propositions. High production and employment within countries should be sought by methods that do not operate at the expense of other countries but are mutually helpful. Economic stability in the leading countries, and particularly in the United States, is a necessary condition of world stability. Economic stability in this country will have to depend primarily upon the domestic policies pursued.

Financing American Prosperity, a symposium by six economists, The Twentieth Century Fund, New York, 1945.

An abridged version of this long paper (somewhat more than half the length of the original), omitting mainly statistical material no longer relevant but retaining all of the analysis.

How much domestic outweigh international factors, so far as this country is concerned, is indicated, for example, by the fact that our export surplus in 1919, when it was abnormally large, amounted to $4 billion, and our total current account surplus, including the invisible items, was only $1.5 billion, while the domestic income-increasing expenditures — for consumer durable goods, inventory accumulation, equipment, and construction — were about $22.5 billion. Comparable figures for a postwar year this time would be an export surplus of over $7 billion and domestic income-increasing expenditures of about $42 billion. It seems obvious from such figures that our chief concern must be with domestic policy and that on this will mainly depend international stability as well.

The problem of production and employment in the postwar period must be viewed against the background of the war and the experience preceding it. The mass unemployment of the 'thirties had no precedent. The significant circumstance is not that unemployment grew from about 3 million in 1929, which is generally regarded as consistent with full employment, to almost 14 million in 1932-3 at the bottom of our deepest depression, but the fact that in the recovery that followed, which was undoubtedly one of the largest recoveries in our history, mass unemployment persisted. By 1939 we had reached and surpassed the gross national product of 1929, though we were still somewhat below it on a per capita basis. But the number of unemployed in that year was 10.4 million, and it was not until 1941, when the stimulus of the war and of our defense program was already pronounced, that unemployment fell below 8 million, for the first time since 1930.

Then came our entry into the war, which affected powerfully both production and employment. The postwar problem would be simpler if we had increased war production by reducing civilian output, assuming that could be done without serious inflation. The problem would then have been the comparatively simple one of conversion of equal magnitudes. But actually our war production was piled on top of the highest level of consumption in our history. Such high consumption in wartime was made possible in part by the virtual elimination of private capital formation, but it was due much more to the rise in government expenditures. The military expenditure did not of course create consumer goods, but it created high consumer incomes, and the expansion of total production under this stimulus gave us high consumption as well as the great output of military goods and services. The postwar problem will be how to contract military expenditure and at the same time fill up the gap in national income sufficiently to avoid large unemployment. One important aspect of the problem is that at wartime levels of national income we generated much more money income than we spent. Liquid assets of individuals and businesses in the form of currency, demand and time deposits, and United States government securities amounted to $193.6 billion by the end of 1944; and holdings of such assets increased $111.5 billion during the three years 1942–4. One of the chief questions is how this large accumulation of liquid assets will affect postwar consumption and investment, and a further question, no less important, is how under normal conditions money incomes will be divided between spending and saving.

It is often said that the challenge of the postwar period is that the war has revealed a hitherto undreamed-of capacity to produce. If we can produce so much in war, why not in peace, with due allowance for voluntary leisure; and must we not do so if all who need jobs are to have them? It is a matter of real importance to determine to what extent programs for the postwar period are based upon wartime phenomena which may be inaccurately measured, or upon wartime relationships without due allowance for changes that may occur under peacetime conditions, or upon developments which are likely to have only temporary, rather than long-run, effects. Most estimates of postwar national product and employment are projections of a prewar year (usually 1940), based on a normal work-week, and with allowances for the growth of population, the rise of prices, and a cumulative annual rate of increase in productivity. If there is any serious error, it would most probably be in the correction for prices, since the forecasting of postwar prices is particularly hazardous; but forecasting changes in productivity also presents difficulties. One question, as some of the recent studies have pointed out, is how much time-lag there will be before wartime technical advances can be applied to peacetime production. One must also take account of Kuznets' view that efficiency in war industries was below that of the most nearly comparable prewar industries, and that the great rise in output in the war was due not so much to increased productivity as to the greater applicability of mass production to wartime output.[1] My own guess, however, is that the postwar period, at least in the manufacturing industries, will be characterized by a rate of technological advance at least as high as that which characterized the interwar period. It will be surprising if the war does not provide a powerful impetus, for war jolts us out of familiar ways of doing things and forces upon us new methods and techniques.

II

Since the great depression of the 'thirties the most widely discussed cure for unemployment has been fiscal policy. It has come to have much the same prominence as central bank policy had in the 'twenties. It has been the history of major ideas about economic policy that there is a warming-up period followed by a cooling-off period, and we have yet to look at fiscal policy in adequate historical perspective.

It is sometimes said that economists know how to prevent or cure unemployment by fiscal means and that the main trouble has been that they have not had their chance.[2] It will perhaps help our perspective to recognize that what we call 'compensatory' fiscal policy was a product of the depression, to which economists turned only after the monetary policies on which they had mainly relied to fight the depression had failed, although they were carried to unprecedented lengths.

Since the depression, theories about fiscal policy have gone through three fairly distinct phases and are still, in my opinion, in process of seeking reasonably firm ground on which to stand. We seem always — and the same was true earlier of central bank policy — to be

---

[1] Simon Kuznets, *National Product, War and Prewar,* Occasional Paper No. 17, National Bureau of Economic Research, New York, February 1944.

[2] Cf. Walter Lippmann, *New York Herald-Tribune,* 26 November 1942: 'Since 1920 men have discovered the principle of prosperity. This discovery is much the most important advance in human knowledge in modern times. It is the discovery that government can by the proper use of public funds create a condition of full employment for all its people. Heaven help the administration which refuses to apply this knowledge in the post-war world.' See also his more recent statements in the *New York Herald-Tribune,* 7 September and 23 September 1944.

Cf. 'The Domestic Economy,' *Fortune,* Supplement, December 1942, p. 7: 'We propose that the government should underwrite permanent prosperity.'

a step behind, the turns in our thinking following the turns in events, rather than the other way around. And yet it is undoubtedly true that fiscal policy will have an indispensable role in any well-rounded program for the postwar period.

The early 'pump-priming' phase of fiscal theory assumed that, apart from business-cycle fluctuations, the economy could sustain itself at full employment. It called for a cyclically unbalanced budget, with deficits in depression and surpluses in boom periods. Though the nature of the reasoning may have somewhat shifted, there is now wide agreement, I think, on the desirability and necessity, at least for major economic fluctuations, of a cyclically unbalanced budget. But the severity of the depression, and particularly the recurrence of depression in 1937-8 at a time when the federal budget came momentarily into balance, led to a growing preoccupation with long-run contractive tendencies toward oversaving and underinvestment which were much discussed in this country under the name of 'mature economy.' [3]

The word 'compensatory' came to be used in a second sense. Deficits would be needed not only to compensate for depression, with offsetting surpluses during booms (though the possibility of boom became for many as remote as that of depression in the late 'twenties), but also to compensate for the long-run contractive tendencies. This opened a prospect of an indefinitely expanding public debt and started a controversy about the economics of public debt which has been continuing ever since. My own view was that on this reasoning the debt charges would be a growing fraction of national income, and in the process the system of private capitalism would disappear.[4]

The war has given the discussion a new turn. With a federal debt in prospect of over $250 billion, the debt takes on a new importance. In a few years we have acquired a debt to which deficits of the size of those of the 'thirties would have carried us only after two or three generations. This has brought a new sense of urgency into our efforts to think through the economic and political implications of a large public debt and to determine our attitude toward its further

[3] The reasoning stemmed mainly from 'Keynesian economics,' and especially from Lord Keynes's book, *The General Theory of Employment, Interest and Money,* Harcourt, Brace, New York, 1936.

[4] Williams, *Post-War Monetary Plans* (Blackwell ed.), chap. 13.

growth. Deficit spending has not been discarded as an instrument of postwar full-employment policy; but, apart from the short-run cyclical aspect, it has been less emphasized. In its place has come a new emphasis on 'developmental' public expenditure, not financed necessarily by deficits, and a much increased interest in the possibilities of using taxation as a compensatory fiscal device.

The new developments in the discussion of fiscal policy do not adequately explain the reduced emphasis on deficits. The main explanation lies in the assumption of a new set of facts. The models prepared to illustrate the composition of postwar national product, breaking it down into the categories of consumption, investment, and public spending, are not simple projections of the prewar composition but are based upon estimates of what might be regarded as 'reasonable' amounts in each category. This is a method which permits of considerable latitude. The larger the amounts estimated for private expenditures, the smaller will be the gap to be filled in by public expenditures. It is an interesting question how much such models are affected by the mathematical necessities of the case. The postwar national income envisaged as essential for full employment is only slightly less than the wartime level, and of a wholly different order of magnitude from the actual prewar level. The wartime national product, moreover, has in it some $80 billion a year of military expenditure and involves a deficit of some $50 billion a year.

The difference between such figures and any practicable program of peacetime public expenditures is so large that there is an understandable tendency to assume as large figures for consumption and private capital formation as can reasonably be devised. I have no quarrel with these estimates when stated as goals that we must try to reach. But the models can do no more than indicate the general order of magnitude of the problem. So much of the discussion has revolved around these purely static *tableaux économiques* that the point should be emphasized that, helpful as they undoubtedly are as a first approach to the problem, they are in no sense a solution.

Probably the chief question to be asked about fiscal policy is whether, like the monetary policy out of which it developed, it is not more useful as an instrument for stabilizing national income at a given level than for lifting it to a new high order of magnitude.[5]

[5] This would not, of course, rule out public expenditures to assist in further growth.

When it was a question of compensating for short-run differences between saving and investment in a full-employment national income of, say, $80 billion, roughly that of 1929, the deficits contemplated were temporary and comparatively small.[6] But the problem as it was posed in the late 'thirties was far more serious, for not only was the deficit spending to be permanent to compensate for the assumed long-run contractive tendencies in private spending, but it was to be applied to a national income which by reason of the strong tendency toward technological advance would have to expand continuously in order to provide full employment.

Thus the problem assumed ever larger proportions. It is small wonder that the advocates of deficits were saying in the late 'thirties and the early war years that the trouble with deficit spending was its small size — it should have been $10 to $15 billion a year rather than $3 or $4 billion — and were pointing to the wartime expansion of output and the accompanying deficits as proof of what could be accomplished.[7] If now we expect that the budget will be balanced, or nearly balanced, in the postwar period and that the wartime level of national income will be nevertheless maintained or only slightly lowered, we must be counting heavily upon other measures, or else — as has happened before — merely projecting a prevailing state of mind.

[6] Prior to the 'thirties, net investment was roughly 12 per cent of national income; see Simon Kuznets, 'Capital Formation, 1879–1938,' *Studies in Economics and Industrial Relations,* University of Pennsylvania Press, Philadelphia, 1941.

[7] Cf. J. M. Keynes, 'The United States and the Keynes Plan,' *The New Republic,* 29 July 1940. He refers to the failure of the deficit spending to produce 'anything like full employment in the United States,' and ascribes the failure to the 'gigantic powers of production' of a modern industrial state. 'Coupled with institutional factors which tend to encourage accumulation and retard the growth of consumption when incomes increase, this means that an unprecedented output has to be reached before a state of full employment can be approached. The full industrial and agricultural capacity of the United States may well exceed 1929 by as much as, or even more than, 1929 exceeded 1914 . . . The conclusion is that at all recent times investment [and public] expenditure has been on a scale which was hopelessly inadequate to the problem . . . It appears to be politically impossible for a capitalistic democracy to organize expenditure on the scale necssary to make the grand experiment which would prove my case . . . except in war conditions.'

III

However it is to be achieved, the maintenance of high employment is being accepted as the basic economic responsibility after the war by both government and business. The discussion of methods here and in England has covered a wide area and revealed a great diversity of viewpoints. Through it all have run the two fundamental questions. How much is it a problem of mitigating cyclical fluctuations, and how much one of creating continuous expansion? How far and in what ways must government intervene?

In England, in the widely heralded White Paper on Employment Policy, issued on 26 May 1944, the Government has officially accepted responsibility for maintaining employment. But apart from the transition from war to peace the White Paper treats the problem as mainly one of cyclical unemployment and directs its recommendations mainly toward offsetting variations in private investment by public works; and, as a second line of attack, stabilizing consumption through cyclical variation of social insurance contributions.

The question of the budget is treated cautiously in the White Paper. Though there is no need, the Paper holds, to adhere to a strict balance, 'none of the main proposals contained in this Paper involves deliberate planning for a deficit in years of subnormal activity.' It insists that the principle of long-run balance of the budget cannot be abandoned; 'the Government will have equally in mind the need to maintain the national income, and the need for a policy of budgetary equilibrium such as will maintain the confidence in the future which is necessary for a healthy and enterprising industry.' [8]

Many people, even in this country where opposition to government intervention is greater than in England, would not regard this as a very bold program, even for its limited purpose.[9] In contrast, Sir William Beveridge in his report *Full Employment in a Free Society* [10]

[8] Cmd. 6527, published in the United States by permission of the Controller of H. M. Stationery Office by the Macmillan Company, pp. 24, 26.

[9] What may be regarded as the American counterpart of the British White Paper is our Employment Act of 1946. See my paper on 'The Employment Act of 1946' in *Post-War Monetary Plans* (Blackwell ed.), chap. 12.

[10] Allen and Unwin, London, 1944, published in the United States by W. W. Norton, New York, 1945. See also Sir William Beveridge's analysis of the White Paper, just mentioned, 'The Government's Employment Policy,' *The Economic Journal*, June–September 1944.

poses the problem as that of planning for continuous expansion. He presents a program that would include:

Abolition of want by social security and children's allowances . . . collective outlay to secure good houses, good food, fuel and other necessaries at stable prices for all . . . regulation of private investment by a national (governmental) investment board . . . extension of the public sector of industry . . . a new type of budget based on the datum of man-power and designed to ensure year by year total outlay sufficient to set up demand for the whole productive resources of the country; control of the location of industry . . . organised mobility of labour . . . controlled marketing of primary products, so as to stabilise overseas demand . . . and international trade arrangements based on acceptance of three fundamental conditions of multilateral trade: full employment, balancing of international accounts and stability of economic policy.[11]

Sir William holds that 'the time calls for total war against unemployment and other social evils, not for a war with inhibitions.' Whatever one's view of his specific proposals, they show the scope and gravity of the problem as seen by one of the most distinguished British economists. His reference to war is significant. It is only in war that we get really full utilization of resources, and his question, which is widely asked also in this country, is: if we can do it in war, why not in peace? The answer suggested is that we can if we are willing to use war methods, and Sir William's own program is in considerable part an adaptation of war methods to peace.

But this raises the question of costs in terms of other values. Many would question whether Sir William's proposals can properly be called an employment program 'in a free society.' It seems true, though so far the world's experience has been confined mostly to war and preparation for war, that in a state-controlled society, with planned and rationed production and consumption and a state-directed labor force, there would be a fuller utilization of resources than there could ever be in a free society. The question is how far we could move in that direction and still preserve our political liberties and the economic freedoms of choice which are the essence of our way of life. The problem, to be sure, is always one of compromise. We have long ceased to have, and probably no one really wants, a *laissez-faire* system. But Sir William Beveridge's program,

[11] Ibid. p. 174.

while stopping far short of a completely regimented society, suggests
it sufficiently as the road along which his kind of planning would
progress (he speaks of it as only a beginning) to put it in the
category of last or late resort, so far as this country is concerned,
after we have experimented further with a war on unemployment
'with inhibitions.'

Two questions about our kind of economic system impress me as
having a special bearing on our problem. The first is that, whatever
its faults, ours has been in terms of productivity a highly progressive
society. That, indeed, is the largest aspect of our postwar problem of
employment; it is because the rate of increase of productivity per
worker has been so high, and will probably continue to be, that we
face the need of greatly expanding our postwar output beyond the
prewar level. Whether some other economic system would be as
efficient, apart from the special stimuli of war, we do not know. The
Russian experiment as yet is not comparable because it is being
applied to a country at a lower stage of development and with a different institutional framework. If efficiency is the test, there is a
strong presumption in favor of retaining and improving what we
have instead of striking out in new directions.

The second question is whether our kind of economic system does
not have to operate on the basis of slacks — slacks in materials, in
plant and equipment, and in employment. This is for me a much
more bothersome question. It has been estimated that even in boom
periods under peace conditions we did not get much above 80 per
cent of full capacity operation. Though this is probably an exaggeration, it illustrates the problem. Failure to utilize resources fully,
including labor, is often referred to as a sign of waste. But full
utilization is not easy to define. The task of the producer in our
kind of system is to produce at lowest possible cost, and his use
of resources, including labor, is governed by this fact. As his output
expands he faces anew, at each step in the process, the question
whether to use more or better machines, whether to use machines
instead of manpower, and whether to use new techniques which are
both capital- and labor-saving. In such a system, under conditions
of rapid progress, there is bound to be a surplus of both men and
resources, continuously being reabsorbed through expansion of output but re-created through further advances in productivity. Of
course, we do in war, when we are straining to get the most output

in the shortest time, and under conditions when ordinary cost considerations do not count, get full utilization of resources by totalitarian methods. But this is not a usable answer in time of peace.[12]

There are some who hold that technical progress and high real income are not our main objectives, and that if we have to choose between high income and high employment we had better choose the latter. But we do not want to choose, if we can help it, between less efficient production, providing jobs for all at low real income, and more efficient production, throwing increasing numbers of workers on to relief rolls and into make-work jobs. Yet for me this is the most perplexing aspect of the subject. One effect it has is to make me want to be careful how we define the postwar problem. The goal can be stated as that of providing high employment or that of preventing high unemployment. The first is the better, but the second is probably the safer, form of statement.

The year 1941 has been much referred to as a model year which showed us what we can do and must strive for. Under the stimulus of the war and our defense program but without as yet much wartime control, we reached a level of national income substantially beyond any previously reached. By any previous standard it was a year of highest prosperity. But it was also a year of 6 million unemployed. The contrast between prewar unemployment and wartime full employment has made us as a nation acutely conscious of the issue. In the political campaign of 1944 the promise made by both sides was 'jobs for all.' Unless people have short memories, a postwar year as good as 1941, after due allowance for growth, will fail to satisfy. How much better we shall be able to do, and at the same time live up to the other campaign promises to sustain democracy and restore free enterprise, will be interesting to watch.

IV

We face two questions. How far will deferred civilian demands go toward filling up the gap left by contraction of military expenditures? What is to take the place of the deferred demand once the process of re-stocking has been completed? Intensive analysis of the deferred demand has been undertaken both by government agencies and privately. Undoubtedly, for a short period this accumulated demand

[12] See my paper 'Deficit Spending' in *Post-War Monetary Plans* (Blackwell ed.), Chap. 13, pp. 227–30.

could be of large proportions. It has been estimated that the deferred demand for consumer durable goods should amount to $4.4 billion a year for four years.[13] Probably a much larger item will be postponed private capital formation. Now almost nil, gross private capital formation averaged $13 billion a year from 1936 through 1941. Not only should it revive, but because of accumulated replacement needs, postponed expansion, replenishment of inventories of civilian goods, and the cost of reconversion it should for a time substantially exceed the prewar volume. There should be also a substantial backlog of demand for housing. There have been estimates that residential construction after the war might amount to one to one and a quarter million units a year, requiring a $5 billion volume of expenditure. These estimates are very high by any previous standards but could well prove true in the aftermath of a war, with its greatly increased marriage rate and greatly reduced residential construction.

In calculations of this kind there is usually added to our own civilian demands accumulated during the war the export surplus representing the needs of foreign countries for rehabilitation and reconstruction. In 1919 our export surplus was about $4 billion and a corresponding surplus this time would have to amount to nearly twice as much. But in regarding the export surplus as an offset to declining war expenditure we must bear in mind that our lend-lease exports are running (1944) at the rate of $11.5 billion a year and our total exports, $14.3 billion a year. To make the same relative contribution to national product, postwar exports would have to be at least three times their prewar magnitude.

If we look at the figures of wartime saving, without asking for what it might be spent, the possibility of filling the gap looks even brighter. But what will happen to these savings is problematical. Very likely the savers will hold on to a large fraction, though no one knows how much; and perhaps the better lead is to stick to estimating the needs (besides unemployment) for which some portion might reasonably be spent. To the point often made that the very existence of these savings will make people more willing to spend their current incomes I shall return later in another connection, but

[13] Sumner H. Slichter, 'Jobs After the War,' *The Atlantic Monthly,* October 1944.

it does not help us here unless we first explain how adequate current income is to be created.

Whether these deferred demands, large as they are, will prove large enough to fill the gap left by the reduction of military expenditures seems to me doubtful. In any case, they will not do so for long. Beyond will lie the question what to rely on when the catching-up process is at an end. To some degree from the start we must depend on growth of new demand, and on this increasingly we must rely as we come out of the transition into normal long-run peace conditions. I conclude again that if after the transition has been passed we find ourselves compelled to fall back upon substantial deficits — and not merely on a cyclically unbalanced budget — we shall have failed to achieve our objective within the limits we have set.

V

This brings us to the long-run problem. The fundamental question is whether we must have a grand plan, with comprehensive government control, or whether, given the short breathing spell of the two-stage war termination and the deferred demands, we can work out an answer consistent with the form and the spirit of the free-enterprise system. As the problem is often put in this country, if business does not succeed government must. To this might be added the question, if business and government combined do not succeed by free-enterprise methods, how far shall we be driven upon some other course — whether that suggested by Sir William Beveridge or some other? As I said earlier, the answer depends in part upon our general scheme of values, political and social as well as economic.

There seem to be three main courses open: (a) the adoption of fiscal and monetary policies to stabilize income and employment, and in so far as possible to expand them, but subject to the qualification that large public expenditure, and especially large deficits, will gradually transform our economic system into some kind of public economy; (b) non-fiscal policies, both business and governmental, to make the private economy function more effectively within itself and respond more promptly to forces making for expansion; and (c) the development of new wants, new products, and new processes. We shall need to rely heavily on all three.

At the core of the problem are the relationships among consumption, investment, and public spending. In much of the monetary literature of the interwar period, consumption was regarded as the passive factor and investment as the factor responsible both for short-period fluctuations of national income and for long-run growth. The role of budgetary deficits was to compensate for variations in investment. The British White Paper on Employment Policy runs mainly in these terms, though, as I have said, it treats budgetary deficits very cautiously.

Even from the short-run standpoint this approach leaves something lacking. The view that consumption is the passive factor ignores the fact that expenditure on consumer durable goods shows quite as wide a range of cyclical fluctuation as expenditure on producer goods. The business cycle is not so much a cycle of investment as a cycle of durable goods, both producers' and consumers'. It is the postponability of the expenditure rather than the character of the goods that seems principally to matter, and since the first war the turns in expenditure on consumer durable goods have led the way into booms and depressions quite as often as those on producer goods. When we consider that since World War I the volume of expenditure on the two types of goods has been of about the same magnitude, it seems doubtful whether there is any more to be said for a policy of stabilizing investment than for a policy of stabilizing consumption of durable goods. Both seem necessary.

But our postwar problem is more a problem of growth than of stability, and from this standpoint especially the concept of consumption, as propped up by and dependent upon the volume of investment, must be re-examined. All the estimates I have cited agree that consumption must expand by at least 40 per cent by 1947, and correspondingly more thereafter, beyond the level of 1939. To what extent must this great rise in consumption, amounting to at least $30 billion, be brought about by policies designed to expand investment and/or public expenditure, and to what extent must consumption be made to stand on its own feet? No doubt we shall need to do both, but it is important to see that there is a fundamental difference in the two approaches.

The view that consumption must be dependent upon investment, or on public spending as a substitute, will always, I believe, leave us subject to the basic worry that the objects of expenditure may not be enough. Thus, before the war, we worried about declining opportunities for investment. It then becomes a short and fairly obvious step to the view that we must look to public investment as the way out — both to encourage private investment and to take its place.

I have no quarrel with this kind of policy, except to raise the question of its adequacy. The desire to avoid spending merely for spending's sake seems now to be general. One of the most difficult questions about public works has always been whether it would be possible to assemble enough worthy projects to provide an adequate prop for a national income which, by reason of the strong tendency toward technological advance, needs to be ever larger to furnish adequate employment. Probably, as the necessity unfolds, we shall do a better job in this regard than ever previously. But the more public spending our program requires, the more we shall need to scrutinize the objects of expenditure. The broad and general view that we can afford whatever we can produce, and that the one thing we cannot afford is unemployment, covers leaf-raking and building causeways to the moon as well as economically desirable expenditure.

What I feel inclined to question is the adequacy of the whole approach. Consumption is roughly eight parts of national income; investment, or a budgetary deficit to take its place, is the other part. If we hope to bring about a great expansion of postwar national income compared with prewar, we shall have to attack consumption more directly. Private investment and public expenditure, important though they are, cannot be more than stepping stones to the final goal. The growth of national income depends only secondarily upon 'income creation' by either private investment or public expenditure and primarily upon the price-cost relationships at work throughout the whole economic structure.

Fiscal and monetary theory has been developed largely on the basis of an assumption of price rigidity as a *force majeure*. It is based on the view that if the price system is not responsive to economic changes we can compensate for its defects. For short-period fluctuations this is often a helpful approach, but when the problem assumes large proportions, as in our present case, we are forced to dig down deeper and remove the defects, if only for the reason that the task of 'compensation' becomes unmanageably large.

What seems needed, more fundamentally than fiscal policies, is to make our economy more responsive and adaptable within itself.

Much attention needs to be given to the question of how the benefits of increasing productivity can be diffused more rapidly through the economic system by downward adjustments of prices and upward adjustments of incomes. If this interflow of income between production and consumption could be made more effective, there would be less need for reliance on public spending and, indeed, even on investment itself. My own view of an advancing economy is one that relies more and more on better technique and organization to increase its output, and more and more upon a rapid diffusion of the benefits through price reductions and income increases to expand consumption correspondingly.

In the economic literature investment has been treated chiefly in two senses: the income-increasing sense, which is its role in Keynesian economics, and the cost-reducing sense, in which the earlier economists regarded it. For the problem of growth and progress there can be little question that the second is much the more fundamental function. From the long-run standpoint, investment is significant not primarily because of the money income and the employment provided by the capital goods industries themselves but because of the fact that by producing consumer goods in more efficient and therefore cheaper ways it releases consumer income for expenditure on other goods and services, and by increasing productivity per worker makes possible upward adjustments of incomes and increased voluntary leisure.

This has been the heart of the productive process under the free-enterprise system. In a task of the present magnitude it seems inescapable that we shall be forced to rely upon making it work rather than upon compensating for its failures. Indeed I think it can be demonstrated that if investment (or public spending) does not have these cost-reducing effects it can never rise beyond being a kind of perpetual pump-priming device, needing always to be renewed and always on a larger scale.[14]

Once the emphasis is shifted to this aspect of the investment process, it becomes just another step to recognize that investment is only one way to reduce prices and raise incomes. In a modern

[14] William Fellner, 'The Technological Argument of the Stagnation Thesis,' *Quarterly Journal of Economics,* August 1941.

highly capitalistic society capital replacement tends steadily to increase relative to new investment, and the question of growth and progress becomes increasingly how to improve equipment and technique through the replacement of old capital. How far this process has gone in England has been shown by Colin Clark.[15] The yearly additions to British home capital have declined since 1875. Clark's figures on net investment as a percentage of national income show a decline from 12.2 per cent in 1907 to 8.1 per cent in 1924, 7.2 per cent in 1929, and 6.9 per cent in 1935. His conclusion is:

I believe the facts have destroyed the view up till now generally prevalent, that the rate of economic growth was primarily dependent upon the rate at which capital could be accumulated. The very rapid expansion at the present time [before the war] is taking place at a time of heavily diminishing capital accumulation. What is more remarkable, practically none of the capital which is being saved is being put into productive industry proper.

Kuznets has shown that in this country in 1919–35 replacement constituted 68 per cent (1929 prices) and new investment 32 per cent of the yearly average volume of gross capital formation.[16] Leaving out public agencies, his figures were 81 per cent replacement and 19 per cent net capital formation.

The main objection that is made to this way of achieving economic progress is that it does not absorb saving. Outlets for saving through investment are reduced and, at the same time through the cost-reducing effects of new technique, consumer wants are satisfied with less expenditure and saving is increased. I discussed earlier the relation of technological progress to unemployment. We have here apparently its counterpart in terms of money income. The more directly and cheaply we seek to satisfy our wants, the more we defeat ourselves by throwing money income out of use. By insisting sufficiently on the intractability of the propensity to save we might persuade ourselves that the higher the cost and the greater the roundaboutness of production, the fuller would be employment

[15] *National Income and Outlay,* Macmillan, New York, 1938, p. 270.

[16] *National Income and Capital Formation,* 1919–1935, National Bureau of Economic Research, New York, 1937, p. 49 and Table 14. In a later analysis covering the longer period, 1919–38, Kuznets found that net investment was 33 per cent of gross capital formation. See his 'Capital Formation, 1879–1938,' op. cit. Table 2, p. 60.

both for labor and for income. The alternative, from this point of view, would be to have the government absorb an increasing portion of the community's money income and spend it on make-work jobs, in order to offset the efficiency of the private-enterprise system. Efficient public expenditure might only re-create the problem by again satisfying wants too cheaply and with too little labor.

I have never been convinced of the reality of the tendency toward oversaving which has been the chief preoccupation of monetary theory for the past decade.[17] Most of the prewar estimates of saving were estimates of real investment, and prove only that, as might be expected, changes in national income have been accompanied by changes in investment. How much of income took the form of idle saving, and to what extent investment may have exceeded or fallen short of saving through accompanying changes in bank credit are aspects of the question usually not covered by the analysis. What the estimates seem to indicate, for this country, is a constant long-run relation between income, investment, and consumption since as far back as 1880.[18] In other words, while national income has risen greatly over this period, standards of living have risen correspondingly, and the great bulk of income has gone into consumption. Saving, at least as measured by real investment, has remained a constant fraction of income. In England, on the other hand, according to Colin Clark's data previously cited, saving has been a diminishing fraction of a growing national income for at least the last generation. Samuelson's analysis of the American data yields the striking conclusion that consumers in the aggregate spent virtually all their increases in money income and that any additional saving accompanying rising income almost wholly took the form of business saving.[19]

---

[17] Williams, op. cit. (Blackwell ed.), chap. 13.

[18] Simon Kuznets, 'Capital Formation, 1879–1938,' op. cit. p. 69.

[19] See Alvin H. Hansen, *Fiscal Policy and Business Cycles,* W. W. Norton, New York, 1941, chap. 11, Appendix, pp. 250–60 by Paul A. Samuelson.

Samuelson's analysis is based on Kuznets' data (1919–35). For consumers he finds a marginal propensity to consume of 0.97, and for business enterprises a marginal propensity to save of 0.49. 'This [business saving] accounts for most of the leakages incident upon net investment: as far as these data go, the leakages incident upon household savings are much smaller and possibly negative' (p. 257). In his conclusion (p. 260) he again emphasizes 'the very sensitive relation of consumption to aggregate income payments.'

For the postwar period concern about the possible depressing effect of saving was heightened by our wartime experience. At the war level of national product we were generating much more income than we spent. One explanation offered was that living standards lag markedly behind income, so that the temporary effect, at least, of a large and sudden rise in national income is a great increase of saving. On these grounds some economists predicted that in the postwar period, even if for a while we spent enough, publicly and privately, to generate a full-employment level of national income, the effects would soon be dissipated by saving. Consumers and business concerns would fail to spend their current incomes.[20] This view was heightened by projections of prewar studies of consumer expenditure [21] which indicated that at a national income level of $140 to $150 billion we might save as much as $30 billion a year.

My guess is that these fears will turn out to be exaggerated. One point, referred to earlier, is that the very fact of accumulated wartime saving may make people more willing after the war to spend their current incomes. But a much more important point is that wartime saving would have been much less if there had been consumer durable goods available to spend it on. In the 'twenties, the last period of sharply rising national income, there was no evidence that consumption lagged markedly behind income, and expenditures on consumer durable goods, including automobiles and residential housing, expanded faster and relatively more than either total income or investment. Consumer durable goods are quite as much an outlet for saving as investment, and when we take them both together the assumption underlying modern monetary theory, that income tends to run to waste in idle saving, seems far less plausible.

VI

In attacking consumption directly, our best hope is to develop new consumer wants and goods to satisfy them, especially the durable goods the demand for which, in response to efficient production as reflected in prices, is highly elastic. The chief generator of national

[20] See Gunnar Myrdal, 'Is American Business Deluding Itself?' *The Atlantic Monthly*, November 1944.
[21] National Resources Planning Board, *Consumer Expenditures in the United States*, 1939; and see also *Family Expenditures in the United States*, 1941.

income in our time has been the automobile. It seems important to note, too, that the growth process to which the automobile gave rise does not lend itself to the conception of consumption as the 'passive factor' induced and propped up by investment. From modest beginnings, first a circus curiosity, then a luxury, and finally a necessity, the demand for which has reached down into lower and lower income brackets, the automobile has generated both consumption and investment on an ever-widening scale. And the accompanying growth of consumer credit shows that it has not failed to make inroads on saving. The history of its successive price reductions, improvements in quality of product, and advancing wage rates, all accompanied by an ever-widening market, mark the automobile industry as the model on which to build our future growth in a far more realistic sense than the models of national income setting forth the proportions of consumption, investment, and public spending which I discussed earlier. If we could repeat this experience with any combination of new and improved products after the war, it would probably be our best means of achieving a high-employment level of national income and consumption.

The war has produced or improved further a number of such products. The airplane, food-freezing in homes, air conditioning on a national scale, nation-wide television networks are some of the things we talk about. But perhaps the chief opportunity on a scale comparable with the automobile would be in housing, if we could impart to it some of the enterprise and ingenuity that have characterized the automobile industry. Here is a market at least equally as large and one that should be equally as attractive as an outlet for saving. In the past we seem to have approached it primarily from the standpoint of public expenditure — how much public housing or public assistance to private housing may be needed as an offset to oversaving. But the characteristic free-enterprise method of solving the problem would be to provide housing, as we have provided automobiles, of a quality and at prices which the community felt it could afford and could not do without. This does not imply that there will not always be an important area for public housing, but it does suggest that one of our greatest needs in preparing for the postwar period is a thorough exploration of the conditions in the construction industry. No industry, as all analyses agree, is more essential to expansion of national income and employment, and no industry today is more characterized by primitive methods, high costs, and monopolistic and racketeering elements. I heartily agree with Beardsley Ruml's proposal that we should have a national commission to study the construction industry.[22]

It is sometimes objected that new products replace old ones. This is often the case, but any implication that consumption does not grow on balance is abundantly disproved by the history of consumer durable goods in our own time, and the reason obviously is that new products have generated new income. On the other hand, we must not conclude that consumers' purchases can be increased only if new products are created. This would imply that the existing needs are fully satisfied. According to prewar studies of consumer expenditures, in 1935-6, 54.9 per cent of all American families (all those earning less than $1250) and 60.7 per cent of single individuals (all those earning less than $1000) *dissaved* in order to cover their current living expenses. These estimates strongly suggest that in order to develop a vigorously expanding high-consumption economy, governmental and business policies should be directed toward modifying the distribution of national income. This is the logical and necessary counterpart of the tendency toward technological advance which, as I said earlier, is the chief explanation of the high estimates of postwar full-employment national income. It points to wage policies, profits, social security, and taxation as areas especially in need of study if we are to accomplish our objective.

A high-consumption economy, i.e. an economy with a high level of income but no excessive saving, should be a high-wage, low-profit economy. Wartime changes have substantially modified in this direction the prewar distribution of income, and in reconverting to peace our aim should be to see how much of this shift it is desirable and feasible to retain. Labor will surely want to retain its pay envelope, despite reduction of hours and loss of overtime rates. Such demands could easily be excessive, but we should recognize that it is easier to achieve a high-consumption economy by holding to a tolerable minimum reduction in wage rates from the present level than it would be under peace conditions to raise them from the prewar level. The great difficulty about raising wage rates as a means of raising national income is the conflict between wages as income and

[22] Beardsley Ruml, 'A Postwar National Fiscal Program,' *The New Republic*, 28 February 1944.

wages as cost. What happens when there is a large and sudden peacetime rise of wage rates was shown in 1937. The rise of wage rates in the first half of 1937 was probably the greatest in our history in so short a period, apart from war. The result was a sharp decline in profits. This, along with the rise of prices and the wave of forward buying (which in turn were related to the uncertainties growing out of wage-rate increases, wage disputes, and fears of strikes) had more to do, I believe, with the renewal of depression in that year than the temporary balancing of the budget. Broadly speaking, wage-rate increases must follow rather than precede advances in productivity and output. But once achieved, as now in war, they must be held so far as possible.

To the maintenance of a high-wage structure I would subordinate the role of public expenditure or any type of what I have called the propping-up method of sustaining consumption. By this I do not mean to deny the importance, even in the longer run, of public expenditure. There will undoubtedly be a growing need for expenditure that can be undertaken only by the community as a whole. I am sympathetic to public expenditure to promote higher standards of health, education, and security. By such means we can help to put a floor under consumption and at the same time increase the productivity and general well-being of our people. I am sympathetic also to the private planning of expenditure, such as that advocated by the Committee for Economic Development. By breaking down the problem, community by community and industry by industry, we should be able to accomplish much toward providing a shelf of private as well as public works [23] to help sustain production and employment through the transition period. But all this, important as it is, is

---

[23] While it is possible and desirable for individual industries and communities to look ahead and plan for, and thus hasten, their necessary and foreseeable capital improvements, on the analogy of the public-works shelf, this seems to me an approach of limited and temporary possibilities. To plan for long-run industrial growth by this method encounters the difficulty, probably inherent in the free-enterprise system as against the state-controlled economy, that we cannot foresee changes in price relationships and in the pattern of production and employment which in a growing economy, particularly following a war, are bound to be great. I expressed earlier my skepticism about the suggestion (see S. Morris Livingston, *Markets After the War*) that business men should break down the postwar projection of national income and employment by individual industries and have each one undertake to do its share.

either temporary or secondary. To the long-run problem we need a more analytical approach. If one may use such a figure of speech, we need an approach that runs more in terms of the biology of the organism of the private-enterprise system — what essentially gives it life and makes it grow? So long as the 'compensatory' approach is kept secondary to this, and is not built up into a device to make the free-enterprise system tolerate more comfortably its organic diseases, it can be a most helpful and necessary secondary method of attack.

I have suggested that a high-consumption economy should be not only a high-wage but a low-profit economy. This is a particularly difficult aspect of our problem. We must not lose sight of the fact that ours is a profit-seeking economy. Profit has been the mainspring of change, both in regard to long-run growth and short-run fluctuations. Profits fluctuate much more than any other type of income. The history of corporate profits in the interwar period was one of large and rising profits from 1922 to 1929, large net losses in the depression, and slow recovery thereafter. Not until 1941 did corporate profits before taxes surpass the peak of 1929. One of the most debated questions in the 'thirties was whether the rate of profits was not too low in relation to the volume of business to induce adequate investment and expansion. The sharp setback in profits caused by the increases in wage rates in 1937, the new social security contributions by employers, and the depression of 1937–8 lent support to this view. But in 1940, when the national income for the first time exceeded that of 1929 on a per capita basis, corporate profits before taxes were about equal to those of 1929, and in 1941 they were nearly double.[24]

Surveying the whole experience, we must ask whether profits were not too high in the 'twenties as well as too low in the 'thirties. Profits are both cause and effect of business-cycle fluctuations. A rise in profits which feeds on itself cyclically results in losses later on. Lower and more stable profits would not necessarily mean lower average profits over the period of the business cycle. A lower rate of profits in a more stable economy would be preferable, even from the standpoint of business itself, if it did not impair long-run growth. The outstanding fact about the interwar experience was the marked stability of the long-run relation between the level of profits and

[24] See Dwight B. Yntema, 'Corporate Profits and National Income,' *Survey of Current Business,* September 1944.

the volume of national income. In 1940–41 there was a substantial identity of the profit-income relation with that of the late 'twenties. But in marked contrast was the change in unemployment. There were 5 to 6 million more unemployed in the later period of high national income than in the earlier one. The growth of both income and profits in 1940–41 was in response to external stimuli. Rising national income, under the stimulus of the war and our defense expenditures, generated profits which, if they had not been increasingly absorbed through taxation, would have been inordinately high. There is a strong presumption that income must increase relative to profits. If the free-enterprise system is to grow from within itself, the rise of profits in response to increasing productivity, new methods, and new investment must be passed on rapidly in the form of higher wage rates and lower prices. Only in this way can the expansion of national income be made a self-continuing process, rather than one that needs increasingly to be propped up by public spending. How to absorb profits into higher wages and lower prices in a steady and orderly manner that business can tolerate without deflationary setbacks or the impairment of investment is the central problem.

One major question involved is the relation of profit to saving. No aspect of the savings problem has been more discussed than that of business savings. Much data and analysis have been developed, especially in connection with the Congressional hearings in 1939 by the Temporary National Economic Committee. The relation of profit to saving stands out strikingly. In 1929, for example, a year of high national income, profit, though only 10 per cent of income, was 46 per cent of saving.[25] But 1929 was a year of high investment, and all that such figures by themselves indicate is that capital expansion was to a large extent financed internally rather than through the securities market. The chief complaint of the 'thirties was that business savings tended to remain idle. It was supported by the contention that improved machinery and technique were financed out of depreciation funds rather than from profits. There was, I think, much truth in this view, though it should not necessarily imply criticism of corporation practice. Under conditions of rapid technological advance, the high rate of obsolescence involved re-

---

[25] See Moses Abramovitz, 'Savings and Investment: Profits vs. Prosperity?' *The American Economic Review*, Supplement, June 1942, p. 65.

quires large replacement funds. But it does mean, as I indicated earlier in reviewing British experience, that in a highly advanced industrial economy, replacement becomes increasingly important relative to new investment, and in consequence the outlets for saving out of current income, whether from profits or from other forms of income, are increasingly reduced.

Reasoning of this sort was responsible for the short-lived undistributed profits tax of 1936. The tax came at a time when business profits were already being undermined by unduly large and rapid wage increases and were about to face a new depression. It represented also a mechanical approach to the problem, emphasizing graduated penalty rate provisions and making inadequate allowance for small and new enterprises. It proved highly effective in forcing distribution of profits through sustained and increased dividends at a time of diminishing profits. In 1937 business dissaved a billion dollars at the very time when, because of wage increases, social security contributions, and renewed depression, idle business saving had for the time being ceased to be a problem. But for the postwar period the question remains one of paramount importance. The central question regarding profits is whether we must tax them away and redistribute them, with due regard for new enterprises and for risk-taking investment in old enterprises, or whether, if business were not taxed, it would itself pass on the benefits of increasing productivity to the consumers in higher wage rates and lower prices.

VII

This brings us to the problem of postwar taxation. There has been, I think, a tendency to oversimplify the subject. Public finance, taking revenue and expenditure together, can theoretically restrict or promote the flow of national income or have a neutral effect. But we have to recognize at the outset that taxation, of almost any sort, tends to be restrictive, and if our objective is to have a balanced, or a nearly balanced, budget, this is a hard fact to reckon with. No doubt we should like to have a tax structure which would promote consumption and investment (particularly of venture capital), encourage new and small enterprises, raise wages and lower prices, and discourage idle saving. But this is asking much of an instrument whose basic tendency is to be restrictive. We have yet to discover how effective taxation can be as a tool of compensatory fiscal policy. But the very size of the postwar budget indicates that the subject must be put high on the agenda of postwar policy.

It has been estimated that, assuming the repeal of the excess-profits tax, our present federal tax structure and tax rates, at a national income level of $140 billion, would yield about $31 billion. Our problem is how much we can reduce the tax burden, and in the process reshape it so as to minimize its restrictive effects on the growth of national income and employment. Many of the tax plans being discussed seem to me to exaggerate the amount of tax reduction that will be possible and therefore the amount of freedom we shall have in revising the tax structure. If we could assume, for example, the widely used estimate of $18 billion of postwar federal revenue (exclusive of social security taxes), we could go a long way in reducing excise taxes and corporation income taxes, and could rely relatively much more than at present on the individual income tax, which students of taxation have long regarded as the ideal form of tax. But even a budget of $18 billion, if it were to be financed exclusively or mainly by the individual income tax, would require a tax with a very broad base, low exemptions, a high normal rate, and a steeply progressive schedule of surtax rates. This would meet objection from those who hold that such a broad application of the income tax to low incomes restricts consumption, and from those who hold that unduly steep progression impairs investment. In a subject about which as yet we really know very little, all generalizations are dangerous, but it seems a cardinal principle of taxation that the amount of emphasis that can be placed on any one kind of tax depends upon the amount of revenue to be raised. If the revenue required is large enough, a simple one-tax structure begins to defeat itself by the restrictions it imposes on the flow of income, and we have to spread out into other kinds of taxes, even though in themselves they may be less desirable. The higher the burden of taxation, the stronger the presumption becomes that to have a balanced tax system we must use different kinds of taxes.

The preoccupation of fiscal theorists with taxation as a compensatory device has been with the absorption of idle saving. Whereas deficit spending is supposed to offset such saving by creating new income, taxation is regarded as a device for absorbing the saving and restoring it to the income stream. Granted that taxation is restrictive, if we could use it to restrict idle saving without impairing either consumption or investment, we could improve the flow of income. If under conditions of high taxation a country were shifting from a system of indirect taxes to a system of direct taxes, consumption could be greatly relieved and saving much reduced. But a number of studies have indicated that, when a country has already a large and progressive income tax, the possibilities of further absorption of saving through the income tax are not great, while the danger of restricting consumption or investment is likely to increase more than in proportion to the yield. The reason is that the great bulk of national income is in the lower and middle income brackets, so that to get a high yield these are the brackets that must be taxed. Thus, under the 1944 rate schedule well over one third of the total yield comes from taxpayers with net incomes of under $3000 and only one-third from incomes above $10,000. One effect that recognition of these facts should have is to make us realize that public expenditure offers no easy road to expansion of national income if it carries a presumption, as I think inevitably it must, that as expenditures increase the tax burden will increase, whether proportionally or not.[26]

[26] See Abram Bergson, 'The Incidence of an Income Tax on Savings,' *Quarterly Journal of Economics,* vol. 56, February 1942; and Gerhard Colm, 'Full Employment through Tax Policy,' *Social Research,* November 1940. See also R. A. Musgrave and E. D. Domar, 'Proportional Income Taxation and Risk Taking,' *Quarterly Journal of Economics,* vol. 57, May 1944. The conclusion that progression of the income tax cannot be relied upon to secure a drastic reduction in savings checks with conclusions reached by an unpublished study of the National Resources Planning Board (*Wartime Planning for Continuing Full Employment,* Interim Report by Full Employment Stabilization Unit, August 1942).

Musgrave and Domar have estimated that in an income tax yielding $16 billion a shift from a flat rate schedule of 30 per cent to the most progressive schedule possible (which would leave nobody with a net income after exemptions of over $2300) would increase the incidence of the tax on savings by only about $3 billion.

Some calculations by Moses Abramovitz ('Savings and Investment: Profits vs. Prosperity?' *The American Economic Review,* Supplement, June 1942, p. 80), based on the estimates of tax burdens and savings by income groups presented by Colm and Tarasov (*Who Pays the Taxes?* Monograph No. 3, TNEC Hearings) indicate that 'a truly enormous shift of taxes from the relatively poor to the relatively rich would be required to effect a substantial reduction of savings.' In the fiscal year 1939, the year to which the Colm-Tarasov figures refer, he estimates that 'a 30 per cent reduction of the amounts people desire

In recent tax proposals the chief subject of discussion and controversy has been the corporation income tax. A rather striking change has occurred from the insistence in the late 'thirties on taxing corporate profits, especially undistributed profits, in order to absorb idle business savings to the present emphasis on the desirability of relieving corporations from taxation. The case for relief from corporate taxation is usually put on two main grounds: first, that the tax absorbs funds which would otherwise go into higher wages and lower prices, that it is in effect a tax on consumption; and, second, that it absorbs funds which would otherwise go into investment. It ought to be pointed out that the first of these grounds rests on the view that the tax is shifted, and the second on the view that it is not. In the past, economic theorists have mainly, though not unanimously, emphasized the second view, but there is probably no subject on which we need more light. One of the chief difficulties is that we have not yet had much experience, under peace conditions, with a very high level of taxation. Very likely the corporate income tax is both shifted and not shifted, depending on the circumstances. But it seems to me doubtful that, to the extent the tax is not shifted, investment would be impaired by a moderate tax rate. On the other hand, even if part of the tax is shifted, the interwar behavior of profits does not suggest that this is a very sure or rapid process, and it seems by no means clear that reduction of the corporate income tax would be the best way to sustain consumption as against the reduction of excise taxes and of the individual income tax on the lower income brackets. As I have said, when the aggregate amount of possible tax reduction is limited, we are forced to think in terms of the comparative merits of reducing different kinds of taxes.

One of the chief arguments for greatly reducing, if not virtually eliminating, corporate income taxation has been that at present we tax corporate income twice, once against the corporation and again in the hands of the dividend receiver. This seems to me a valid argument, not because of the double taxation involved (we have many

to save (aggregate income being constant) would have involved the extinction of all taxes on the incomes of families earning less than $2000 a year and the distribution of this burden among higher income groups. The groups so relieved of taxation contributed in 1939 no less than 45 per cent of total tax revenues. Moreover, since the taxes on the lower income groups are levied mainly by states and local governments, what is involved is nothing less than the stupendous task of local rather than national fiscal reform.'

forms of double taxation) but because we are discriminating against equity financing as compared with fixed indebtedness and thereby impairing both stability and growth of national income. But this leaves the question of what to do about undistributed profits, which last year were about half the total. I have already reviewed the prewar discussion of undistributed profits as a main source of saving. Various suggestions have been made as to how the undistributed portion of corporate income could be reached by a tax on the stockholders. But this, even if it could be done, and I have not yet seen a suggestion that sounds practicable, would not meet the point about taxing idle corporate saving. The conclusion seems warranted that if distributed profits are to be exempted or substantially relieved from taxation, a fairly high rate of taxation of undistributed profits must be retained.

But this is the most puzzling aspect of the subject. We must bear in mind that financing out of undistributed profit is an important source of new investment. The view often expressed that business should be compelled to face the test of the security market when it contemplates expansion overlooks the fact that for new and small businesses this is often not a practical possibility,[27] and even for larger companies with widely fluctuating earnings may be unwise if the financing involves an increase of indebtedness. A tax policy which virtually forced the distribution of earnings to stockholders regardless of circumstances and left to business management little discretion regarding its reserves against possible future losses or its methods of financing future expansion would surely be too mechanical. It could have a paralyzing effect upon the attitude of business both toward new investment (or any sort of innovation involving risk-taking) and toward the policy of wage increases and price reductions so essential to a progressive system of free enterprise. I therefore find it hard to say whether a heavy tax on distributed profits or a more moderate tax on total profits would be the better compromise toward achieving the not easily disentangled aims of forcing idle business savings into use, on the one hand, and encouraging busi-

---

[27] See especially the studies by J. Keith Butters and John Lintner, *Effect of Federal Taxes on Growing Enterprises:* Study No. 1, The Lockheed Aircraft Corporation, April 1944; Study No. 2, Polaroid Corporation, November 1944, Research Division, Graduate School of Business Administration, Harvard University.

ness enterprise and initiative, on the other, as a means of expanding national income and employment. But in any case such a low over-all rate as the 16 to 20 per cent tax recommended by the Committee for Economic Development or the 5 per cent franchise tax (plus 16 per cent normal tax) proposed in the Ruml-Sonne plan seems unrealistic, at least on any other basis than that federal expenditures will be as low as these plans assume. There is one further important distinction between the amount of corporate income taxation and the way it is applied. I entirely agree with the suggestion made in many of the current tax plans that the corporate income tax should include liberal provisions for averaging income over a period of years by carrying losses forward and back.[28] To encourage risky investment, the application of the averaging principle to irregular personal incomes also deserves careful study.

The results of this brief survey of the tax problem are depressing. We are dealing, as I have said, with a restrictive instrument. Granted the importance of having the best tax system we can devise, the point to emphasize is that, inescapably, it will be a burdensome system. When we add in state and local taxes, the total burden will be some $30 billion or more, or between a quarter and a fifth of a full-employment national income. Against the tax burden we should, of course, put the possible expansive effects of different kinds of public expenditure. Without denying that with the right combination of expenditure and revenue we might achieve some net expansive effects, it does seem true that the economists have scarcely begun to analyze the problem in this way. Instead (because of their preoccupation with the over-saving theory) they have been regarding public expenditure and taxation as alternative methods of correcting the flow of income. My own view is that unless we frankly accept budgetary deficits as the means of income expansion, an approach of which I have long been skeptical and from which there seems now to be a general desire to back away, we are forced to work primarily in other directions than fiscal policy to develop a satisfactory theory

[28] See J. Keith Butters, 'Discriminatory Effects of the Annual Computation of the Corporation Income Tax,' *The Quarterly Journal of Economics,* vol. 54, November 1939.

To encourage rapid technological advance, we should also permit adequate deductions for depreciation and obsolescence.

and policy of the growth of income and employment in a free-enterprise system.

This brings me back to a view I expressed in an earlier section of this paper: that fiscal policy is a better instrument for business-cycle stability than for growth. A policy of cyclically unbalanced budget combined with tax reductions in depression and tax increases during booms could probably accomplish much to stabilize national income, if such a policy is politically and administratively feasible. For business-cycle purposes, it would be desirable to have a sufficiently simplified tax structure so that with few changes in the rate schedules up or down we could effect the desired changes in the revenue and in the budgetary deficit or surplus. It does, however, seem an oversimplification to suppose that we could fix once and for all upon rates that would automatically produce the results desired as the national income fluctuates. Finally, for the reasons I have given, it seems to me an oversimplification to suppose that we can get away from a mixed tax system including the individual income tax, the corporation income tax, and excise taxes. With a need for revenue as large as seems to be in prospect, the mixed tax system probably offers the best assurance of a balanced system resting as lightly as possible on consumption and investment.

VIII

Our postwar problem of income and employment is many sided. I have been trying to discuss the core of the problem rather than to make a comprehensive survey. There are many aspects which, for want of space or knowledge, I must omit. But two sets of questions seem to me hardly less central to our whole attack upon the problem than those I have discussed. One is monetary and banking policy, and the other our relations with the outside world. Both deserve fuller treatment than my remaining space permits.

Taking the war and the interwar periods together, there have been revolutionary changes in both central and commercial banking. These changes have stemmed chiefly from the growth of the public debt. The commercial banks have become mainly dependent for assets and for earnings upon the public debt, and in the process central bank policy as an instrument of control of economic fluctuations has been largely supplanted by fiscal policy. The larger the public debt becomes and the more of it the banks hold, the less feasible it becomes to exercise a general monetary control.

Monetary policy in the past has worked mainly through the effect of central bank control over reserves and deposits upon the rate of interest, which in turn was supposed to influence investment and employment. In the early 'thirties monetary and fiscal policy were regarded by economists as complementary. If the problem had remained that of business-cycle control, on the assumption of a budget balanced for the cycle as a whole, a combination of general monetary control affecting interest rates and the money supply, with fiscal policies working through deficits and surpluses to affect the volume of expenditures, might have offered possibilities of more effective stabilization of national income and employment than we had ever previously attained. Perhaps a moderate and gradual long-run growth of the public debt, if the debt were held mainly by non-bank investors, would not have interfered seriously with this kind of control policy. But when the debt is large and the bank share of it substantial, stability of interest rates becomes increasingly essential and general monetary control has to give way to a policy of 'maintaining orderly market conditions' for government securities.

These changes in the character of central and commercial banking, already apparent in the later 'thirties, have gone much further under the necessities of wartime financing. The maintenance of orderly market conditions developed into a conscious maintenance of a fixed pattern of interest rates, stabilized at a level lower than ever before in the history of this or any other country. To fight wartime inflation earlier economists would have put monetary controls first, fiscal controls second, and direct controls last, but in World War II the emphasis was precisely reversed. This was a striking but a correct and necessary change; it occurred in all the countries at war. In wartime the banking system should provide an assured market of last resort for Treasury financing, and the only kind of control appropriate is through limiting the banks' participation to what is necessary (after adequate effort is made to finance government expenditures through taxation and borrowing from non-bank sources) and limiting the rate of interest on securities sold to banks to prevent undue bank earnings at the government's expense. In the early part of the war much concern was felt over the fact that our Treasury was borrowing more from the banks than from the public, but in the last two years this tendency was progressively corrected.

Looking to the postwar period, we face the facts that the federal debt will be large, some $250 billion, that the banks have acquired about one-third of it, and that in the process total deposits and currency have had a huge growth — from about $61 billion in June 1939 to about $151 billion in December 1944. There may well be a further large increase in the banks' government security holdings and hence in the money supply after the war. Those who anticipate an inflationary rise of prices in the transition period stress these possible monetary changes. Such a development could occur in the interval of reconversion while civilian goods are still scarce. This indicates the need not only of speedy and orderly reconversion but of retention of wartime controls until such a danger is passed. I have long believed that the quantity of money, by itself, has a permissive rather than a positive effect on prices and production, and our whole experience since 1929 has seemed to show that the relation is much looser than almost anyone had previously supposed.

I can see no prospect of a revival of a general monetary control in the postwar period. This is not merely, or perhaps even mainly, a question of the vulnerability of the banking system to a rise in interest rates. In the last two war years the banks pursued a prudent policy regarding the maturities of their security holdings; their holdings of maturities beyond ten years have not increased and nearly two-thirds of their holdings mature or are callable within five years. This does not mean, however, that a rise in interest rates would not find the banks very sensitive and might not precipitate a wave of government security selling by banks, as happened in 1937 in response to the raising of reserve requirements.[29] But the larger fact, I think, is that as the debt increases the whole economy becomes vulnerable to any substantial change in interest rates and the public and the Treasury, as well as the banks, develop a strong vested interest in stability of rates.

How much room there may be for other types of monetary control is problematical. With the great decline in excess reserves that has

---

[29] To stabilize bank holdings of government securities, the device of a government securities reserve against deposits has been suggested by Lawrence Seltzer and others.

occurred during the war there might be some room for monetary control through variations in the shorter rates of interest. But the logical alternative, if a general monetary control is no longer feasible, is more direct controls, such as those we now have over the stock market use of credit and consumer credit. Both of these, I think, should be permanently retained and some other possibilities, such as control over urban housing and farm mortgage credit, carefully explored. But this kind of monetary control has, I am inclined to think, a limited range of application; it seems best suited to control of the use of credit in organized markets providing a standardized collateral for loans. I doubt, for example, whether it would be an effective method of control over business inventories, which have been one of the chief elements of business-cycle fluctuations. There is also the question how far we want to go in this direction. The rationing of credit for specific purposes does not go so far as the rationing of private spending or even as Sir William Beveridge's suggestion of public direction and control of private investment, but it is not unlike in kind and raises similar questions about the meaning of a 'free society.'

The public debt and the banks' holdings of it raise important questions also about the future of the commercial banking system. Though interest rates have been low, bank earnings have become abnormally high because of the great volume of financing. Meanwhile the great growth of deposits has produced a marked decline in the ratio of capital to deposit liabilities. This puts an increasing premium on comparatively riskless bank lending and investments, such as government securities. It is the kind of process which feeds upon itself. It could raise the question whether banking should become a public function, or at least the question of how much its services in holding the public debt should cost the Treasury. Interest will be one of the chief items in the postwar budget. There have been already a number of proposals for reducing the interest on the part of the debt held by banks. My own view is that the amount of interest that could be saved by any reasonable proposal would not be great, and that steps taken in this direction could arouse fears in the rest of the community about the goodness of the government's promises to pay. For the future of the banking system, as well as for stability and growth of the economy, what is most to be desired is that we should get more and more of the debt into private hands and free the banks to take a larger share in serving the credit and investment needs of private enterprise.

IX

In concluding this paper I can comment only briefly on the international aspects of our postwar problem. As I have said, national income and employment will have to depend primarily upon domestic policies and conditions. But our economic and financial relations with other countries will have an important secondary influence upon our own market, and may well be the decisive factor in determining whether and when international economic stability can be achieved.

The international and the domestic sides of the problem raise some similar questions. The cessation of lend-lease now the war has ended will be the foreign trade counterpart of the reduction of military expenditures here at home and, like the latter, will raise the question of how the gap is to be filled under peacetime conditions. In answering the question we shall again have to distinguish between the period of transition from war to peace and the longer-run conditions. Undoubtedly in the years immediately after the war the foreign demand for American exports will be large. We can foresee something of its character. There will probably be important amounts of lend-lease goods in process of production which could serve civilian needs abroad if satisfactory arrangements, possibly through the Export-Import Bank, could be made for long-term financing. There will also be the supplies to be financed by the United Nations Relief and Rehabilitation Administration. There will be demands for goods to assist in reconstruction, as distinct from relief. It seems very desirable, in our own interest, to define reconstruction broadly and even generously, as meaning, for example, that the capacity of foreign countries to produce and export should be restored as rapidly as possible and with as much emphasis as is prudently feasible upon external aid rather than at the expense of the internal standard of living, which has been so greatly depressed in many countries. There will be also, as here at home, large deferred demands for consumer durable goods. Besides all these, there will be demands from the young and from the less-developed older countries for capital goods to assist in development of their resources.

Without pretending to be exhaustive, I have said enough about the foreign demand to suggest that it will be large. How large it will be depends to a great extent on the financing. To a greater degree than seems generally realized foreign demands for our goods can be financed by the importing countries themselves. The war has greatly increased the gold and foreign exchange resources of many countries. One important problem will be the wartime accumulation of sterling balances in London, which at the end of 1944 amounted to about $12 billion.

Undoubtedly, however, there will be important demands for reconstruction and development which will have to be financed by foreign investment, and the capital will have to come primarily from the United States. Our experiences after the last war indicated that foreign investments misdirected are worse than none at all. We greatly need to develop improved standards and procedures and to differentiate more carefully between the kinds of expenditures which should be financed at home by the borrowing country and those which should be financed with foreign funds. There is a tendency, I think, to exaggerate both the amount of capital that could effectively be spent abroad and the speed with which the expansive effects upon our own economy could be generated.

There is a widespread belief, born largely of our unfortunate experiences in the 'twenties, that foreign investment of private capital will involve some kind of insurance. It was from this point of view that I first came to recognize the desirability of the Bank for Reconstruction and Development proposed at Bretton Woods. The Bank agreement faces up squarely to the fact that the bulk of the lending would have to be done by the creditor countries, and mainly by the United States. The capital of the Bank would serve mainly as a contingent guarantee fund to guarantee issues marketed either by the Bank itself (its own debentures) or by other public or private agencies. To have the insurance take an international form would have many advantages. Besides the fact that it is equitable that all countries should share in the risk, it opens up the possibility of developing, through the collective action of borrowers and lenders, the standards and procedures of sound investment to which I have referred. The Bank, according to its provisions, would avoid the practice of 'tied loans,' would require written reports by its own committees on loan projects, would control the loan expenditures and confine loans, with rare exceptions, to the financing of capital goods actually needed from abroad. In these and other ways it could serve as an agency for continuous international consultation and co-operation.

My special interest in this section is in the contribution that American foreign trade and investment can make to the solution of our postwar problem of employment. This contribution will be through the export surplus. Despite what I have said about the large foreign demands, especially in the transition period, it will be a mistake, I think, to count very heavily upon the export surplus to fill up the gap that will be left by the cessation of war expenditures. There is, first, the point I mentioned earlier, that even though postwar foreign demand is large it will have to be very large indeed to make the same relative contribution to national income and employment as is now being made by lend-lease exports. There is the further consideration that in the future, if we wish to see a proper balance restored in the world, we must increasingly emphasize imports. We have seen the evil consequences of a mechanical propping-up of our economy by one-sided trade involving either a draining from the rest of the world of its monetary resources or a foreign 'investment' that does not eventuate in a flow of goods from the borrowing countries. We have seen also the conflict generated at home when, as a consequence of large-scale foreign investment, we have to face up to the logic of the process and ask ourselves which industries and which workers are to meet the competition of the foreign goods that are the only means whereby in the end the investment can be justified.

The propping-up of our national income and employment through the export surplus represents the same kind of mechanical approach to national income and employment which I discussed in connection with budgetary deficits. I favor the development of international trade through the freer flow of goods and capital on the same grounds as I have argued for the revitalizing of the private-enterprise system here at home. They are the logical counterparts of each other. But this view emphasizes the volume of trade as a whole, and the cost-reducing effects that can be achieved through a better utilization of the world's resources, and not the export surplus, which suggests instead a desire to get leverage for our own employment at the expense of the outside world.

It should help our perspective to recognize that this country produces almost half of the world's manufactures and uses more than half of the world's raw materials. It follows from this fact that the solution of our own problem of employment must be predominantly domestic.[30] It follows also that the greatest contribution we can make toward international economic stability will be to solve our problem domestically and to maintain a high, stable, and growing level of production, income, and employment. Under these conditions we should need large amounts of foreign goods and could most readily afford to take the lead in reducing barriers to the international flow of goods and capital. It seems no exaggeration to say that not only will postwar international economic and monetary stability be primarily dependent upon the success of American domestic economic policy but the character of the program we adopt and the success we have with it may go far toward determining what kind of economic and political system will prevail in the world. In the postwar world we shall find the nations strung out at various points along the way between the private-enterprise economy and some sort of state-controlled economic system. Perhaps our most important new problem in international trade and financial relations will be the question of how countries so different in economic and political character can work out mutually beneficial relations. Will it be possible under such heterogeneous conditions to restore the system of multilateral trade which is the logical counterpart of the free-enterprise national economy or will the balance swing the other way? It would be rash to attempt an answer to this question, but it does seem clear that the greatest contribution we can make toward the preservation of our kind of economic system, both here and elsewhere in the world, will be through the achievement of high national income and employment by methods directed primarily toward making the private-enterprise economy function more effectively.[31]

[30] As I indicated earlier, after the last war (1919–20) the export surplus, though abnormally large, represented only about one-seventh, and domestic factors about six-sevenths, of the aggregate of income-increasing expenditures.

[31] For lack of space I have omitted reference in this paper to the International Monetary Fund, which had been a leading preoccupation of mine. For my views, see *Post-War Monetary Plans* (Blackwell ed.), chaps. 6–11 inclusive.

11

The Monetary Doctrines
of J. M. Keynes

A REVIEW of so comprehensive, closely reasoned, and provocative a work as Mr. J. M. Keynes's two volume *Treatise on Money* must be to a greater degree than usual selective. It is of course a substantial contribution to the literature of the subject. It exhibits a rare combination of penetration in theoretical analysis, grasp of mathematical statistical method, and felicity of expression. I cannot hope to give a just impression of its scope and richness. That it could have been written piecemeal over a period of years in intervals between other activities and still retain so much vitality and spontaneity is astonishing. As one who has rather a prejudice against big books I can merely say that I have seldom read two large volumes with as much pleasure. At the same time, partly from its length and partly perhaps from the way in which it was written, it appears to suffer somewhat at times in consistency and in clarity; and I agree with Mr. Keynes that he may find a shorter and better way to say it.

The book contains what seems to me — I do not feel competent to pass judgment on the statistical analysis — a brilliantly successful treatment of the problem of index numbers and the plurality of price levels. There is also a survey of the English and American statistics on banking and the volume of investment which are most pertinent to his monetary theory, a survey which not only reveals much ingenuity in estimating but shows also how inadequate our present data are for the banking policy which he proposes. Other principal features of the *Treatise* are an extensive comparative analysis of central bank operations and methods in the leading countries; a

The Quarterly Journal of Economics, August 1931.

most impressive discussion of the theoretical significance of, and the statistical problem of measuring, industrial working capital; a study, for purposes of verification of his price theory, of certain historical periods of prosperity and depression; and an analysis of the causes of the current depression.

The introductory section includes a wonderfully compact description of the mechanism of deposit credit creation on the lines of Phillips' 'able, if prolix' analysis of multiple loan expansion. This characterization of Phillips, though true, hardly makes it clear that he was the first to straighten out a major error that had appeared quite uniformly in the earlier books and had been taught to generations of university students; by now, I have no doubt, Phillips has found a shorter way to say it. There is included also the suggestion that in England the unused portion of overdrafts should be regarded as bank credit equally with the deposits, which raises the old question where credit ends and wealth begins. Mill included in purchasing power book credits, bills of exchange, and promissory notes, which clearly suggest double counting.[1] In the United States the English overdraft is regarded as the counterpart of our customer's loan, particularly that made under line of credit. Should one, on this reasoning, include with actual deposits the unused portion of the line of credit, and if so, why not customers' securities in safe-keeping accounts, which could be pledged automatically for new loans; and from there the mind runs on to the buildings and lands on which one can borrow money.

II

In its main argument the book contains a theory of the value of money and a theory of price control by central banks. Turning away from old versions of the quantity theory, including that which he had set forth in his earlier book *A Tract on Monetary Reform,* Keynes seeks an understanding of the price level in a study of the purposes and processes of spending, a point of view which in general suggests such writers as Hawtrey, Robertson, the 'over-savings' theorists, and, farther back, J. S. Mill.[2]

[1] But Mill had in mind the distinction between loan instruments exchanged for money and those exchanged for debts; only the latter would he call purchasing power; e.g. bills of exchange as circulated in Lancashire. See *Principles* (Ashley edition), p. 514.

[2] Ibid. Book III, Chap. 12, pp. 524, 532, 539.

It is a theory of the relation of saving to investment, which attempts to get closer to the money-goods relationship by splitting up both money and goods into categories which reveal causal relations and thus permit the formulation of equations of exchange that may become in use something more than mere identities. He divides goods into consumption and investment goods, and money into what is spent and what is saved. The central purpose is to explain the price level of consumption goods, as the function of the ratio of the community's earnings to its output. The complicating circumstance is that not all income is spent for consumption goods, and not all output is offered for current sale. Saving decreases income, and the cost of producing investment goods increases income without increasing current output. Investment goods comprise all 'non-available' goods, whether fixed capital, inventories of goods in process, or surplus stocks of finished goods withheld from market. An excess of investment raises prices and an excess of saving lowers prices. Given efficiency earnings, the rate of pay per unit of output, the single necessary condition for stability of the price level of consumption goods is therefore that saving equal investment; and it is the function of the banking system, through its control over the price and the quantity of money, to maintain the equality of investment and saving.

This influence must be exerted, however, upon the value (price level) of investment goods, as well as upon saving and the volume (cost) of investment. For the price level of investment goods can affect the price level of consumption goods, indirectly, in two ways: by affecting the relation of cost of investment to saving; and by affecting, in the end, the rate of earnings of the productive factors. If value of investment goods exceed their cost, the difference will be profit. Profit is neither part of normal income of the community nor part of saving; its spending is therefore a source of disturbance of the equations of exchange. If, as would characteristically occur,[3] the profit of producers of investment goods were spent on production of more investment goods, cost (expenses) of investment goods would exceed saving, so that the community income would exceed current output at the previous price level, and prices of consumption

[3] If profits were spent directly on consumption goods, income would exceed current output by the amount of profits, and prices of consumption goods would rise.

goods would rise, yielding in turn a profit to producers of this class of goods. Profit is thus the 'mainspring of change,' producing an inflation which proceeds spirally until the competition of producers for the factors of production raises the rate of earnings ('income inflation') to the point where profits disappear. If at this point a new equilibrium is not established, but the process continues until losses appear, there will follow 'profits deflation,' 'commodity deflation,' and at length 'income deflation.' To preserve an equality of investment and saving it is therefore necessary to prevent profit or loss; [4] and therefore to maintain the price level of investment goods equal to the cost of investment goods; or as Keynes puts it algebraically, when S (savings) $= I'$ (cost of investment) $= I$ (value of investment), q (profits) $= o$, and P (prices of consumption goods) $= \dfrac{E \text{ (earnings)}}{O \text{ (output)}}$.[5]

Recognizing that all short statements are wrong, I hope this very simple summary does not do serious injustice to Keynes's intricate analysis. As an explanation of the cyclical behavior of prices, his theory represents a distinct advance [6] over others that resemble it in general type. It is, for example, essentially different from the 'over-savings' theorists [7] with which its affinity appears closest. It does not occupy at all the same ground as Foster and Catchings' statement that prices fall because 'money is used twice in production for once in consumption.' In the latter view, saving and investment are the same thing; what is saved is invested, with the result (according to this theory) that current income cannot carry off the enlarged output of consumption goods at the previous price level. In Keynes's

[4] Leaving only wages of management, a part of normal community income.

[5] The fundamental equations of exchange are:

$$P = \frac{E}{O} + \frac{I' - S}{R}; \text{ and}$$

$$II = P + P' = \frac{E}{O} + \frac{I - S}{O}, \text{ where } R = \text{current output of consumption}$$

goods and $P' = $ price level of investment goods, and the other symbols are as given in the text.

[6] Keynes mentions the recent work of German monetary theorists on similar lines.

[7] E.g. Bouniatian, Hobson, Foster and Catchings, Martin; some of the basic ideas go as far back as Sismondi, 1819.

view, savings may not be spent at all; 'it is a volume of saving which does *not* lead to a corresponding volume of investment (not one which *does*) which is the root of the trouble.' [8] Since producing investment goods and saving are frequently the acts of different individuals, differently motivated, there is no reason why they should be equal. In terms of the banking system, if banks are loaned up to the limits of their reserves, as is characteristically the case, a shift of deposits from demand to time deposits will not affect the aggregate of loans; [9] but it will represent a decrease of consumers' spendable balances, the substitution of an idle for an active deposit. The concept of the idle savings deposit, and the consequent distinction between saving and investment, underlie Keynes's whole treatment and constitute a valid claim to his having broken new and significant ground in monetary theory.

Nevertheless, I am not certain that his distinction does not leave unsolved the 'dilemma' with which the oversavings theorists are concerned. Keynes does say: 'In so far as those theories are capable of any reconciliation with mine, it is at a later stage of events; for in certain cases a tendency for the rate of investment to lag behind the rate of savings might come about as a result of a reaction from oversaving in the above sense.' [10] I interpret this statement to mean — there is no discussion of it at the point where it occurs — that when investment exceeds saving there may at length be over-investment, in the sense of a difficulty of disposing of the consumable products of investment goods, which may cause subsequent investment to lag behind saving.[11] Keynes's statement in itself somewhat mars the

---

[8] I, ch. 12, p. 179.

[9] Except to the extent of a difference in reserve requirements, as in the United States.

[10] I, ch. 12, p. 178.

[11] Such passages as the following perhaps indicate his meaning: 'We thus have (in the secondary phase of the business cycle) under the influence of the windfall profits accruing from the price rise consequent on the primary phase of the credit cycle, a secondary stimulus to an increased volume of production, which, this time, is of an all-round character and affects *all* types of goods which are the object of general consumption.' I, 288. 'Now, since the secondary phase necessarily stimulates the production of consumption-goods, it follows that even where the primary phase is caused by an increased production of capital-goods, the secondary phase brings with it the seeds of a reaction, which will germinate as soon as the increased supply of consumption-goods is ready for the market. Thus, sooner or later, consumption goods will be coming on to the

precision of his theory, for it occasionally leads him to mention over-production of consumption goods, as well as the more usual 'income inflation,' as bringing prosperity to an end. It does not, however, really touch the point of the oversavings theory, which is that even when saving equals investment, over-production will result.[12] If a producer borrows from savers $100,000 to buy a machine which costs $100,000 to produce, and if these operations are concurrent or proceed at a uniform rate, saving = value of investment = cost of investment, and the conditions of price equilibrium are fulfilled. But there is a new productive instrument which in the *next* production period will increase output without correspondingly increasing income, so that prices will fall. In other words, in the second production period, the first of Keynes's fundamental equations is upset, for while $I' = S$, O increases relative to E, and P must fall (of course, as with any mathematical identity, the equation will still solve). It is true that if now savings decrease in precise equality with the increased output of consumers' goods, trouble will be avoided; but there is no reason to expect such an occurrence. It would be possible, assuming at all times an equality of saving and investment, to carry this process to the point where either saving ceases entirely or, failing that, prices fall toward zero, which suggests another method than the failure of entrepreneurs to invest savings whereby calamity may visit the inhabitants of Keynes's banana plantation.

For general economic theory, this situation presents no difficulty,[13] since the justification for increased supply of capital goods must al-

---

market which can no longer be sold at the previously ruling price; so that the downward price phase of the Cycle now commences.' i, 289.

These passages indicate that it is not only (as in his usual statement) an increase in the rate of earnings caused by entrepreneurs' competing for the factors of production which brings profit inflation to a close, but also the stimulation of production of consumption goods. But in both cases it is profits making, arising from an excess of investment over saving, that causes the result, and certainly not the equality of saving and investment.

[12] Foster and Catchings, for example, recognize that investment can exceed savings by the extent of new bank loans, and conclude that in this case there is first a rise of prices for essentially the same reason as Keynes gives: current earnings exceed current output. They do not, however, perceive the opposite possibility, that savings may exceed investment, which seems to me Keynes's distinctive contribution.

[13] But see A. E. Monroe: 'Investment and Saving, A Genetic Analysis,' *Quarterly Journal of Economics,* August 1929, pp. 586–7.

ways be its ability to lower unit costs. The general and familiar answer of monetary theory would be a secular increase in the supply of money. But it would be necessary to show by what process the increase of money occurs, to whom the money goes, and how it affects the relation of saving to investment. An increase of capital goods, whether financed by saving or not, is in itself a dynamic phenomenon, involving changes in value relationships: earnings must rise with prices stable, or prices fall with earnings stable. Whether this process proceeds smoothly in the actual world or by jerks is a pertinent question; an equality of saving and investment cannot from this viewpoint be regarded as affording stable equilibrium, except in an immediate and rather superficial sense. Moreover, there are considerations of quality as well as quantity; not all investment effects a fall of unit costs sufficient to cover the fall of prices which its output entails; and losses to producers, other things equal, could upset the balance of saving and investment. Thus far, depressions have served to weed out inefficient users and producers of investment, as well as other, goods.

There is a further difficulty arising out of over-production of specific types of investment (or consumption) goods. I see no reason why this could not occur consistently with the condition that total saving = total investment. Specific maladjustments tend to be lost sight of in any general theory, or to be minimized. They do not lend themselves readily to the broader logical processes. Yet over-production in a dominant industry could readily affect an entire situation. Given varying degrees of elasticity of demand-supply for individual goods, and given friction in the adjustment of productive factors to the changing conditions of demand, a general effect on prices is likely to be produced. When, for example, the American automobile industry was producing at the rate of six to seven million cars a year in the first half of 1929, or some two to three millions beyond the normal (a condition which can readily occur in a highly competitive industry with a productive capacity of e.g. eight million cars), it became apparent by early summer that the output was excessive. Shutting down this particular industry produced a profound effect on others. Until, in such a case, we are able to move the factors of production out of over-active industries into under-active industries, with the same speed and ease with which demand can shift, or with which a banking system can alter the terms of lending and the supply of money, specific maladjustments will always be a major cause of instability of the price level. The difficulty is that of economic friction. The effective cure for over-production of automobiles, buildings, or any durable good, once it has occurred, is under-production, which involves the lapse of time.

I have a further difficulty, arising from the distinction between profit and anticipation of profit. Profit is described as the 'mainspring of change,' which causes investment to exceed saving and prices to rise; but on the other hand profit is caused by the excess of investment over saving and the consequent rise of prices. There is thus a difficulty as to how the ball gets rolling. Keynes has apparently little use for the optimism-pessimism theory of the cycle, and is usually careful to say that business expectations have no significant result unless based on correct forecasting of economic and monetary fundamentals. But on the point here raised he says that as production takes time and business men must foresee what effect the relation of saving and investment is to have on demand for their own product,

strictly we should say that it is the *anticipated* profit or loss which is the mainspring of change, and that it is by causing anticipation of the appropriate kind that the banking system is able to influence the price level . . . Thus entrepreneurs will sometimes begin to act before the price-changes which are the justification of their action have actually occurred . . . Widely held anticipations will tend for a short time to bring their own verification, even if they have no basis outside themselves.[14]

The question raised here is the one which is always the most perplexing in economics, and perhaps peculiarly so in the field of money, the question of emphasis. What is 'a short time'? The cycle is itself a short-time phenomenon. How important expectations can be for Keynes will appear when we come to his analysis of the effect of 'bullish' and 'bearish' sentiment on the price of investments and through this on the price level of consumption goods. Here the point seems to be that anticipations have no effect unless they are 'right'; and the difficulty is that to some extent they can make their own rightness. To some extent, surely, anticipation of profit will cause excess of investment over saving, and thus produce rise of prices, profits, and more rise of prices. Keynes's only specific reference to Pigou is a rejection of the latter's contention that bank rate depends

[14] I, pp. 160–61.

for effectiveness on its power to influence business anticipation,[15] Keynes's rejoinder being that the expectation would have no effect if it were based on an illusion. But evidently 'for a short time' illusion can produce very real results. The case is even more perplexing when the bank expects one thing and the business community another. The difficulty may often be made worse by the conflicting general and individual aspects of the problem:

When for any reason an entrepreneur feels discouraged about the prospects . . . he can reduce his output or lower his costs by reducing his offers to the factors of production. Neither course, if adopted by entrepreneurs as a whole, will relieve in the least their losses as a whole . . . whilst both courses are likely to aggravate their losses by reducing the cost of investment. Nevertheless these courses will in fact appeal to them, because, in so far as any class of entrepreneurs is able to adopt either of these courses to a degree greater than the average, they will be able to protect themselves.[16]

The matter could hardly be better put; the difficult question is what emphasis to give it. Keynes's general answer to this and other qualifications (including, I should suppose, those which I have previously made) is apparently that

it is sufficient that the general tendency of a disequilibrium between saving and investment is in the sense described and that if the cause persists, the tendency must materialize sooner or later. Nor do any of the qualifications . . . affect in any way the rigour or the validity of our conclusions as to the quantitative effect of divergencies between saving and investment on the price-levels ruling in the market.[17]

But one question is whether 'sooner or later' is sufficiently precise for bank control, and another is whether the 'rigour of our conclusions' does not suggest that same dependence upon a mere quantitative identity for which Keynes criticizes the quantity theory.

III

Mr. Keynes points out that most theories of the business cycle fail to relate their analysis adequately to the money mechanism; partic-

[15] I, p. 199.
[16] I, pp. 160, 161.
[17] I, p. 161.

ularly is this essential for a theory which proposes central bank control of prices. Though careful to state that he does not, like Hawtrey, regard the cycle as a 'purely monetary phenomenon,' he aims especially to put his explanation into terms of the banking mechanism. His division of income into spending and saving requires logically a division of money into income deposits and savings deposits. Our statistics divide merely into demand and time deposits. The question becomes how nearly the one division fits the other. Keynes recognizes two classes of demand deposits, — income and business deposits; and also that deposits are used for industrial and financial purposes; so that his scheme becomes: 'industrial circulation' comprising income deposits and business deposits A, and 'financial circulation,' comprising savings deposits and business deposits B. At the same time, it is necessary to account for changes in velocity; savings deposits are idle, but demand deposits may be more or less active or idle. He finds, however, that velocity of income deposits changes but little, that industrial business deposits in the main interact with income deposits, and that while velocity of the financial business deposits is extremely variable the amount of such deposits is small. Thus he concludes that the significant changes in consumers' spending and saving are shown by changes in the *relative amounts* of demand and time deposits. An increase of time relative to demand deposits, for example, would show an increase of saving relative to investment, for money invested would feed back into income deposits through expenses, so that a relative increase in time deposits would indicate that, on balance, money was being held idle, which would depress the price level. Keynes examines the statistics of demand and time deposits in England and the United States to show what light they throw on the behavior of prices.

In some respects this is an important advance. Fisher's equation, for example, deals exclusively with demand deposits. So far as I know all theories previous to Keynes's have failed to make use of the statistical division of deposits into demand and time. I am interested also in the attempt to get closer to velocity of circulation by splitting deposits into parts and examining the velocity of each; for it is on velocity that both our thinking and our facts are vaguest. There may, however, be a danger of overstressing the distinction between the active and the *wholly* idle deposits, and understressing the greater or less activity or idleness of demand deposits themselves and the duality of their composition. The chief difficulty lies in the handling of business deposits and their relation to income deposits.[18]

The importance of the question is indicated, for example, by the fact that Hawtrey's theory of the price cycle turns peculiarly upon the behavior of 'traders'' balances of money, and goods. Indeed, though Hawtrey makes special use of the point, nothing has been more familiar than the view that business men, besides borrowing more from banks in active times and paying off such debts in depression, make more active use of their own balances at the one time and convert goods into comparatively idle balances at the other. This involves changes not only in velocity but in size of business deposits. That Keynes appreciates the difficulties involved in business deposits is shown by the grounds he cites for rejecting his own earlier version of the quantity theory: the community's balances of money held represent far more than command over 'consumption units.' It is shown too by his introductory description of demand deposits. There he points out that the volume of speculative transactions in capital goods or commodities is 'subject to very wide and incalculable fluctuations,' and that 'unfortunately' they are also large enough 'compared with ordinary transactions arising out of production and consumption to confuse the statistics'; indeed the latter transactions are 'swamped by business transactions of other kinds,' and 'the proportion, K_2, of the average level of the business deposits to the volume of the business transactions may be quite different from K_1, the proportion of the income deposits to the income transactions. Also it is likely both to vary differently and to be much more variable.' [19]

---

[18] To put the matter into equation form, when S (saving) $= I$ (investment), the equation for prices is $P = \dfrac{E}{O}$, which in monetary terms is $P = \dfrac{M_1 V_1}{O}$, where $M_1 V_1$ is quantity times velocity of income deposits, time deposits are represented by S, and business deposits are not accounted for. (Bank notes are included as part of income deposits.) If the quantity and velocity of business deposits merely interact with, and thus bear an unchanging proportion to, income deposits, there is no problem, but there will be a difficulty to the extent that this is not the case. How complicated Keynes's money equation becomes when he endeavors to account for *all* demand deposits, instead of income deposits alone, is shown by his formula $P = \dfrac{M}{O} \cdot \dfrac{wV_1(V_2 - V_1)}{V_2 - V_1}$, of which, so far as I have found, he makes no further use in the book.

[19] I, p. 48.

I am not certain, however, whether the point receives its due value in his subsequent more detailed discussion of business deposits, and more especially in the logic and the statistical demonstration of his theory. To my mind the difficulty is not due entirely to the speculative and financial transactions, but also to the cyclical movement of ordinary production and consumption, which involves a net flow of balances to consumers in active times, and a net flow to producers in quiet times, a movement which, though likely to be greatly enhanced in depression by liquidation of speculative stocks of commodities, would occur in any case. The speculative and financial business transactions Keynes classifies as affecting 'business deposits B,' which he says are small in amount though highly variable. This would suggest that such transactions create their own funds, so to speak, by velocity changes within business deposits B; and that these deposits, remaining small at all times, would not impair his conclusion that changes in *amount* of demand deposits reflect essentially changes in amount of income deposits. He has already said, however, that business transactions 'confuse the statistics,' and in the second volume says that we have no direct evidence of either the size or the velocity of business deposits. The familiar division of bank debits in the United States as between New York and 'outside' is intended to segregate the effect of speculative transactions, though everyone recognizes that it does so very imperfectly; and of course New York deposits as a total are far from small. In calling business deposits B a small fraction of total demand deposits, Keynes is evidently thinking of the economy of stock exchange clearance. Yet the funds used to clear security transactions in New York are but a small part of funds used throughout the country for security transactions; moreover they do not include balances used for speculative commodity transactions, which he also includes in business deposits B; and in any case do not touch the question of size and variability of 'business deposits A,' which is part of industrial circulation.

Keynes's discussion of business deposits A [20] points out, first, that obviously part of such deposits merely interact with income deposits (remuneration to the productive factors feeding sales to consumers) so that the two bear the same proportion to each other in size and in velocity; and second, that 'in equilibrium' prices and volume of transactions of unfinished goods (working capital) and fixed capital

[20] See I, Chap. 15, section 2.

goods will move parallel to and reflect the prices and the rate of
flow of finished goods, so that the quantity of this 'part of business
deposits . . . will also tend in these conditions to vary in the same
proportion as do the income deposits.' But these conclusions only
suggest that if there were no business cycle there would be no difficulty, which I grant. Keynes does then recognize: (1) that changes
in *relative* prices upset the ratio between the two classes of deposits;
(2) that when business is active and bank rates high, firms will
economize in balances held, and vice versa (whereas consumers' outgo
is tied to size and regularity of consumers' income so that 'short
period fluctuations of income deposit velocity are inconsiderable');
and (3) that business balances may be influenced by profit or loss
'which . . . can affect price levels . . . out of proportion to the
change, if any, in the volume of income deposits.' These are very large
qualifications, but he concludes: 'Nevertheless, in the main the
volume of the industrial circulation will vary with E, the aggregate
of money incomes, i.e. with the volume and cost of production of
current output.' Does 'in the main' mean apart from the business
cycle? Thus Keynes reaches his general conclusion, which the logic
of his theory requires, that changes in the demand deposits (essentially in the income deposits) are

generally a good index of changes in the industrial circulation; and,
similarly, changes in the savings deposits of changes in the financial
circulation — which fortunately brings us back to classes of deposits
of the magnitude of which we have in practice moderately good
statistical indications.

The matter is partly one of emphasis, and shows how important
such questions can be when a writer like Hawtrey can make one
element in the case an important feature of his analysis,[21] and another, though recognizing that element as a qualification, begins
and ends with an essentially opposite view. At bottom the question
is one of fact. To the extent that business deposits, when idle, are
transferred to time deposits, and when active merely interact with
income deposits, Keynes's case becomes stronger. It is probably true
that idle business deposits are so transferred in England to a greater
extent than in the United States, and to a greater extent here at
present than before the war.

[21] Variability of business balances of money (and goods) relative to income
balances.

The pronounced growth of time deposits in this country is a post-war phenomenon not yet fully understood. In part it is thought to represent a growth of thrift deposits. In part it undoubtedly represents the changed financial practice of corporations, especially since 1921 when the presence of large inventories financed by bank loans was perhaps the worst feature of the depression. Not only because inventories have since been most closely controlled but also because of a changed attitude toward bank loans in general, it has become the familiar practice of the larger corporations to finance their requirements out of their own funds (or funds secured directly from the public) and to maintain a stronger cash position. That this development has been accompanied by so large a growth of time deposits is hardly a coincidence, and it fits into Keynes's view. On the other hand, there is little evidence of cyclical variation in these deposits. In part, also, these deposits represent, as Keynes points out, the competition of banks for deposits, and the effort to get around the greater reserve requirements of demand deposits; moreover, interest is often paid upon demand as well as time deposits, though at a lower rate, so that the distinction between the two sorts of deposits becomes in actuality rather blurred. It is not possible to believe, in any case, that *all* idle business deposits by any means are transferred to time deposits. The demand deposit is the more available and convenient, interest is paid on both, and particularly in periods of generally low rates the difference will not always be regarded as worth while.[22] It should be noted too, as a practical matter, that even when

[22] While the available statistics do not tell us much on the point, they perhaps permit one to draw the inference that idle business demand deposits are in depression an important magnitude:

(In billion dollars)

Call Dates	Time Deposits	Total Demand Deposits Unadjusted	Adjusted United States	Demand New York City	Deposits Country Member Banks
Feb. 1928	12.9	18.2	16.1	4.1	5.8
Mar. 1929	13.3	19.5	16.4	4.2	5.8
Mar. 1930	13.5	18.2	16.2	4.4	5.5
Feb. 1931	13.7	18.4	15.9	4.5	5.1

Demand deposits are adjusted to include individual demand deposits plus certified checks and travelers checks, and to exclude bankers' balances due to and due from other banks, and all items in process of collection. Column 3 includes also government deposits, while columns 4 and 5 do not; the inclusion of

idle deposits are actually transferred from demand to time deposits the former will not, under American conditions, be greatly reduced, owing to the difference in reserve requirements. A transfer of $1000 would release, for example, $70 of reserves and permit an increase in loans and demand deposits of $700 in the banking system. What this means is that transfers to time deposits are largely offset by an increase in total deposits, and transfers from time to demand deposits by a contraction of total deposits, a circumstance which strengthens one's feeling that, so far as this country is concerned, the more significant changes, as regards their effects on the price level, are those which occur within demand deposits themselves. In England, the same reserve ratio is applied to both demand and time deposits.

Of course to the extent that idle business deposits are not converted into time deposits, they can still be included for theoretical purposes in Keynes's savings; [23] but from a statistical point of view the theory then becomes less clear-cut and less useful. The awkwardness would be that, so far as idle business deposits are demand deposits, they bear an *inverse* relation to income deposits; in prosperity they feed into

government deposits in New York would not change the nature of the result; the figures would read, 4.1, 4.4, 4.5, 4.7; they are omitted in order to get as close as possible to business balances. From the active year 1929 to the depression bottom in 1931 total time deposits increased $400 million which is about in line with the secular growth since 1914 and especially since the war, and does not therefore necessarily show that idle balances went into time deposits. Adjusted demand deposits (= the actual means of payment) declined $500 million; county bank deposits declined $700 million and New York deposits increased $300 million. (I have not at hand the intermediate classification, reserve city banks.) Since bankers' balances ('due to' and 'due from') are omitted, their concentration in the center in quiet times is abstracted from, and also the holdings of government deposits. The assumption is, I think, warranted that New York deposits are affected by business balances to a greater degree than are country deposits, since large corporations would keep their balances primarily in the financial center where their headquarters are. It therefore seems a fair inference from the opposite changes in the two categories that, as suggested in the text, during the business cycle business deposits and income deposits, both comprised within demand deposits, vary inversely to each other. The corrections of demand deposits, designed to show the true community means of payment, have been made by L. B. Currie, on his own formula, from data derived from the Abstract of Member Bank Call Date Reports.

[23] But it is really not so simple as this; it is not merely a matter of what happens to *wholly* idle business deposits, but a question also, as Keynes's three qualifications show (see p. 237 above), of quantity and velocity of business deposits that are *not* wholly idle.

income deposits, and in depression feed back into idle business deposits. The result is that the *total* of demand deposits may undergo little change from prosperity to depression, while yet the volume of consumer spending may be profoundly affected. I incline to agree with Keynes that the velocity of income deposits is not much changed in the course of the cycle,[24] outgo depending mainly on income, so that changes in *amount* of such deposits are chiefly significant, but the difficulty would be to *see* these changes, disentangled from opposite changes in business deposits.[25]

How much importance Keynes attaches to the distinction between time and demand deposits, as expressing essentially the difference between saving and consumers' spending, and how possible, to my mind, it is to overstress the point, is best seen in his extended discussion of a speculative security boom. This analysis, I must confess, I find very confusing. Its main purpose is to explain the price level of investment goods, and the effect of this upon the price level of consumption goods. Up to this point the references to investment have been in terms of goods and goods prices; and the price level of investment goods has been explained as reflecting the rate of interest and the prospective demand for the utilities (or products) of such goods, a low rate of interest, for instance, being capitalized into a high price of investment goods and this result being modified up or down by entrepreneurs' judgments of prospective demand. But now the price of investment becomes the price of securities representing title to such investment goods. (I am not sure whether it is intended that the reader should infer that because United States Steel common goes from 100 to 250 the prices of steel goods or of steel plants necessarily rise correspondingly; in our recent boom that was far from being the case.) Also, instead of considering, as hitherto, the relation of *current* saving to current new investment, attention is directed to *all* saving and all investment, and particularly to old securities; for the effect of the boom on new security issues and new investment goods, is discussed as a distinct and separable point.

Keynes sets forth four phases of a security market cycle. Securities

---

[24] Though there are important changes in circuit velocity.

[25] There is the equal difficulty of disentangling business deposits. Data on corporations' cash balances would throw some light, but would usually include securities and would not distinguish between demand and time deposits.

may go up by common consent, in which case savings deposits are transferred through securities to demand deposits, and commodity prices rise. Or securities may go down by common consent, in which case the opposite shift occurs, and a fall of commodity prices. These two phases are simple, but two other phases remain: sentiment may be divided, some people bearish and others bullish. With security prices still rising, some holders may sell out and establish savings deposits. These he calls 'the bear position.' If, as they sold out, the banks bought securities, the increase of savings deposits would be offset by new demand deposits created by the banks, and commodity prices would not be affected. This, I believe, is what he means by the often recurring statement that the banking system can influence and control 'the bear position.' The operation would, of course, require new money from the central bank and would mean an increase in *total* deposits. Or the banks could make new loans to individual buyers of securities, with the same result. But there is a way, according to Keynes, for 'the bear position' to make itself felt in an increase of savings deposits relative to demand deposits at the same time that security prices are rising. This way is provided by 'loans for the account of others'; and here he is obviously thinking in terms of our security boom of 1928-9.

The savings depositors, having sold out, now lend directly to the new buyers. Keynes evidently satisfies himself that in this case savings deposits have increased on balance, so that commodity prices will fall; and this notwithstanding that the deposits are loaned out again and thus transferred, one might suppose, to active circulation. The point apparently is that such loans will not affect the quantity of *deposits as a whole,* since they are not loans made by banks, and that therefore, the security sellers having established saving deposits, and deposits as a whole being unchanged, the proportion of savings deposits to demand deposits must be increased; so that commodity prices fall. But, so far as I can yet see, the savings deposits were, in effect, never made if they were loaned out again by their holders: the holders cannot have them and not have them at the same time. That deposits as a whole do not grow, in such a case, while loans do, is perfectly true, a point to which I shall come back later. The fourth phase of the security cycle is the opposite of this: security prices are falling, but with sentiment divided; savings depositors are buying securities on balance, presumably from margin holders who have debts to pay. Savings deposits decline relative to demand deposits and commodity prices rise.

The points that interest me most in this analysis — there is not space to describe it in detail — are his treatment of 'loans for account of others,' and especially his demonstration that money that comes out of savings deposits must go into 'industrial circulation,' and hence must cause a rise of commodity prices; and contrariwise. The essential point in Keynes's proof is that security speculation cannot absorb credit, so that there is really nowhere else that credit can go except into savings or income deposits, depending on the phase of the security cycle. It therefore follows that the banking system by its power to offset changes in savings deposits through its own lending (and resultant creation of demand deposits) has the key to the commodity price level. Except to this extent, and for this purpose, the banking system has no interest in controlling a security boom.

The contention that security speculation does not tie up credit and deprive industry has been made by a number of monetary writers in recent years, and has been the principal ground for criticism of Federal Reserve policy in 1928-9. Besides Keynes, one thinks of Reed, Calvin Hoover, Rogers, Cassel, Foster and Catchings, and others. Keynes, I believe, goes farther than any of them in that he contends that security speculation positively increases industrial circulation and raises commodity prices; and this not through expansion of bank credit as a whole or through its effect on new security issues and consequent investment goods expansion (though he makes that point as well), but through releasing savings deposits, old as well as new, into active consumer spending. The explanation is of the same kind that other writers have given — the extraordinary economy of the machinery of financial clearance. Professor Calvin Hoover has shown that deposits were not diverted from the country to New York, and Professors Reed and Rogers have demonstrated how little net movement of deposits is involved in margin trading through brokers.

While impressed by the apparent unanimity of opinion, I have felt that economy of clearance and failure of deposits to be diverted to New York do not dispose of the question. A rise in security prices suggests that in some sense or other more aggregate spending upon securities is involved. The analogy with the ordinary money-goods equation is obviously indicated. Higher prices would there mean more money exchanged for the same goods, or at least a relative increase in money spent. By analogy with the language of the recent debate over speculative use of credit, this fact could be expressed as the 'tying up' of money in goods, which would not be thought to mean that the money actually froze upon the first act of purchase, but only that, in the given period of time, the money was absorbed continuously in the exchange for goods. Moreover, if the trading involved, for example, buyers and sellers in Chicago and Boston and the payments were cleared through New York, and if the two-way transactions were equal, as would be the normal expectation, there would be no reason to expect either a diversion of deposits to New York or a great amount of transfer of deposits between the two trading centers, while at the same time *some* clearing balances in New York would clearly be necessary, and if transactions were numerous these would show a high velocity of circulation. Still it would be clear that a higher price level of goods could occur, and that it would be due to greater spending of money relative to the volume of goods traded. The greater spending would represent a greater use of deposits in the two trading centers, rather than in New York, and a greater use of deposits *by the traders,* not necessarily a shifting of deposits on balance from bank to bank between the trading centers. The spending by depositors would explain the rise of prices completely. Moreover, with banks loaned up, the total of deposits could not be increased (barring new money), and this particular use of deposits by their customer owners would prevent any alternative use to which the deposits might have been put.

I am unable as yet to see why the analogy with the security market is not complete. To the extent that individuals all over this country, and abroad, bought securities with their bank deposits, and that the process was continuously repeated during the period of the boom, there was, in precisely similar fashion, a particular use made of bank deposits and a precisely similar result expressed, in the rise of security prices; and to the extent that this process occurred the deposits were not put to some other use; and with banks loaned up (quite apart from the fact that total deposits were actually curtailed by Federal Reserve action) no other deposits to perform such other uses could be created. It would follow that money attracted out of savings deposits would neither have to lodge in Keynes's 'financial business deposits' (the New York clearance fund) nor be conceded to have been added to consumers' spending; it would be 'tied up' in securities. Moreover, security markets could absorb money, in the same sense, from income deposits themselves, representing an alternative to their transfer into savings deposits. Both of these possibilities, incidentally, raise questions about the banking system's ability to control the commodity price level by reference to the behavior of savings deposits; and also as to the conclusion that the central bank has no concern with a security boom except as the relation of savings deposits to industrial circulation is affected.

The treatment of loans 'for account of others' is a related point. These loans show how an increase of loans can occur without an increase of deposits. The deposit is merely transferred to another user, but since it is transferred by the depositor, the banking system being already loaned up, it constitutes a net addition to loans. In this particular case, since the (time) deposit is loaned by one who would have kept it entirely idle to one who puts it to use, the significance of the transfer depends upon the kind of spending to be done. It is of course quite possible that the deposit will go through the security market into some industrial use, but to the extent that such loans are being made continuously they indicate one particular sort of spending, whereas (a) there would have been no spending at all had the savings depositor retained his deposit, or (b) there would have been some other sort of spending had the depositor loaned to a different type of borrower. The fact that when these loans are called for payment by the lenders, security holders must sell, thus depressing security prices, or transfer their loans to the banks, involving a net increase in total deposits though not in total loans, and requiring resort by banks to the central bank for new money, would also seem to indicate in what sense security speculation ties up credit.[26]

[26] I wish to make it clear that I take no position here on the question of *fact*, whether in 1928–9 speculation deprived industry of credit; I am dealing only with the theoretical questions raised by Keynes's analysis. For one thing, new issues represent a means whereby deposits could and did go into industrial circulation. But Keynes has distinctly barred out new issues, which he treats separately and in the same sense that I do. Moreover, new issues would not account for the rise of security prices but would tend to depress these prices. I recognize, too, that to the extent that speculation was by traders, through brokerage accounts, Professor Reed's point about the economy of the whole process has force. But this does not touch my own point, which rests on the

IV

Bank control of the price level is the dominant theme of Mr. Keynes's book. He calls it 'the crux of the whole matter.' Yet I am not quite sure what he finally thinks about it. It is here that one really feels the length of the book and the piecemeal character of its preparation, which have inevitably resulted in some shifting of emphasis as first one and then another part of the complicated analysis has come up for intensive examination. Over the whole period the writer's attitude on the general question may, very naturally, have undergone some degree of change. Since Keynes has had the courage to combine in one book proposals for practical policy and a fundamental theory of value, there is raised the question how consistently the two are combined. The warmth of the reformer and the cold logic of the theorist may sometimes make a lumpy solution unless very thoroughly stirred. Toward the end of the second volume Keynes quotes the adverse testimony of the late Governor Strong and of Walter Stewart before our Congressional committee on the stabilization bill in 1926 and concedes considerable weight to their objections; but he points out that they had not the benefit of a theory which explains the effect of bank rate on investment and saving. Yet, though now equipped with such a theory, he confesses to have 'more sympathy today than I had a few years ago with some of the doubts and hesitations . . . expressed.' On the whole I feel that he thoroughly believes in the ability of central banks to control prices, but is more impressed by the complex nature of the problem, and more inclined to limit his claims and to recognize important qualifications, than when he published the *Tract* in 1925.

The literature of price stabilization is already extensive; indeed since the war no monetary subject has been so much debated. Keynes thus writes against a very large background. That he has significantly advanced the discussion is not to be doubted. The usual statement of the case for bank control of prices proceeds directly out of the quantity theory of money. Bank rate controls the quantity of money which controls the price level. To elaborate a little, the central bank by its rate controls the size of member bank reserves (if necessary

---

fact that securities were bought by people all over the country through their bank accounts. The whole subject is beclouded by the fact that Reserve Bank action was contracting the total of deposits.

it can control reserves by open market operations); since member banks are always 'loaned up' to reserve limits, a change in reserves will mean a change in the amount of loans, which will mean a change in the amount of deposits; a change in deposits will produce a change in the price level. But this explanation is too simple and begs some important questions. Like the quantity theory, it assumes 'other things equal.' Only if velocity remains unchanged will a change in deposits mean a corresponding change in the effective quantity of money, and only if goods remain unchanged will a change in that quantity produce an equal change in prices. Since velocity is subject to change during the business cycle, that proviso is extremely important. And since the change in quantity of deposits proceeds out of a change in quantity of bank loans, the presumption is that more deposits rest on more goods. The simple quantitative comparison of money and goods provides no explanation of how money is spent. If to have more money we must have the banks make more loans, who borrows and for what purpose? Different kinds of transactions require different amounts of money and have different degrees of effect upon the price level.

In one of his most interesting chapters Keynes traces the different strands of thought regarding bank rate. Hawtrey, he recognizes, gets closer to the matter than most others by attempting to find the borrower. In Hawtrey's view, the 'trader' is peculiarly sensitive to bank rate, because bank interest is his principal cost; and since (according to Hawtrey) the trader occupies the key position in industry, giving the orders which induce the manufacturer to employ the consumer in production, more borrowing by the trader means more consumer spending. Moreover, if the rate is low, the trader will be more willing to carry stocks of goods on borrowed money, which will mean an increase of consumer income and spending relative to current sales of consumers' goods. Keynes makes the familiar, and I think entirely sound, criticism that the trader is more sensitive to prospective demand for goods than to the cost of borrowing. On similar grounds, he rejects Marshall's explanation that the new money gets into circulation through borrowing by speculators, and cites Tooke's criticism of a similar suggestion made by Petty — speculators who think in terms of 10 per cent or more are not controlled by a change of bank rate from 3 to 6 per cent.

Keynes then produces his own *deus ex machina*. The sensitive borrower must be someone for whom a small change in bank rate will mean a large change in cost or price and to whom, moreover, bank cost is really vital. This is the investor. Keynes's case is strengthened by the fact that the saver also, though to a less degree, is sensitive to bank rate, and in an opposite direction; [27] so that a higher rate will mean less investment and more saving, and vice versa. Thus the central bank, controlling the relation of saving to investment through the rate, prevents profit or loss and maintains the equality of community earnings and output at the stable price level.

Among the many questions which this analysis raises, we may start with two. Keynes's 'investor' seems better than Hawtrey's 'trader,' but the questions to be answered are the same: how sensitive to bank rate is the investor and how sensitive to other influences? The answers are complicated, as I shall point out later, by the fact that Keynes himself designates Hawtrey's trader as one type of investor, and presents elsewhere a most impressive analysis of working capital and liquid stocks of goods which I cannot but feel considerably increases the difficulties of analyzing bank control; yet in his final summing up, he appears to forget this analysis, or at least to emphasize it very differently.

It is unnecessary to present Keynes's proof in detail. He recognizes that bank rate affects directly only short-term money rates, but says that money flows over into the long-term market. The essential fact is that banks are always 'loaned up,' so that when the rate is lowered and reserves are increased, the decline in profit on short-term loans will lead banks to buy bonds.[28] Bank buying puts up bond prices and reduces yields, and the movement broadens as other investors, afraid to 'miss the bus,' also buy. Speculators, anticipating investors and encouraged by low carrying charges, give an impetus to the movement. Issue houses assist, holding off new issues when rates are rising for fear of spoiling the market for previous issues, and

[27] Then there is the fact that quite apart from, or in addition to, effects of bank rate on current investment and saving, the banking system can 'offset' changes in *total* savings deposits caused by security speculation, by itself buying or selling securities and thereby affecting the ratio of demand deposits to savings deposits. Since I have dealt with this point in Part III, I make no further mention of it here.

[28] Keynes cites W. W. Riefler's, *Money Rates and Money Markets in the United States,* Harper, New York, 1930, as showing the sensitiveness of long-term rates to short-term.

stimulating new issues when conditions are favorable. Meantime, since bond borrowing involves comparatively large amounts and is made for long periods, slight differences in rates represent important differences in cost, and rate changes can therefore hasten or retard bond issues. Also, there is always an 'unsatisfied fringe' to whom the banks can lend, so that the matter is not merely one of sensitiveness of borrowers to the rate. Finally, bond rate affects *value* of investment relative to cost, a low rate being capitalized into a high price of investment goods. Thus value of investment can be controlled relative to cost of investment, and therefore profit or loss, while at the same time saving is oppositely affected; hence the price level of consumption goods is controlled by the central bank.

To this line of reasoning there is one large objection. The price level is affected by demand for money as well as by price and supply of money. It is a two-sided matter. While insisting, I think rightly, that his investor is far more sensitive to bank rate than Hawtrey's trader, Keynes recognizes that he is sensitive, also, to 'prospective demand' or what we may call people's judgment of the business outlook. Indeed Keynes's 'value of investment,' the crucial point of his whole structure, is determined not only by the capitalized rate of interest but by 'prospective demand' for capital goods or their products. He insists, quite rightly, on this dual determination and points out the commodiousness of his theory, since from this side it embraces such theories as Schumpeter's 'innovations.' Prospective demand is the rock on which many theories of bank control finally break; it is the rock that, according to Keynes, has wrecked Hawtrey and Marshall.

Keynes's solution is that suggested by Wicksell in 1898. Prospective demand helps to determine the 'natural rate' of interest; the central bank controls the market rate. The natural rate is that at which investment and saving are equal; it varies with the community's judgments of the changing business outlook and with the supply of savings. Over this rate the central bank has no control, except of a secondary nature. Its task is therefore to adjust the market rate to the natural rate, putting it above if the need is for contraction of investment and below in the opposite case. I cannot help feeling that this distinction between market rate and natural rate does not advance us at all. It sounds like a solution of the difficulty, but amounts merely to another way of stating the difficulty. If the natural rate were visible, the case might be different, but only the market rate is known. The natural rate is an abstraction; like faith, it is seen by its works. One can only say that if the bank policy succeeds in stabilizing prices, the bank rate must have been brought into proper line with the natural rate, but if it does not it must not have been. If bank rate is lowered but fails to stimulate investment relative to saving, it will be because the natural rate has fallen still lower, which sounds suspiciously like saying that people do not want to borrow and spend in view of the business outlook.

I believe it is Mr. Robertson who has said that you can raise bank rate to any desired extent (though it is difficult to know in advance how high and how rapidly to raise it), but you cannot reduce it below zero. Some of Keynes's points about the effectiveness of bank rate seem to cut both ways. For example, as to the 'unsatisfied fringe' of borrowers, it is true that discrimination and rationing of borrowers are important influences in the money market, but both in prosperity and in depression they seem to work in the opposite way to that which Keynes suggests. In prosperity bankers are less conservative and in depression more conservative. The result is that credit is most readily expanded when it should not be, and least readily when it should be. Nor is this entirely due to a state of mind. As a central bank official recently remarked to me, the trouble with our bond market in the past year (1930–31) has been that companies whose bonds people want will not borrow, and bonds of companies who will borrow people do not want. This condition affects no class of bond buyers more acutely than the banks. The result is a concentration of bank investment in highly seasoned (mainly government) securities. This condition is also in line with the remark, often made by the bond houses, that while highest grade issues reflect the price of money, most issues reflect earnings and prospective earnings. For the most part, in the past year the state of earnings appears to have dominated our bond prices; the general average price has ruled lower than a year ago despite extreme ease of money, but the bonds of those public utility companies whose earnings have been maintained have risen in price. Moreover, new issues have been less than in the previous year.

Of course, with a bank rate unprecedently low the difficulty — on the reasoning just stated — must be that the 'natural rate' has been still lower, and the presumption would be that the market rate was not low enough. Criticism of central bank policy usually takes this form. If the central bank had not acted, or had acted in the wrong direction, the criticism would be obviously pertinent. But the more usual case is that the central bank did not go far enough; or though it did act in the right direction, it failed to do so at the right moment, the critics having the benefit of hindsight. While there is frequently merit in such criticism, there must also come a point where its ridiculousness becomes apparent. There are times when business activity and prices are not primarily matters of money rates. Pumping money into the bond market through the banks does not insure a better bond market (still less a greater aggregate, or a right kind, of spending), if as the banks buy more bonds others buy less. In monetary terms, the crux of the matter is that, while banks control the physical quantity of deposits, depositors control the spending of them, and changes in quantity may be offset by changes in velocity or in direction.

Keynes several times mentions the 'awkwardness' of new money's getting into the 'wrong hands.' He mentions especially the possibility that money intended for home investment may go into foreign investment, which has been one of England's chief difficulties. But there is also Hawtrey's trader, who though rejected must not be forgotten. Just because the trader and the speculator are more concerned with prospective demand, as they see it, than with bank rate, they are apt to prove a hindrance rather than a help; they will borrow in spite of high rates and will not borrow though baited by low rates. And the trader is 'one kind' of investor. There is the possibility, also, that high rates, while depressing bond prices and bond issues, may not depress stock prices and stock issues, so that investment in capital goods goes on despite central bank policy, the speculators shouldering the cost while industry expands at slight expense. Then too there is the fact that cheaper borrowing, 'since it lowers the cost of production of all types of entrepreneurs' may stimulate all alike to increase their output. Keynes mentions this possibility, but adds that 'with correct forecasting this should not be the case'; the money should go only into capital goods; but he adds further, 'Since entrepreneurs are not always acquainted with such reasoning, easier credit is, it is true, liable to provoke mistaken forecasting.' [29]

I do not question the fact that bank control of the price and the supply of money is an important factor in determining business con-

[29] I, p. 211.

ditions and prices, but I do not know how to determine *how much* of a factor it is relative to others, or within what time interval or to what extent a change in monetary conditions will affect general business conditions and the price level. In ordinary times, the problem is mainly one of smoothing out minor variations and presents no special difficulties. It is in connection with the great 'conjunctures' that the questions about ability to control are acutely raised. I have no firm conviction that in any one of the six major depressions since 1875 (excluding the outbreak of the war) money was or could have been *the* dominant factor in the situation, though it was an important factor in all; while another factor, the question of the standard, was certainly very prominent in this country in 1875–9 and in 1893–6.

Keynes discusses at length some of these periods. He is especially troubled by the period of the 'nineties. He finds that it presents, in the terms of his theory, a severe and prolonged commodity deflation, 'developing and persisting in spite of a great increase in the total volume of bank-money.'

Could the Bank of England have prevented the deflation? In the matter of Bank-rate it did what lay in its power to make credit easy. Between 1890 and 1896 the total stock of gold in the Bank of England was doubled, the Bank's reserves were nearly trebled, and its deposits nearly doubled. For two and a half years the Bank-rate stood unchanged at 2 per cent. Meanwhile the deposits of the banks other than the Bank of England increased by 20 per cent. In short, the period was marked by extreme ease of credit.

He says the trouble was that people would not invest:

There was a prolonged withdrawal of entrepreneurs from undertaking the production of new fixed capital on a scale commensurate with current savings.

Foreign investment was at a standstill, owing in large part to the Baring Crisis (which, of course, was a sheer case of over-expansion in Argentina, not to be cured except by digestion and growth involving the lapse of time); meanwhile there were no *'new inventions* to absorb the redundant savings at home.' He says 'it is not obvious what further action the Bank of England could have taken.' Of course, 'open market' policy had not been heard of, and the purchase of securities by the bank 'might have done something,' but 'the Bank's "proportion" rose to 70 per cent in 1893 and 1894' and 'consols were already high in price and it must be doubtful whether purchases of consols by the Bank of England would have done anything material to stimulate investment.' He gives it up finally, and falls back on the suggestion of 'strenuous measures' by the government, 'large programmes' of public works and 'government guarantees,' evidently overlooking the fact that it had been just such 'programmes' and such 'guarantees' (to the railroads) which had caused the Baring Crisis in Argentina.[30]

There is not space to review Keynes's treatment of later periods. He evidently finds England's difficulties since the war to be deeper than the monetary alone; in particular, wages will not come down along with prices, and investment goes abroad instead of into home industry. This is one of the 'awkwardnesses' previously mentioned. He suggests that if the reason is that investments earn more abroad, England should give three per cent bounties to home investment, which I think means in effect that investors should receive from the Exchequer checks for the difference between home and foreign coupons. To my mind this is like sweeping back the ocean with a broom, and a broom badly frayed already by high taxation. England's trouble is a bad balance of productive factors, too much labor and capital for her natural resources; a condition which represents a late phase of the whole cycle of change which began with foreign investment in the sixteenth and seventeenth centuries. Since the war, British trade has not responded sufficiently to British foreign investment, and the more true this becomes, the more the incentive to foreign as against home investment. The cumulative effects are just the opposite of those which prevailed in the nineteenth century, when England, possessing both a surplus of capital and industrial advantages over other nations, concentrated in decreasing cost industries and bought from abroad products of increasing cost industries, largely developed with the aid of her own capital; with the result that the more capital she applied to foreign investment the more she had for home investment.

Keynes finds the fundamental cause of the current depression to be a persistent gap between long-time interest rates and short-time interest rates, particularly since 1925. It will be recalled that his theory of price control rests on the contention that there is no such gap, that money flows over from the short-term market to the long-term mar-

[30] II, pp. 164–70.

ket, which is very sensitive to bank rate. Evidently, then, there have been some non-monetary difficulties, affecting 'prospective demand,' which are not sufficiently amenable to monetary action.

The war, the post-war reconstruction, the epoch of 'artificial' borrowing have kept rates up for fifteen years to a level which would have seemed a generation ago quite beyond reasonable probability. Consequently a first-class bond yielding 4½ to 5 per cent, at a time when the short-term rate is not much above 2 per cent, does not strike the modern financier as the outstanding bargain that it would have seemed to his father.

He thinks that 'in time' the gap will disappear, 'in time the multitude will move'; and that if banks would reduce the rate of interest allowed to depositors to one-half per cent and central banks would engage in open-market operations 'à outrance,' the process would be hastened.[31]

Many of the qualifications I have made to bank control of prices Keynes, I think, would grant; indeed a number of them I have quoted from Keynes himself. But I cannot think that we agree as to emphasis; nor do I think the qualifications are consistent with such statements as that the 'banking system . . . can by the terms of credit influence *to any required extent* the volume of investment.' [32] Keynes agrees that booms and slumps, particularly the latter, are difficult and perhaps to some extent impossible to control by bank policy. The real problem is to prevent their occurrence. But this, as he points out, requires action 'at the right time,' which is in advance. This was the point of view of the Federal Reserve Report of 1923, which pointed out that prices are symptomatic of processes already under way, and that, since to control a price movement once started is difficult if not impossible, control would have to begin sooner; its view was that such action by anticipation is hardly possible and might even do harm in the absence of more certain foreknowledge than now seems obtainable. The late Governor Strong's opposition to price control was based partly on the same ground, though he dwelt also on the complexity of prices, and the difficulty of correcting some prices without doing injury to others.[33] To my mind, also,

[31] II, ch. 37.

[32] II, p. 346.

[33] There are many such situations, e.g. as between manufacturing and agricultural prices.

Keynes's very interesting discussion of the cyclical behavior of working capital provides another illustration of the difficulty of controlling booms and slumps by bank rate, once they are under way. Bank rate, in his view, can control fixed capital investments, and his final reply to his own treatment of working capital would seem to be that if you maintain stable prices such difficulties will not arise. But action in advance requires correct forecasting. It cannot be denied, I think, that thus far the record of the professional forecasting services has been far from perfect. The problem becomes harder rather than easier if action must be in advance. The point may be illustrated by another quotation. Keynes concludes his discussion with the words: 'I am writing these concluding lines in the midst of the world-wide slump of 1930 . . . Thus I am lured on to the rash course of giving an opinion on contemporary events which are too near to be visible distinctly.' But if one doubts one's ability to diagnose this depression now, how can one expect the central bank to have diagnosed it correctly in advance?

There is not space for further discussion. I have left out entirely Keynes's treatment of the international side of price control. He recognizes this to be the principal stumbling block under present conditions. It is necessary to maintain an equality of the balance of foreign lending and the balance of foreign trade, as well as of saving and investment at home, in order to maintain stability of prices. But almost no central bank, acting by itself, can do both things at once, and nations really have to choose between internal and external stability. Changes of bank rate may have opposite external and internal effects. This is profoundly true, and is a sufficient reason why bank policy in the future must be based on international co-operation. He discusses very interestingly the possibilities of 'supernational management.' Again, while I agree with very much of it, I feel less optimistic than he does. Perhaps the chief advantages to be hoped for from a supernational bank and close co-operation between central banks are such things as economy in international clearance (relieving pressure on gold reserves and more especially the unreasonable fears which arise therefrom), smoothing operations, even sometimes of emergency character, and perhaps an educational advantage in disseminating through the world better knowledge of, and a greater desire to achieve, banking economy in the supply of money. The young countries, especially, could revise their banking systems to good purpose. Of more exalted claims I am rather skeptical. Particularly in international markets do we find friction, heterogeneity, unequal development, differences in business organization, unequal sensitivity to monetary, and other factors. Keynes seemed to feel this sort of thing particularly (indeed to a much greater degree, I should have said, than myself) in his controversy with Professor Ohlin about reparations, where he emphasized the 'stickiness' of Germany's foreign trade situation and the danger of applying the theory of liquids. England's foreign trade since the war is another good illustration. So long as friction and heterogeneity are found between and within countries, the realization of the goal of world price control even by a supernational bank will, I fear, be imperfectly realized.

In concluding this extended interview, I wish to express again a sense of my shortcomings. These two volumes contain much difficult reading, and it may well be that on further study some of the points which have bothered me, difficulties which I have here sought to express, may become clear or be removed by other writers. I recognize, too, that in giving emphasis to certain phases of the analysis, I am omitting others perhaps equally important. In particular, I am giving no attention to index numbers and their availability for guiding monetary policy; a most perplexing matter, as Keynes brings out in his first volume. The *Treatise* provides room, indeed, for half a dozen reviews; no better tribute can be paid to its substantial character. It is very probable, moreover, that in selecting some points on which I feel a difference with the writer, as perhaps one inevitably will do in reviewing a work that really interests him deeply, I have been guilty of a distortion by no means intended, and have failed to express adequately my appreciation of one of the most stimulating and attractive books I have read in recent years.

Appendix

Testimony on Post-War Recovery Program

[Friday, 27 February 1948]

Mr. Williams: My name is John H. Williams. I am a professor of political economy at Harvard University and economic adviser to the Federal Reserve Bank of New York.

My statement will be brief, but I shall be glad to discuss any questions which the members of the Committee may wish to raise. I have from the beginning been heartily in favor of the Marshall Plan. Many aspects of it have now been thoroughly discussed, and a great deal of constructive work has been accomplished. At this late point in the discussions, I cannot do more than emphasize some aspects that seem to me especially important.

I shall not attempt to say anything on the much-debated question of the amount to be appropriated, except to express my approval of Senator Vandenberg's suggestion that the appropriation should cover twelve months from 1 April rather than fifteen. It seems very desirable that Congress should have an opportunity early next year to resurvey the whole matter in the light of experience. I have followed with great interest the discussions as to how the program should be administered. My own view is that the appointment of an Administrator who would be directly responsible to the President and at the same time a member of the National Advisory Council, provides the best line of solution. But I feel strongly that, possibly by reason of our absorption in these two very difficult matters — the amount to be appropriated and the American administration of the Plan — we have failed as yet to give adequate attention to the equally important question of how the Western European countries can best be organized to carry out the purposes of the Plan.

We need, I think, a more analytical approach to what the European problem is and how to deal with it. Secretary Marshall, in his speech last June, emphasized European co-operation and self-help and made American aid contingent thereon. Our experience after both wars has been that piecemeal aid to individual countries is of doubtful effectiveness; and it was from this kind of procedure, as I understood, that we sought to get away. But I have the impression that since the Committee of European Economic Co-operation reported last

Hearings, U.S. House of Representatives, Committee on Foreign Affairs. *United States Foreign Policy for a Post-War Recovery Program.* H.R. 4840, H.R. 4579. 80th Congress, 2nd Session, Part 2, 17 February–10 March 1948.

September little or no progress has been made on this most essential aspect of the problem.

The sixteen-nation report was an impressive document, considering the short time in which it was prepared, but despite much excellent analysis and much emphasis on the need of European co-operation, what has mainly emerged from it is the amount of aid required from us. This is understandable, since we had asked for such an estimate; but what is really needed is an integrated plan. Such a plan could not of course be worked out in a few weeks, and the Committee emphasized the desirability of establishing a continuing organization. It has been reported that some of the countries have taken tentative steps, or indicated their willingness to take steps, in this direction, and one of the questions uppermost in my mind, about which I have no knowledge, is whether our Government has encouraged or discouraged such suggestions. That we should be vague on such a point raises, I think, the largest question still unexplored with respect to the European recovery program and its chances of success.

The method adopted by the European Committee last summer in estimating the amount of American aid was to aggregate the international deficits of the sixteen countries over a four-year period. I understand that our State Department has since submitted to Congress more detailed projections. Though everyone who has attempted to make such estimates knows how much guessing is involved, there probably is no other way to reach a first approximation. In arriving at its estimates, the Committee tried to take account of the nature of the European problem as a whole and how much intra-European co-operation could be expected, including such difficult questions as the recovery of Western Germany and its future role in the European economy. The danger, nevertheless, in this approach is that it may put the whole matter of American aid on a bilateral basis as between this country and the individual European countries.

Perhaps initially this procedure will be unavoidable, particularly in view of the fact that the European Committee has not been functioning since its report was made. I recognize also that the question of dealing with Western Europe as a whole, rather than with the individual countries, is most complex. There have been many suggestions — economic, political, military — looking toward some kind of Western European integration, but if the recovery program is to go into effect as scheduled on 1 April, it does not seem realistic to insist on these — or any one of them — as a necessary condition. It would involve the further loss of time during which the situation in Europe would deteriorate further, and time is the essence of the problem. It does, however, seem essential for us to recognize that, until some kind of over-all integration is achieved, our program of assistance to Europe will be more in the nature of an extension of interim aid than a genuine program of European reconstruction.

It seems unnecessary to discuss at length the nature of the European problem. There have been a number of excellent analyses, including the studies made by the Select Committee on Foreign Aid, and others submitted in the course of these hearings. We should recognize that much progress toward recovery has already been achieved. Industrial production in the United Kingdom, Belgium, Denmark, Norway, and Sweden was higher in 1947 than in 1937, France and the Netherlands were approaching prewar levels, and only in Italy, Austria, and Western Germany was production still far below the prewar level. With wise management, full recovery should be feasible.

But we must recognize also that European production and trade will need to be substantially higher than before the war because of the profound maladjustments in Western Europe's international position — the loss of foreign assets and markets, the loss of shipping services, the interruption of east-west European trade caused by the iron curtain, and the chaotic conditions in the Far East on which Western Europe formerly depended to defray its debit balance to the Western Hemisphere. Added to these changes, and to the internal destruction of resources, is the partition of Germany and the loss of German territory to the east, which has not only disrupted the German economy itself but thrown badly out of balance that of Europe as a whole. Not the least serious aspect of the German problem is the fact that Western Germany must now rely to a much greater extent than previously on export-import trade, a factor that comes on top of the general European international derangement.

These problems must be dealt with under conditions of inflation which thus far have been world-wide, but most severe within Europe itself. One main object must be to correct the European inflation, while at the same time preventing the program's having inflationary effects here at home or elsewhere. But conditions are different in the different European countries. In some the rise in prices has much outrun the increase in the money supply, while in others the reverse is true. There are varying conditions of 'open' and 'repressed' inflation. In some countries inflation is closely connected with budgetary deficits while in others it exists despite a condition of balanced budget. The relation between internal inflation, international deficits, and exchange rates varies from country to country.

Regarding Western Europe as a whole, there are certain key situations which, if corrected, would go far to promote recovery throughout the whole area. Of central importance are Western Germany and England, the former from the standpoint of the internal European economy, and the latter by reason of its central position in the network of world trade. What can be done to correct Britain's foreign deficit is far from clear. Perhaps the main hope lies in a fall in world agricultural prices which would improve Britain's terms of trade; and, apart from that, in British internal policy, directed toward correcting inflation and increasing productivity. But in the meantime American aid seems essential.

In Western Germany, the decisions lie not with the sixteen countries but between the French, the British, and ourselves. We have taken a long step forward by the decision to go ahead despite the Russians. We have made slow but definite progress away from the concept of the 'pastoral state.' But we have still very far to go before Germany can be made ready to play her necessary role in a reconstructed Europe. Granted that the problems, political and military as well as economic, are difficult, it seems not too much to say that Western European recovery is more dependent on our policies in Germany than on any other single factor. One of my chief misgivings has been the reparations program which we are still pursuing.

In most other countries the difficulties seem less fundamental. The Nether-

lands and Belgium, both of which have made substantial progress, would benefit greatly from German recovery. France has normally a well-balanced economy. From a purely economic standpoint, if her inflation were corrected, and
assuming better crops than last year, her external problem should not prove
intractable. In Italy, though production by last fall was only three-fourths of
prewar, reconstruction is now proceeding well, in spite of the great physical
destruction and the political disorder wrought by the war. The greatest immediate obstacles to further expansion of output have been the lack of imported
raw materials and fuel. A revival of trade with Germany, and with the Bal-
kans, would go far toward rehabilitating the Italian economy.

The conclusion to be drawn from this brief survey is that the European
countries interact upon each other. Each has an interest in the monetary, fiscal,
and general economic policies of the others. What is needed is an integrated
program of recovery, based on mutual self-help among the Western European
countries and supported by American aid directed, not toward the individual
countries but toward Western Europe as a whole. As I indicated earlier, the
chief lack in the European recovery program, as we approach the decisive stage
of Congressional action, is the failure to develop further the movement toward
European co-operation, which seemed last summer to be the essence of the
Marshall Plan, and to give it more effective expression in the present program.
I am strongly in favor of the suggestion that has been made by Mr. McCloy,
that we should urge the European countries to give serious consideration to
the creation of a Western European organization which could serve, in some
sense, as the European counterpart of our own Economic Co-operation Administration. I am uncertain how far such an organization should have actual powers
of direction and how far merely powers of planning and consultation. But even
on the latter basis, it would, I think, be an important step toward assuring a
better integrated plan, and might go far to meet the charge that we are interfering unduly in the internal affairs of individual countries.

One other matter that has especially interested me is the handling of the
foreign currency funds, which are to be set aside by the participating countries
in amounts equivalent to the dollar costs of goods supplied as grants-in-aid. The
uses made of such funds will be a major determinant of the success of the whole
program. But the problem is complex and delicate, and could easily be a chief
source of friction and confusion both at home and abroad. I would prefer to
avoid not only taking title to such funds, but also rigid provisions as to their
use, and to leave a large measure of discretion to the Administrator.

The general purpose should be to correct inflation and promote production
and trade. But with conditions so different in the various countries it would be
difficult to say in advance either what the operations should be or how they
should be timed. Perhaps the simplest and safest general rule would be, as
Winfield Riefler has suggested, to sterilize the funds as an anti-inflationary
measure until such time as they can be expended for capital purposes without
inflationary effects. But even such a rule might be less desirable than a clear
statement of purpose and intent. One point, however, that ought to be insisted
upon is that the funds should not be expended in any way that might reduce the
supply of dollars that might otherwise be available to the participating countries,

a reservation that should hold against even such an otherwise helpful and desirable purpose as stockpiling.

A question of perhaps equal difficulty and importance is how American aid should be financed here at home, whether exclusively by taxation or by a combination of taxing and borrowing from non-bank sources. So long as the inflationary danger in our own economy remains acute, taxation should be recognized as one of our most effective anti-inflationary weapons, because of both its direct restraint upon spending and its indirect monetary effect, through the use of the budgetary surplus, to restrict the money supply and raise short-term interest rates. The conclusion seems to follow that, in such circumstances, the European recovery program should be financed entirely by taxation. But quite apart from the political urge to reduce taxes in an election year, the recent drop in food and farm prices has introduced a new uncertainty as to whether the inflationary pressure may not have run its course. If this proves to be the fact, I think we should be prepared to finance the European program in part by borrowing from non-bank sources.

On longer-run grounds, it seems to me imperative that taxes should be reduced whenever the relaxation of inflation will permit, because there is probably no other way in a democracy to put effective pressure on government expenditures. One of our greatest dangers, from a long-run view, is that we may accept the high level of expenditure to which the war has brought us, and regard this as a base from which inevitably as time goes on expenditures will rise. One has only to read the ten-year program in the President's Economic Report, and to consider the many demands even now being strongly brought forward for education, housing, health, and welfare generally to appreciate the seriousness of the issues involved. In the aggregate, such projected expenditures — many of them very worthy in themselves — raise a question whether the nature of our economy will not be profoundly affected by this developing tendency to do more and more of the nation's spending collectively rather than privately. One issue it raises, I think, is whether, as Senator George has suggested, we shall not have to differentiate between ordinary expenditure, chargeable against current income through taxation, and extraordinary expenditure to be financed by borrowing. From this point of view, I think a good case can be made out for regarding the European recovery program as capital expenditure, or at any rate as emergency expenditure analogous to war expenditure; and once we are sure that the inflationary pressures are lessening, I would favor financing part of the program by borrowing from non-bank sources.

As to the future impact of the European recovery program on our own economy, it seems to be not unlikely that the effects will be more helpful than harmful. Added to the still large unsatisfied demands here at home, we shall have the assurance of a large volume of foreign demand, but with perhaps less acute inflationary pressures therefrom than hitherto. The worst aspect of the situation in Europe has been the continuing low level of agricultural output, which is still some 20 per cent below prewar. There seems a fair prospect that European crops will be better this year than last, and at the same time the agricultural outlook here and in other parts of the world seems to promise some improvement. No doubt it was this changing statistical picture that was partly responsible for the dramatic drop in our own primary food and farm prices in January and February. Perhaps nothing (along with an improvement in the European coal situation) would exert a more favorable influence on Europe's international position, and go further to reinforce the recovery program, than a rise in world agricultural output and a fall in agricultural prices. With this acute aspect of the problem relieved, we would be in a much better position to go forward with a genuine program of European reconstruction, with results beneficial not only to Western Europe but to our own economy.

I should like to conclude with some brief comment on the longer-run implications of the European recovery program. The basic purpose is to raise the output, and thus the exports, of the participating countries on a scale that will reduce their over-all deficit by 1952 to a level that will obviate the need for further United States Government aid. To achieve this objective in so short a time, consumption will probably have to be held to a low level, perhaps substantially lower than before the war, while investment will be concentrated upon the export industries. So long as the present condition of sellers' markets continues, the emphasis will probably be on the aggregate volume of production and trade, rather than on their character. But tremendous changes have occurred during the past decade in the underlying structure of world trade and of world demand and supply, changes in tastes, in growth of secondary production in newer countries, and in productivity; and when the present abnormal demands for goods have abated, these changes may well have an important effect upon the trade position of the European countries. It will be a mistake, therefore, to assume that by 1952 the European problem will have been entirely solved. For some time thereafter there probably will be a continuing need for investment in Europe to raise living standards, increase productivity, and help reshape the European economies to meet the changed conditions of trade.

How these longer-run problems are to be met we cannot now foresee, but the general objective, I think, should be to prepare the way through the European recovery program for a flow of private foreign investment. This flow should eventually be directed not merely, or perhaps mainly, toward Europe itself but toward the less-developed parts of the world on whose trade Europe formerly relied to cover her debit balance with us. This larger aspect of the world problem points also to the need of thinking in broader terms than the European recovery program itself, strategic though that is, and taking account of other parts of the world and their potential economic development.

In my prepared statement I have tried to indicate the different nature of the problem in the different countries. I could go on with them one by one. What I think it boils down to is this broad, general situation: That there are certain key difficulties in the European situation. The most serious is that in Western Germany and another, almost equally serious, but quite different in kind, is the British problem. The others are not nearly so serious, and I think they could be handled by means of a program of this sort without too much difficulty if the general inflation can be checked.

The main point I have tried to make is that there ought to be a provision for a Western European agency. My most keen disappointment in this whole matter is that the mutual-aid co-operation aspect of it seems to have become submerged somewhere along the line last summer.

Mrs. Bolton: What happened to it? We were told — and it was in the press, I believe — that the State Department had to sort of soft-pedal it. Do you know anything in regard to that?

Mr. Williams: I think we have been losing time — or, I might say, wasting time — on this most important aspect of the question, and I do not know what could be done about it at this late date, but I do know that if I were in Congress I should want to call attention to it.

Mr. Judd: Is there any real hope that that will be taken up again and pushed vigorously by them unless it is at American insistence? Otherwise they are likely to shift to America carrying the load — that is not criticism of them; that is just human nature. There is not much likelihood of a return to that primary condition of success unless there is rather firm insistence upon it. It is not because we do not want the program to succeed, but because we do want it to that we must require such mutual aid.

Mr. Williams: That is right. I should not like to make the passage of this bill dependent upon a full-blown plan for European co-ordination or integration, but I think there should be a stronger reference to the desirability of it in the bill than I have as yet seen. I should think that we might go as far as to suggest the creation of at least a consultative body for the Western European countries.

I do not know what the possibilities are, or how possible it is to give them powers of direction over the expenditure of funds — the large foreign currency funds, for example, the working out of the program, the decision as to where the funds should be spent — but I feel very strongly that we must get beyond nationalities. It ought to be possible for the Europeans to say to each other: 'This money ought not to be spent necessarily in France, but, for example, in Western Germany, or somewhere else.' That is the kind of thing I have felt in reading over the bills.

There has been much discussion of Western European integration. Sometimes it takes an economic line; sometimes political, and sometimes military. I can think of nothing more concrete to take hold of in the beginning than to give some Western European agency a prominent place in this program, whether with merely consultative or directive powers I do not know. I would not like to make that a condition for passage of the act at this time, but it seems to me we should be able to work that in in much stronger terms than any terms I have yet heard.

If you did a thing of that sort, I can see the kind of uses to which such an agency might be put. They might make studies of the possibilities of co-operation in Europe, such as along the lines of customs union, although my experience is that that is a pretty slow and complicated matter. They could study the possibilities of intra-European monetary clearance. They could draw up plans and make allocations of these funds in consultation with our administrator, and they could have a voice in the management of the foreign currency funds that will arise as a result of our grants-in-aid.

All of that, I think, would make a very good beginning, and then, as we went on over the four years, we could build that agency up into a legal agency of co-ordination in the Western European economy. That strikes me as more concrete than the suggestion that there should be some kind of a political federation. Not that I am against that at all, but it remains rather hazy always. They want to know what they can do. Well, here is something for them to do. They can get together in connection with this program.

I think that is the principal suggestion I have to make this afternoon. As I say, I do not know whether it is too late for that or not, but it ought to be discussed, in my opinion.

Now, for the rest, I have been much interested in the handling of the foreign currency funds, and the more I have thought about that question, the more I have come to the belief that it is a very complex and delicate matter. There might easily be complaints of invasion of sovereignty. It might even give the Russians a handle to take hold of. We might find ourselves interfering unduly in the internal economy of these countries. We might give rise, here at home, to expectations of some sort of *quid pro quo* on the part of our own people, wanting to know what is being done with our money on the other side. And it might get to be a very delicate matter, something like the interallied debt of the First World War.

Mr. Judd: On your number one point that you just covered, we had testimony the other day from a business man, here, that it was thought that the recovery aspects of this should be handled by the RFC. And then he suggested a subsidiary RFC in each of these sixteen countries. Following a question from the gentleman from Ohio, he said there may be an advantage to having one RFC in Europe. We would take the preferred stock and they the common stock. It was an attempt to get into this problem you are discussing. Each country would then be interested in restoring Europe as well as itself. Could you discuss the feasibility of that?

Mr. Williams: Whether it should be an RFC or not raises technical questions which I think we are not ready to go into. I have not thought enough about it myself. It was my feeling that if we had an administrative agency on the other side, more or less a counterpart of our Administrator — if there is to be an administrator — it is the kind of suggestion Mr. McCloy has made, for example — and if the personnel of that agency was selected so they could rise above merely national considerations, that would be more important than the financial aspects which the RFC suggests.

I am also fearful of our getting too much entangled in European finances. That is why I get back to the foreign currency funds. I do not like the idea of our taking title to those funds or specifying what the use of those funds ought to be because the situations are so different in the different countries. If there were an agency over there responsible to all of Western Europe and not to one country, I should think that we could talk it over with them and make wise decisions as we went along, so we here could confine ourselves perhaps to a general statement of the purposes and our intent with respect to these funds.

As a general statement of principle, I liked the one that Mr. Riefler worked out in one of the pamphlets prepared for the Select Committee on Foreign Aid — that is, holding the funds during the early period when the inflationary pressures are heavy, with a view to spending them for capital purposes later on. That is perhaps the best short and simple rule that could be laid down. However, I would not like to put even that down as a rigid rule because I think what you are going to find is very different conditions in different countries. Some of these countries have open inflation and some have suppressed inflation; in some the rise in prices had been more than the increase in money, and in others it is reversed. Some are having inflation on an unbalanced budget and some on a balanced budget. The inflation is different in all the different countries.

I think the time-schedule of recovery will be different in the different countries, and it will be very difficult to lay down a rule as to what should be done and when it should be done. I think that is a matter for wise administration, but I would like to see it handled between our Administrator and some corresponding agency on the other side that could think in terms of all of Western Europe and not of any one country.

Mr. Jonkman: Might I interrupt there? How does that square with the thought that I have, that in the legislation you must at least make some provision as to in whom will rest title to these funds? Because, after all, they will be largely the proceeds of grants, once those grants have been made to the participating countries. Will you not be raising a question, unless you define in the legislation in a general way, at least, who shall have title to those funds, as to what disposition could be made? And would there not be some claim, on the part of the participating country, that it would belong to them?

Mr. Williams: My lawyer friends always take your point of view, and I always feel helpless. They say the funds have to belong to someone and I cannot get around that. I guess they do.

Mr. Jonkman: I was very much interested in your opening statement to the effect that we had not waited long enough for them to respond to what was, after all, General Marshall's request in his speech, if he had anything in mind, because he has stated frankly many times before he made that speech that he had no plan at all.

In other words, it seems to me that the practice for us has been to almost break a leg getting the money over there before we ask them to do anything.

Mr. Williams: I feel, on that, that time is pressing. Indeed, we are already engaged in this program of interim aid, and we can only follow it up with another one and another one, and I do feel that we cannot let time go by. What I do object to is that we have now let six months, more or less, go by without having done anything further in the way of setting up a co-operative agency in Europe.

Mr. Jonkman: And yet there is universal agreement — and I have not heard one witness to the contrary — that we cannot help them unless they first help themselves, and that they must do the co-operating and reconstruct and co-operate with each other.

Mr. Williams: I have talked to some of the experts on the sixteen-nation committee, and I think they did a conscientious job in that short period of time, and under very great pressure. But what has really amazed me is that ever since that report came in there has been just silence.

Mr. Jonkman: Is it true that the only thing they did quickly was come back and say, 'We want 29 billions more or less'?

Mr. Williams: That is right, but we more or less asked them that.

Mr. Vorys: According to the newspapers, one reason they have not done anything is because they have been told by the State Department not to meet and now they have been given the green light and are planning to get together.

Mr. Williams: That is right, but could not some provision be made in such a bill for such an agency? Of course, there are references in here, not only to individual countries but groups of countries, but that is a different thing from providing there be such an agency. It seems to me we could go that far, even though perhaps in the early months of this program we should have to go along bilaterally with the individual countries. Yet we could plan to have that agency progressively take over and deal with our corresponding agency over here, and I think we should get a much better integrated program and a great deal more for our money if we do it that way.

Mr. Vorys: Will the gentleman yield?

Mr. Jonkman: Yes.

Mr. Vorys: Your suggestion, following Mr. McCloy's suggestion that there be some joint agency over there has appealed to me. Every witness who has appeared has said that unless there is some form of unity and union in Europe comparatively soon, this whole operation is 'Operation Rat-Hole.' I wondered about providing that the title in these currency deposits should remain in the United States until there is a European union or organization, or duly appointed official committee, representing the entire group, and that the law would then provide that title to the funds, or title to a substantial part, say, one billion dollars or so, go to the new organization.

In this way we would offer a tremendous inducement to Europe to unite. It would be the first time in all history of which I have heard where you would offer a new union a treasury with which to start business.

Mr. Williams: Yes, and a function to perform in the management of those funds.

Mr. Vorys: I mean many unions have had a function to perform, with challenges and threats to them, and so forth, but I never heard of one which had presented to it an advance a treasury with which to operate, and the only thing they had to do would be to unite on the basis of pledges or undertakings, we will say, that they had already made. I had in mind the statements that each of these nations have made at the Paris Conference. What do you think of that possibility?

Mr. Williams: I should think that could be a very good way out. There is language in this bill:

In concluding arrangements with the various recipient countries, the Authority shall endeavor to secure the inclusion of provisions to the effect that all disputes in respect to the use or administration of local reconstruction funds shall be submitted forthwith for final determination to a designated international agency or arbitral tribunal.

Now, there is an agency that would make what I have been talking about capable of performance.

They should have a responsibility in the matter that is over and above that of the individual countries. That follows right along your line, I think.

That, I think now, is the greatly-to-be-desired objective and a great deal has been said about it, as we all know. However, it is vague all the time. I do not believe it will be enough to get them to establish customs unions or currency unions or anything of that sort.

When you suggest a political federation, the question comes up: 'What will it do and what is it going to be about?' Perhaps the military approach is more concrete. Of course, I know nothing about that.

I do think I see a starting point here. We have said we want to deal with these nations — not individually but as a group — and then we have appeared to forget all about that and let them forget about it; but here is a way, I think, of reviving the most essential feature of this plan. If that means that we should carry right through on the matter of title and responsibility of holding, handling, and using these funds, I think we ought to give very serious consideration to it. However, I would not at this late date make it a condition such as would perhaps hold up the whole business. I think if you do that you will be involved in another interim-aid program before very long.

Mr. Vorys: Could I say on that point that the Senate bill has an interim provision, a 30-day provision, with reference to the appointment of an Administrator, and a 90-day provision with reference to entering into bilateral agreements and also a billion-dollar provision with relation to the Reconstruction Finance Corporation, so that if a bill is passed, it can function the day after, while the organization is forming.

Mr. Williams: Yes; I think that is very helpful.

Mr. Vorys: Could I ask this question? We have had a number of witnesses urge some form of guaranty for individual transactions and private enterprise. The Senate bill provides that five per cent of the appropriations can be used for that purpose. We have had two or three witnesses who have urged that guaranties be substantially unlimited, the guaranty being that of guaranty of convertibility out of the foreign currency into dollars. Some of us have felt that to do that without controls would mean that there would be practically no direction to the program at all, and that it would be enormously expensive as an operation. On the other hand, to have controls would be no different from what is already in the bill.

Have you given thought to these guaranties?

Mr. Williams: I think the two approaches are not really very compatible. You guarantee a foreign investment in order to encourage someone else to make the investment and take the risk out of it. I feel that comes really at a later stage. Europe really is not a fit place now for private investment, conditions being what they are. I think we went too far after the First World War by encouraging private investment in Europe. It turned out badly before we got through with it.

I think there should be a period of preparation, perhaps in the next four years, wherein we can create a state of affairs in Europe in which our capital might legitimately become interested. I think that even then there might be some necessity of a guaranty, but I do not have much interest now in trying to induce capital to go into Europe because I think it might turn out badly, and, if it did, it would be a setback as it was after the last war. I am not much interested in that aspect.

With respect to these foreign currency funds, I feel more and more that this may turn out to be the most difficult feature of the whole plan. Everybody abroad and at home is bound to be interested in that money. It will run into large sums and everybody will have an idea about what ought to be done. On the one hand, there is a danger of too great an invasion of European sovereignty and laying us open to the charge of imperialism and trying to colonize Europe and all that sort of thing. On the other hand, there is the danger that if we do not exercise adequate control, it will be money down the drain; and we have to hit in between somehow. One way to go at it is along this line of retaining title, spelling out specific rules, and so on. The other way would be to leave it to the administrator, and the corresponding agency on the other side, with powers of review over here so that we can check up on what we are doing. I should rather see it done that way, all under some broad statement of purpose such as that the funds shall not be expended in inflationary ways, and that as far as possible at the right time they should be spent for capital purposes. It should be a broad statement like that and then leave it up to the Administrator.

Mr. Jonkman (presiding): Are there any further questions?

(No response.)

Mr. Jonkman: Thank you very much, Mr. Williams.

Index

27-28

182-83